COMMON SENSE ECONOMICS

The Mises Institute
2010

*The propensity to work,
and not the propensity to spend,
is the foundation
of national income and wealth*

COMMON SENSE ECONOMICS

by

L. ALBERT HAHN

ERRATUM

Page 131, first line of the second paragraph should read:

As inflation progresses, even the least inflation-conscious

Page 172, last line of the second paragraph should read:
tious have to be liquidated. Over-speculation ends in deflation.

Page 198, fifth line should read:
smaller part of total earnings was then distributed, expressing

© *Copyright 1956 by L. Albert Hahn*
Library of Congress Catalog Number: 56–5919

PRINTED IN GREAT BRITAIN BY JARROLD AND SONS LTD, NORWICH,
FOR THE PUBLISHERS,
ABELARD-SCHUMANN LIMITED, 404 FOURTH AVENUE, NEW YORK 16, N.Y.,
38 RUSSELL SQUARE, LONDON, W.C.1, ENGLAND.

FOREWORD

As the English version[1] of this book goes to press the economy of the United States, as well as that of many European countries, has reached a state which can be described only as that of a highly inflationary boom. All pertinent data—total investment, demand deposits, consumer credits and production —show clearly a steep upward trend. And many characteristic signs of an overstressed economy, such as bottlenecks in employment and raw materials, backlogs for deliveries, exaggerated stockmarket booms, have made their appearance.

The inflationary character of the American boom is now recognized by an increasing number of economists but is still denied by some. The main argument in support of the latter's opinion, and therefore of a *laissez-faire, laissez-aller* attitude, is based on the relative stability of the general price level in the United States.

The consumer price averages have indeed remained entirely, and the wholesale price averages almost, unchanged since 1953. However, the picture is very different when one examines the prices of the single groups of commodities upon which the price averages are based. One sees immediately that the prices of industrial finished goods have risen substantially since 1953, and those of industrial goods, especially building materials, since 1954. These increases are offset in the price averages by the decline in agricultural prices. But this decline is merely the result of the liquidation of over-production during the World and Korean wars. Viewed from a quantity theoretical standpoint these lower prices appear to be due to a temporary over-supply from the side of goods; this, however, does not change but only conceals the over-demand from the money side. The price movements in the industrial sector alone show all the features of inflation. And this is decisive. For crises are nowadays—this should not be forgotten—industrial and not agricultural crises.

But apart from this it seems very doubtful that much importance can be attributed to the stability of the price level in

[1] The first German edition appeared in 1954, the second in 1955 (Verlag Fritz Knapp, Frankfurt am Main). A French edition is appearing shortly (Editions M.Th. Génin, Librairie de Médicis, Paris).

times of marked increases in productivity. Higher productivity without inflation leads to lower prices. If prices remain stable in spite of rapidly increasing productivity, this can be only the result of an inflationary credit expansion. Such a monetary inflation without, or with only little, price inflation is in principle not less dangerous than an inflation with strong price inflation. Whether inflation profits are the result of prices going up while costs lag, or of prices remaining stable while costs decline through an increase in productivity, a dynamic process is stimulated which is bound to end in crisis and depression—if for no other reason than because every stimulus must finally exhaust itself.[2]

Was the present inflation unavoidable, or avoidable only at the cost of permanent unemployment? I do not believe so. When, in 1953, the Republicans took over the administration they endeavored—successfully—to interrupt the inflationary post-war boom[3] by the classical means of tightening money and credit. As a result unemployment had risen substantially by the end of the year. The Republican administration found itself faced with the dilemma of correcting this unemployment —which was essentially a stabilization and not a deflation phenomenon[4]—through renewed inflation or through enforced adjustments of costs to the no longer permanently inflating price level. The administration chose—to the regret of conservative and to the satisfaction of Keynesian economists—the first method. As was easily predictable,[5] unemployment disappeared, but at the price of continued inflation.

Recognizing the danger of inflation the authorities have, since the beginning of 1955, allowed the interest rates to go up somewhat. But the boom has not decreased and has even increased in vigor—see, for instance, the movement of prices for steel scrap and certain metals in 1955.

This is not surprising. For the measures adopted are adequate only for dampening but not for stopping inflation. What the authorities are doing, in order to keep the economy

[2] See also pp. 127–128 and Appendix I, p. 223.
[3] For a description of the period before 1953, see Appendix I, p. 220.
[4] For details see Appendix II, p. 233.
[5] See my prognosis in June 1954, Appendix II, pp. 236–237.

FOREWORD

running at a high level of production and employment, is to tighten the reins when inflation seems to be getting out of hand, and to loosen them—thus resorting again to inflation—as soon as the boom appears to be weakening. One must concede that this policy of "leaning against the wind" is carried out with ability and—considering the strong political pressure in favor of inflation—with remarkable courage. But will this policy which is nevertheless one of inflation, even though that inflation is a slow and regulated one, succeed in the long run? I doubt it. It is the tragedy of every boom created and carried forward by inflationary credit expansion that it never leads to stabilization but always to reaction.

Thus there is only the choice: either one tolerates further inflation, then the boom continues until a saturation point of demand is reached—at that point a depression will inevitably set in, the more severe the longer the boom has lasted; or one stops inflation, then the reaction sets in immediately—a very unwelcome occurrence especially in an election year.

This whole paradoxical situation of the economies of the United States and of most Western countries is, I think, in the last analysis the logical consequence of an economic policy which in theory overstresses the importance of *effective demand* for the attainment of full employment, and in practice recommends the correction of any sign of unemployment by more and more credit expansion, using for its justification the old purchasing power theory and all the other semi-scientific arguments advocated for centuries by inflationists.

The present book is, from the first to the last word, nothing but an endeavor—perhaps inadequate—to demonstrate the theoretical shortcomings and the practical danger of this philosophy by stressing the importance of the *supply* of production factors for the maintenance of a high and stable level of economic activity.

My grateful acknowledgments are due to Mrs. Elizabeth Henderson of London and Rome, whose editing improved the English manuscript and purged it of a number of inconsistencies.

Paris, June 1956.　　　　　　　　　　　　　　　　　　A. H.

PREFACE

My book, *The Economics of Illusion,* published in 1949[1], was essentially a critique of the late Lord Keynes' *General Theory of Employment, Interest and Money.* My conclusion was, briefly, that what is new in Keynes' work is not good, and what is good is not new.

Since then I have often been asked to add to my negative critique of Keynes' theory the positive exposition of an economic theory which offered a more correct explanation and description of economic reality. The present book is my answer to this request. I have called it *Common Sense Economics* in contrast to Keynes' theory, which I regard as *illusion economics* since its underlying factual assumptions seem to me to rest on illusion.

I approached this work with mixed feelings. On the one hand, I was fully aware of the fact that professional economists have more experience and a better technique in the exposition of economic relationships than a person whose main activity has consisted in making business decisions. On the other hand, I had long been tempted to try, at some time, to describe the economic model which I myself, after more than thirty years of activity in economic theory and practice, regard as adequate because close to reality. Also, I have often asked myself how I would rewrite today my *Economic Theory of Bank Credit,* which first appeared thirty-five years ago.

The arrangement of the present volume is in deliberate contradiction to that usual nowadays, particularly in English and American literature, following Keynes' *General Theory.*

In my view, the Keynesian theory is original, but also fatal in its peculiar, almost paradoxical, decisions as to what is to be regarded as constant and what as variable in the economy. The workers' nominal wage demands, for instance, are

[1] Squier Publishing Co., New York, distributed through New York Institute of Finance.

assumed to be relatively constant, while aggregate purchasing power is assumed to be continuously fluctuating and the economy therefore continuously exposed to inflation and deflation. The ensuing picture of the economy appears to the non-Keynesian as a sort of trick film. Everything happens in a manner that is exactly the opposite of what he is used to. It is no longer the supply of labor, but the propensity to consume which determines the volume of production; the old and oft-refuted under-consumption theories—of which Keynes' theory is no more than a replica—once more become respectable. I am firmly convinced that this allegedly revolutionary progress in economic science is really retrogression compared to classical economics. The *long-run* economic forces, such as the propensity to work, are completely eclipsed by less important factors, such as the propensity to consume; and, notwithstanding occasional assurances to the contrary, Keynes' theory, as a general theory, also purports to be a theory of secular developments. Nor does Keynes provide a satisfactory theory of *short-run* developments, and in particular no business cycle theory. There is no explanation of the dynamics of the cycle, and such indications as are given—note for instance the under-employment equilibrium which allegedly comes about when savings become excessive and which disappears when savings contract—are unrealistic and untrue.

The present work tries to avoid the dangers of overestimating the importance of "effective demand." To this purpose it starts, in an old-fashioned manner, with the description of a stationary economy, i.e. one which ever repeats itself without any changes in data. Next comes the description of a changing economy, in which, however—and this, too, is decisively old-fashioned—the monetary system is assumed to be entirely inelastic. Here new credits are granted only to the extent of new savings. Such a monetary system is presupposed in order to demonstrate the changes occurring in the economy when changes from the money side are eliminated. The next section, on the contrary, is concerned with an economy with an elastic monetary system, that is an economy where inflationary credit expansion and deflationary credit contraction are possible. The business cycle is then treated as a special case of the economy in inflation and deflation. Finally, Part V is a substantially unaltered reproduction of a lecture given in 1952, in which I examined the laws of price formation on the stock markets, on the basis of developments on the New York Exchange during the last twenty-five years.

Part I begins with a description of the Robinson Crusoe economy. This may appear superfluous or elementary to the professional economist. I included it, first because the principles which I consider essential are most clearly seen in the case of the isolated producer; second because in publishing this book I had also a secondary purpose in mind: it is meant as a sort of minimum economics for the business man, banker and investor who is interested in theory. For this reason I have also included, at the end of each section, some practical conclusions with regard to stock prices.

I know, of course, that theoretical knowledge is despised by many practical business men. I can only say, in justification of my secondary purpose, that on the few occasions I have been successful in my own business life I have been so not because of any superior practical ability, but simply because my studies of monetary and business cycle theory had disclosed to me earlier than to many others the consequences of the initially inflationary and later deflationary monetary and credit policies of European governments.

I would like, however, to add a word of warning. Although I consider a knowledge of the fundamentals of economics essential for any business and investment management, I do not consider it sufficient for success. Our economy is subject to constant changes. These changes, whether they are technical, legal, institutional, political, or simply in consumer taste, are uncertain and as unforeseeable as is the whole future. Business men and investors have to judge the relative strength of the forces that will bring about future changes and adjust their dispositions accordingly. In order to do so they will have to draw upon everything they have ever read, thought, or experienced. Even so they will often be wrong. In no case, however, can future change be predicted scientifically.

Therefore, business and especially investment management is an art and not a science, and the concept of scientific method of investment is nonsensical.

As regards my method of presentation, I would like to make the following remarks.

Many contemporary presentations of both a specialist and a non-specialist nature suffer, in my opinion, from trying to embody too many details and eventualities, with the result that the fundamentals are obscured. One no longer sees the forest for the trees, and not even the trees are always described correctly. The custom of examining what happens if one curve shifts while others remain fixed—e.g. in the graphical description of supply and demand at various price levels—is very useful for theoretical analysis, but has led, in many instances, to the belief that this is what actually happens in reality. But the economic world is not divided into variable and fixed data. All relevant economic data are variable.

Furthermore, the mathematical language of modern economics has led many an economist to describe not so much what actually happens but what possibly *could* happen—for instance what *could* cause the boom to turn into depression. But any resemblance of these descriptions and explanations to reality seems to me purely accidental. Nor is this situation likely to be changed by objections raised by men in the practical business world. It is a regrettable fact that most of what is written nowadays in our field moves in such esoteric spheres and uses such technical language that it can no longer be read or understood even by a business man interested in economic theory.

On my part I have tried to describe in everyday language a model of an economy that is simple enough to clarify the fundamental relationships between various economic data, while, at the same time, it is not so simplified and abstract as to become completely unrealistic. I know that other methods of presentation are possible and may be useful. But I can say in favor of my model that it has very often proved useful and helpful to me when making business decisions.

I cherish no exaggerated hopes that my theory—if I may so

term my modest picture of the economic world—may find the approval of my colleagues who have been reared in the spirit of Keynes. Anyone who sees the cause of most short-run and long-run disturbances of the capitalist economy—and in particular the cause of unemployment—in an excess of saving, and who therefore recommends higher public and private expenditure as a means for the permanent maintenance of prosperity, will read this book only with abhorrence.

There are not only cycles of business activity but also cycles of economic theory, and particularly of business cycle theory. We are at present in a phase of exaggeration of the importance of effective demand. However, while there are cycles of theory, there are, obviously, also phase-lags within these cycles. I have a feeling that German economic theory just now displays such a lag as against Anglo-American theory. The former seems to be entering a phase of enthusiasm for modern economics of the Keynesian pattern and to indulge in orgies of formally correct equations, however unrealistic the underlying factual assumptions may be. The latter, on the other hand, seems to have already passed the peak of enthusiasm. It is increasingly recognized that the simple basic principles of the neo-classics lead further—and make avoidance of errors easier—than the "modernistic stuff." A counter revolution to the Keynesian revolution seems to be originating.

If my *Common Sense Economics*—the German edition has preceded the English for technical reasons—should have the effect of somewhat shortening the phase of enthusiasm I should be well pleased with the result. I am not optimistic in this respect, but I have patience. It took fully eight years for my *Economic Theory of Bank Credit,* which was a reaction against money being looked upon as no more than a veil, to win through. I assume that it will take as long for the present work, written as a reaction against exaggerated views of the role of money as a motive force, to gain acceptance.

CONTENTS

FOREWORD v

PREFACE viii

PART I THE STATIONARY ECONOMY 1

The Isolated Producer—Some Preliminary Consequences —A Multitude of Products—Differences in Utility Judgments—Differences in Production Costs—Exchange of Goods—Exchange and Profits—The Entrepreneur—Money—The Time Element—Expansion of Production Dependent on Capital Accumulation?—Amount of Capital Dependent on Volume of Production?—Amount of Capital and Roundabout Ways of Production—What is a Stationary Economy?—Production Exchange and Consumption Exchange—The Fundamental Problems of Economics—Production Exchange: Production by Labor Alone—Production by Labor and Capital—The Law of Diminishing Marginal Returns—Production Factors are Remunerated according to their Marginal Utility—Production with Land—Is Land a Third Production Factor? —The Price of the Services of Land—The Price of Land—Differential Rents and Differential Prices—Land Prices, Wages and Interest Rates—Variable and Fixed Capital—The Size of the Firm—Variable and Fixed Costs. Total Costs. Unit Costs and Marginal Costs—The Consumption Exchange—The Purchase of Intermediate Goods—Equality of Production and Consumption—Equality of Costs and Revenue—The Profits of Entrepreneurs—Profits, Interests, Rents—Security Prices.

PART II THE CHANGING ECONOMY 64

J. B. Say's Law—Changes in Consumption—Changes in Production—Unemployment, a Vague Concept—The Basic Law of Employment—Changes in the Supply of Labor—Reasons for Scarcer and Costlier Labor Supply —Minimum Wage Laws. Laws Limiting Labor Supply. Union Action—The Demand Curve for Labor—Effects of Changes in Labor Supply—Reaction on Profits and Interest—Changes in the Demand for Labor—Changes in the Productivity of Labor—Changes in the

xiv CONTENTS

Productivity of Capital—Changes in Production Coupled to Changes in Income Distribution—Changes in Supply of Capital—The Reasons for Saving—Changes in Demand for Capital—Changes in Capital Supply and Demand Influence Demand for Labor—Personal and Corporation Taxes Influence Capital Supply and Demand—Changes in Use of Capital Coupled to Changes in Income Distribution—Changes in Consumption and Investment do not Affect Aggregate Demand—Underemployment as such does not Invalidate this Statement—Deflationary Effect of Increased Employment—Wage and Price Level and Increase in Productivity—Changes in Consumption and Investment do not Change Employment—Facts and Expectations—Maladjustments to Future Changes—Profits Result from Correct Anticipations—Do Profits Disappear in the Long Run?—Security Prices and Changes in Demand for and Supply of Capital—Corporation Taxes and Share Prices—Personal Income Taxes and Share Prices.

PART III THE ECONOMY IN INFLATION AND DEFLATION   105

The Preconditions of Inflation and Deflation—The Myth of the Small Death Traps—The Large Death Traps—Involuntary Rigidities—Deliberate Maladjustments—Budgetary Deficits and Surpluses, as such, do not Create Inflation or Deflation—Death Traps Open when the Credit Demand is Extremely Weak—Cyclical Deflation—Secular Deflation (Stagnation)—Checking Accounts and Cash—Circular Flow and Sequence Analysis of the Effects of Inflation and Deflation—Effects of Inflation and Deflation on the Capital Structure—Effects of Inflation and Deflation on Employment—Are these Effects Lasting?—Does Saving Equal Investment?—The Banks and the Central Banks are the Savers—Inflation and Deflation and the General Price Level—The Demand for Products of the Current Production Period—The Supply of Products of the Current Period—The Price Level for Products of the Current Period—Must or Should Growth be Financed by Inflation?—Should Increased Productivity be met by Inflationary Credit Expansion?—Cumulative Effect of the Original Inflation—Inflation Profits are Mostly Apparent Profits—Prices and Production in Deflation—Waiting and Hurrying—Credit Supply in Inflation is Enhanced by Waiting and Curtailed by

CONTENTS XV

Hurrying of Buyers—Velocity of Money Turnover during Inflation—Inventories during Waiting and Hurrying—Credit Demand in Deflation is Enhanced by Waiting and Curtailed by Hurrying of Sellers—Genuine Saving in Times of Inflation—Multiplier Theory and Acceleration Principle—Compensating Reactions of Factors of Production—Compensating Reactions of Creditors—Compensating Reactions of Labor—Do Wage Increases lead to Inflation?—Wage Rigidities Downward—Wage Increases during Deflation Increase Unemployment. The Purchasing Power Theory—The End of Inflation—Who Gains and Who Loses by Inflation?—The Banks—Earners of Wages, Salaries and Fixed Incomes—Entrepreneurs—Debtors and Creditors—Deflation Profits and Losses—Share Prices in Inflation—Profits due to Lagging Production Costs—Windfall Profits and Share Prices—Interest Rates and Share Prices—Idle Money Boom—Hurrying and the Stock Market—Stock Prices in Deflation.

PART IV THE BUSINESS CYCLE 159

Business Cycles are Alternating Inflations and Deflations—Maldistribution of Monetary Demand over Time—Under-consumption Theories—Over-investment Theories—The Theory of Unnatural Interest Rates—Psychological Business Cycle Theories—Psychological Cycle Theories are Realistic—Error about the Reversibility of Price Movements a Necessary Condition for the Cycle—Liquidity Preference not a Helpful Concept—Multiplier Theory, Acceleration Principle and Business Cycles—Responsibility of Money-Issuing Institutions—The Start of an Upswing—From Recovery to Boom—The End of the Boom—Delayed Deflation—Interest Rates during the Cycle—Money Circulation during the Cycle—Cyclical Phenomena are Results of Maladjustments—Changes in the Capital Structure—Changes in Employment—Significance of the Elasticity of Labor Supply—Unliquidated Inventories and Idle Fixed Capital—Decreasing Unit Costs—Profits and Losses during the Cycle—Is There Still a Cycle?—Stabilizing the Business Cycle—Business Cycle Consciousness as a Stabilizing Factor—Does Economic Growth Guarantee Lasting Prosperity?—Easy Money Policy and the Cycle—Stabilizing Interest Rates—Stabilizing Low Interest Rates—Securities during the Cycle—Money Market Rates during the Cycle—Bond

CONTENTS

Prices and Capital Market Rates—Common Share Prices—Sequence of Interest Rate, Bond and Share Price Movements—Fluctuation in the Yield of Common Shares—Earnings, Dividends and Share Prices—Independent Share Price Cycles.

PART V PRICE FORMATION ON STOCK MARKETS   192

Significance of the Problem—Shares as a Source of Long-Term Income—Corrected Price Curves—Dividends, Net Earnings and Share Prices—The Significance of the Past for the Future—Expectations as the Cause of Market Distortions—Model of a Typical Stock Market Movement—Are the Market Expectations Correct or Wrong?—Uncertainty and Error as Price-Forming Factors—Purchases of Stocks are Purchases of Chances—Mathematical Probabilities?—Weighing the Chances—Facts or Expectations as the Basis of Stock Price Formation—Is the Economy a By-product of a Gambling Casino?—Interpersonal Differences of Expectations—Shifts in the Distribution of Securities—Emancipation from Mass Opinion—Mass Opinion as an Objective Datum—The Basic Principle of Successful Investment—Only Minority Forecasts are Useful—Forecasts are always Highly Subjective.

APPENDIX I PROSPERITY BY INFLATION   217

APPENDIX II THE ECONOMIC SITUATION IN THE UNITED STATES   229

INDEX   238

Part I

THE STATIONARY ECONOMY

The Isolated Producer

Everybody tries to live. In order to live one has to consume goods. Goods for consumption are not generally obtainable without work. They are the products of labor. This holds true for individuals, for communities and for the whole of humanity.

When somebody produces consumption goods by his own work he exchanges, so to speak, work-hours, of which he has plenty but which he cannot consume directly, for goods which he can consume but which he lacks until they are produced. This is exchange in its simplest form. We have to understand it thoroughly in order to understand other forms of exchange which, though somewhat more complicated, are all based upon the same principle.

Our ability to exchange work for goods, to produce, rests upon the fundamental fact that nature offers the technical possibility of transforming work into goods—say of transforming one hour of work into ten apples. Given this technical possibility there arises the question of how many hours men will actually use to produce the apples they wish to consume. The answer is that each individual decides how many hours of leisure he is willing to sacrifice in order to satisfy his appetite for apples. It is up to each individual to decide when the point has come at which the *disutility* of work is no longer compensated by the *utility* gained by more apples.

If a man considered the utility of every additional apple, as compared with the disutility of every additional hour's work, to be the same as that of all previously acquired apples and previously worked hours, he would obviously work himself to death—provided he started out by wanting any apples at all. He would be killed by an insatiable appetite for apples and a flagrant disregard for his physical limitations. He would never stop working, and we could never know his relative valuation of apples and work-hours.

Fortunately this never happens. The famous law of diminishing marginal utility, or better, the law of diminishing valuation of additional quantities of goods, comes into play. The utility of each new apple which even the most passionate lover of apples acquires appears to him less than the utility of apples previously produced. On the one hand the need for apples becomes less pressing and is finally limited by the individual's consumption capacity. Even utmost greed is satisfied. On the other hand the remaining rest and play hours become fewer and therefore more urgently needed. The individual's valuation of leisure increases. This means that our man will demand an increasing amount of apples for each additional work-hour; or, looking at it from another angle, his supply price of work in terms of apples will be higher for every additional hour. If the working day is to lengthen, nature must pay him a higher price for each working hour. Inevitably the price at some point will be more than nature can pay.

Our man may be prepared to work one hour each day in return for only two apples. This one hour is needed neither for rest nor for play, whereas he values the apples highly because they are his first. He may be willing to work the following hour for a return of four apples, the next for six apples, and so on. The eighth hour, maybe, he will sell only for a return of say sixteen apples. He may not be prepared to work at all the ninth hour, even for much greater compensation, because his appetite for apples may be satiated by those already obtained and his desire for rest may have become very urgent.

It is usual to represent willingness to supply work by a graph in which the quantities offered are measured on the horizontal axis, and the price at which they are offered on the vertical line. The resulting supply curve then slopes upward from the left to the right.

The assumptions referred to above can thus be represented by the supply curve shown in Figure 1.

THE STATIONARY ECONOMY

The supply curve slopes upward to the right up to the eighth hour. It shows how the hours of work offered increase with the price paid. From the eighth hour onward the curve rises vertically: the supply of work-hours no longer increases with rising prices. No matter how much the price is raised it no longer has the power to lengthen the working day.

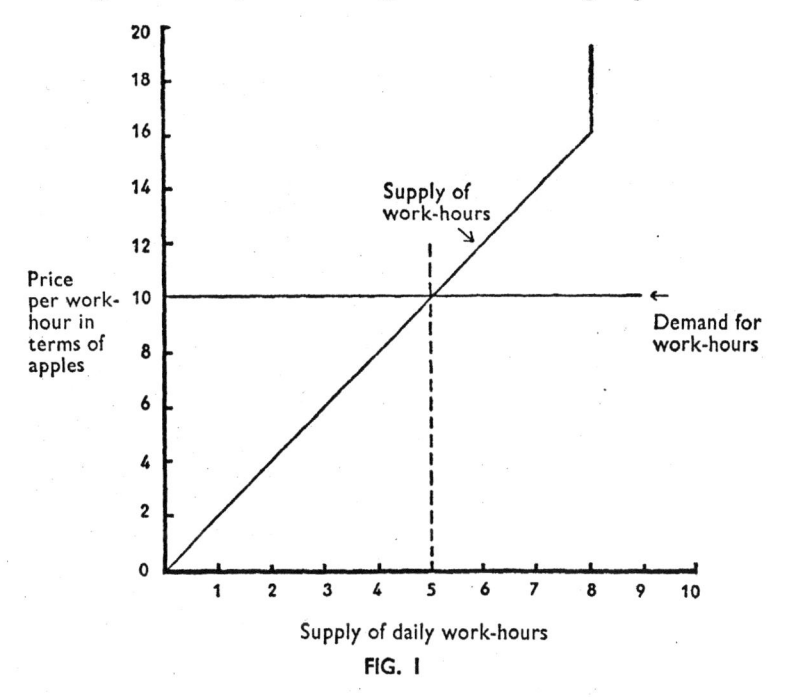

FIG. I

Our assumption that until the eighth hour the supply of labor increases with the wage demanded is broadly in conformity with reality. According to the general law, the higher the price the greater the supply.

In the particular case of labor supply, however, we must note a peculiarity. A higher wage level, and the resulting higher living standard of the workers, may cause a change in their value judgments. The workers may prefer additional rest to additional consumption goods. We then speak of the supply curve of labor moving upward or to the left. This indicates that less work is now forthcoming at each of the various compensation levels. On the other hand when the wage level, and with it the living standard, falls the workers may prefer to have more consumption goods rather than more rest. The supply curve of labor then moves downward or to the right, indicating that more work is forthcoming at each of the various compensation levels. This renders the effect of wage changes somewhat unpredictable, especially in the long run. History shows that the higher wages resulting from the increased productivity of the economy have been used by labor partly to increase leisure and partly to buy more goods. In insisting on shorter working time labor went without a certain amount of consumption goods which it could otherwise have obtained. We shall, nevertheless, assume that in the general case higher wages lead to an increase in the supply of work-hours.

Let us return to our diagram. How many hours will our man actually work on the assumption underlying our curve? The answer obviously depends upon the price, in terms of apples, which the demand for labor is prepared to pay. In our simplified model it is nature herself who demands labor in exchange for apples. But nature, working neither at a profit nor at a loss, offers for a work-hour exactly what an hour's work produces. Suppose this is ten apples. Then nature offers ten apples as a reward for every hour of work. We represent this demand situation in our graph in the usual way by a horizontal line at the wage level of ten apples an hour. We immediately see that on the given assumptions our man will work five hours and produce fifty apples—not more and not less—because nature's offer of ten apples for an hour's work is exactly the compensation which our man demands for his fifth hour. In other words his work stops at the so-called marginal work-hour where the price, at which its supply is offered, is still just covered by the price which the demand is prepared to pay.

Some Preliminary Consequences

This is, of course, a very simplified model of what would happen in the real world even within an isolated economic unit. Yet for all its simplicity it shows quite clearly certain fundamental facts about the economic world which we will encounter again and again as we proceed to the examination of the more complicated real conditions:

(1) Production never expands beyond the point where the worker demands more for his work-hour than he produces during this work-hour. Any expansion of production depends upon the worker not demanding more in payment than he produces.

(2) At a given schedule of prices at which the worker offers various quantities of work-hours, that is at a given particular supply curve for labor, production can expand only if the productivity of labor increases. Higher productivity of labor enables nature to pay greater compensation, in terms of product units. The extra-marginal work-hours, which had so far been too expensive, can now be used.

In our model the work-hours were supplied by one single worker. If there are several workers it is now possible also to use work-hours of other workers, who had so far not been employed at all because even their first hour was too dear. Higher productivity, therefore, leads not only to longer working time for individual workers, but also to the employment of more workers.

(3) At given productivity of labor, and hence given demand for labor, production can expand only if the supply price of labor decreases. This will happen if the workers either value the utility of consumer goods *more* or the disutility of work *less* than they did in the past. Workers will then offer the same amount of work at lower prices, or more work at the same prices. Individual workers' hitherto idle hours or hitherto idle workers will be drawn into the productive process.

This means that a population can consume more if it is willing to work more and to rest less. This truth is often forgotten nowadays, although it is self-evident to common sense. The comparatively low living standards of tropical countries are admittedly at least partly due to their peoples' greater appreciation of rest and lesser appreciation of the comforts of life to be produced by work.

(4) The over-production problem, one of the major problems

that has intrigued economists, does not exist in our simplified Robinson Crusoe world. So far as it occurs in reality, overproduction has its roots in conditions not present in the case of the isolated producer. Here there can never be separate decisions on consumption and production. Production and consumption are so closely linked that neither can ever exceed the other. Never can anything be produced that is not consumed. Jean-Baptiste Say's law, according to which any production creates a corresponding consumption, is unconditionally valid. As soon as the utility of consumption goods no longer compensates for the disutility of the work of producing, production stops.

(5) Our model also allows us to make certain preliminary remarks on the important subject of profits. Our man receives a uniform compensation of ten apples for his work-hours, although it is only for the fifth hour that he demanded this compensation. He demanded substantially less for the first, second, third and fourth hours. He receives in fact more than what he considered sufficient to compensate him for his work. This is his good fortune and results from the fact that nature, exercising demand for his labor, values one work-hour at ten apples. For this reason nature pays, for *all* hours, more than the minimum compensation which he required for his first intra-marginal work-hours. But this surplus is not a *profit* in the usual sense of the word.

A profit is a phenomenon of distribution. It is a surplus arising when part of the output is withheld from other production factors for special reasons. No such surplus exists in the case of an isolated producer. His own input (of work-hours) is always both necessary and sufficient to produce the whole output (of apples). The two are always equal, and neither can exceed the other. Even if more is produced through improved techniques, there will still be no surplus. A given input can always result only in the output corresponding to the technique employed. If our man were to save or hoard his output, the apples, he would indeed end up with a stock of apples. But this would be not because he had made a profit from his production but because he had saved or hoarded part of the output.

An isolated producer can never make a profit, nor as we shall see later (p. 16) can an economy as a whole. We shall have to keep this in mind in our later examination of the true nature and origin of profits.

A Multitude of Products

We have so far assumed that our man has the choice only between rest and producing a single product, apples. In our example he was prepared to work five hours to produce fifty apples.

We now take a small step away from the simplest model of economic life toward the enormous complexity of the actual economy by assuming that he can produce and consume more than one product. In order to simplify the presentation, however, we shall assume that our individual has only the alternative of producing and consuming one more product, pears. So far it was a choice between rest and work; now there is the additional choice between the production and consumption of several goods. In analyzing the basic principles of this choice we are faced with one of the most important problems in economics—namely the problem of how mankind allocates available resources to various possible productions.

In our example our producer worked five hours to achieve a total production of fifty apples. Let us suppose that he wants to work neither more nor less than before. To what extent will he replace the production and consumption of apples with those of pears, now that he has the choice between the two? The answer depends on the one hand upon his valuation of the relative utilities of pears and apples, and on the other hand upon the relative production costs of apples and pears. The question arises whether more or less time is needed to produce pears rather than apples.

When the choice is between work and rest, the utility of the products of work is, as we have seen, valued exactly according to the law of diminishing marginal utility: the utility of additional apples appears less as their number increases. The same law governs the decisions relating to the consumption of two products, apples and pears. Our man will, therefore, value pears lower in relation to apples, as soon as the quantity of the former increases. This also because the utility of apples now appears greater to him. For if we assume that our producer wishes to produce pears only by sacrificing some of the time hitherto employed in the production of apples, the latter become scarcer.

Our man might, for instance, consider the utility of the first 5 pears as equivalent to that of 15 apples (1 pear = 3 apples); the utility of the next 5 pears as equivalent to that of 10 apples (1 pear = 2 apples); and the utility of the next 5 pears as equivalent to that of 5 apples (1 pear = 1 apple). The next 5 pears might drop in his valuation to less than 5 apples.

These valuations are, of course, the result of the psychological fact that the appetite for pears decreases with increasing satisfaction, whereas the appetite for apples increases with decreasing satisfaction. We are assuming that the individuals are aware of this fact when making their production plans for a certain time period.

Anyone who is prepared to forgo apples if he can produce pears instead, demands from himself, as it were, pears in exchange for apples. The valuation of pears in relation to apples can, therefore, be represented by a demand curve in the usual way. On the assumption just mentioned, this curve will have the shape pictured in Figure 2.

It has become usual in recent years to present the distribution of a given income (or effort) between two consumption (or production) possibilities with the help of so-called indifference curves. Since this technique is generally less accessible to laymen than simple demand and supply curves, we have tried to do without it, especially as we believe that the introduction of the indifference curve technique does not involve any substantial change or progress. The method of presentation adopted here reaches essentially the same results.

Now how many pears will actually be produced, and how many apples sacrificed? This obviously depends upon the supply of pears. Pears are, so to speak, supplied by nature when work previously devoted to the production of apples is transferred to the production of pears. The supply of pears in terms of apples is, therefore, dependent upon the relative production costs of apples and pears—in other words upon how much more or less time it takes to produce pears rather than apples.

Our graph with its several supply curves shows how many apples and pears our man will produce, provided the assumptions underlying the demand curve remain unchanged.

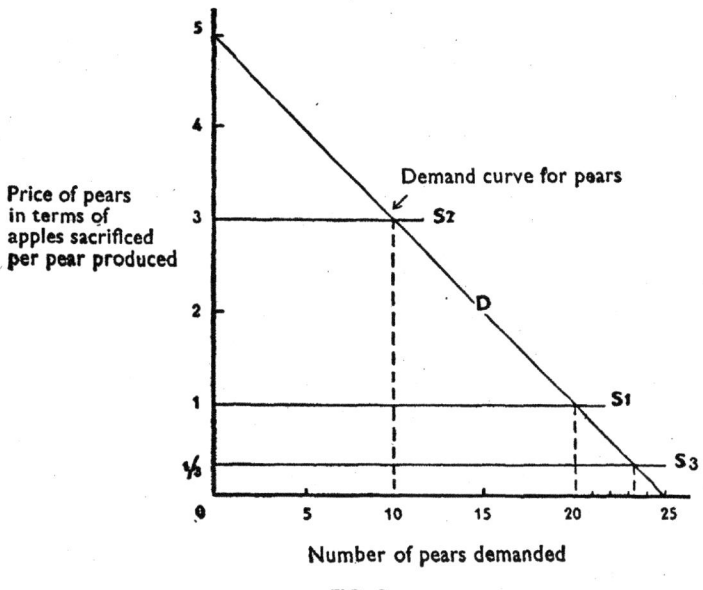

FIG. 2

If we assume that it takes the same time to produce pears and apples, the horizontal supply curve is situated at the price of one apple, or curve S_1. If it takes three times as much time to produce a pear as it does to produce an apple, the horizontal supply curve will run at the price of three apples, or curve S_2. If to produce pears takes one-third of the time that it takes to produce apples, the supply curve will run at the price of one-third of an apple per pear, or curve S_3. The position of the intersection points between the demand curve and the three supply curves immediately provides the answer to the question of how many pears and apples will be produced on our various assumptions. In the first case (represented by S_1), our man produces 20 pears and sacrifices 20 apples in order to do so. Instead of having 50 apples he will now have 30 apples. In the second case (represented by curve S_2), 10 pears are produced at a sacrifice of 30 apples. Instead of 50 apples there will now be 20 apples. In the third case (represented by curve S_3), where only one-third of an apple need be sacrificed for the production of each pear, 23 pears will be produced at a sacrifice of nearly 8 apples. Instead of the original 50 apples there will now be 42.

Differences in Utility Judgments

We have so far been analyzing the behavior of a single producer or Robinson Crusoe. However, an economy does not consist of a single producer but of innumerable producers. If all made the same value judgments and produced goods at the same costs—meaning, in our simplified model, that each producer would be devoting the same number of hours of work to the production of the same goods as every other producer—then the output of all producers would have the same composition. The whole economy would be no more than the sum of all the similar, even if separate, activities of its members. No new problem would arise. But men do not all have the same tastes, nor do they all produce the same goods with the same expenditure of work-hours.

Let us, therefore, turn to an examination of an economy with more than one single producer-consumer. For simplicity's sake we assume that there are two, A and B. Our single producer valued pears in terms of apples in the manner shown in Figure 2. Suppose that the value, in terms of apples, which A attaches to pears is *less* than our single producer's. Producer B, on the other hand, attaches *greater* value to pears in terms of apples than did our single producer. This situation is pictured in Figure 3. The curve D_a (A's demand for pears in terms of apples) now runs to the left of curve D, the demand curve of our single producer. The demand curve D_b of producer B runs to the right of the former demand curve D.

We can now immediately see how many apples and pears A and B produce, if we assume that the production costs of apples and pears are the same (supply curve S_1), and if we also assume that the original work-rest choice remains valid, i.e. that each works the number of work-hours that is required for the production of 50 apples. A then produces and con-

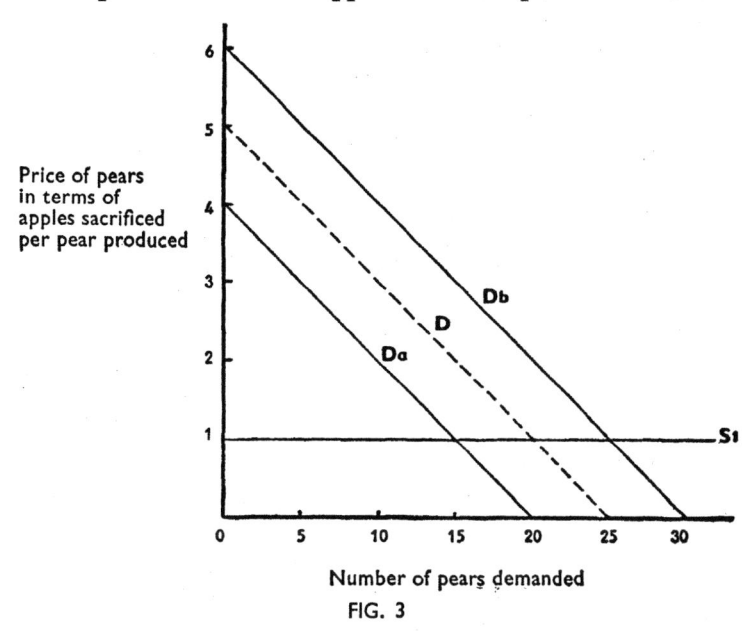

FIG. 3

sumes 15 pears and 35 apples, while B produces and consumes 25 pears and 25 apples. Our single producer produced and consumed 20 pears and 30 apples. A now concentrates more on the production of apples, B more on the production of pears. Even though the production costs of pears, in terms of apples, are the same for both, differences in taste have resulted in a different proportion of pears to apples in each of the two producers' total output.

Differences in Production Costs

We can now take another small step towards reality. It is most unlikely that production costs will be the same for two or more producers. Differences in the ability to produce various goods may be the result of tradition (a man learns the art of producing apples from his father), or of natural conditions (apples grow better on his land than pears). But whatever the reasons, the fact remains that the cost of production of goods in terms of work-hours normally is different for different people.

Figure 2 has shown us what a single producer would produce and consume at various production cost levels, given a certain demand curve, i.e. a certain judgment of the comparative utilities of apples and pears. Suppose now that A can produce pears only at higher cost, i.e. by more work, than B. A may, for instance, be working under conditions represented by the supply curve S_2 in Figure 2 (1 pear can be produced by sacrificing 3 apples), while B may be working under the conditions of supply curve S_3 (1 pear can be produced by sacrificing $\frac{1}{3}$ apple). If the demand curve for A and B were that of our original single producer (D), producer A would now do as the single producer did when faced with supply conditions S_2, i.e. produce 10 pears and 20 apples; at the same time producer B would do as the single producer did when faced with supply conditions S_3, i.e. produce 23 pears and 42 apples.

But the demand curves of A and B differ from those of our single producer; the demand curves now are as D_a and D_b in Figure 3. To demonstrate what will happen, we have only to amalgamate Figures 2 and 3 in Figure 4, which shows: Producer A, with demand conditions D_a and supply conditions S_2, produces 5 pears. To do so he must sacrifice 15 of the original total of 50 apples, leaving him with 35 apples. Producer B, with demand conditions D_b and supply conditions S_3, produces 28 pears at a sacrifice of just over 9 apples, leaving him with nearly 41 apples. A thus produces only 1 pear for every 7 apples—a result of his being both a man with a weaker taste for pears and a poorer producer of them. B produces just over 7 pears for every 10 apples, the result of both greater liking for pears and greater proficiency in their production.

Exchange of Goods

So long as both *A* and *B* produce at the same cost, each sacrificing the same number of working hours for the same quantity of the same product, no exchange takes place between *A* and *B* no matter how different their individual relative valuations of apples and pears may be. Production simply

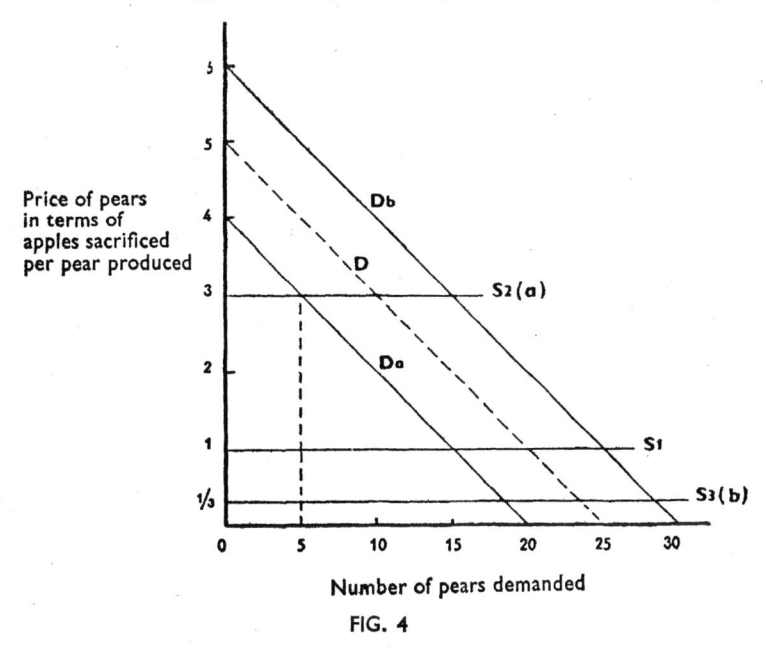

FIG. 4

follows the demand and consumption of the individual producers. But if the production costs of *A* and *B* differ, exchange will take place as soon as they are no longer isolated from each other but able to exchange goods.

As an isolated producer, *A* could produce 5 pears only by exchanging 15 apples *with nature*, since his production costs for pears are those shown by curve S_2 in Figure 4 (1 pear for 3 apples). It would obviously be advantageous for him to produce no pears at all but only apples, and to exchange some of the latter for pears *with B*, whose production costs for pears are those shown by curve S_3 (1 pear for $\frac{1}{3}$ apple). So-called division of labor would be the result. No one any longer produces everything. Labor is divided according to what is to be produced. It should be noted that in our example both *A* and *B* produce apples at the same cost. What differs is the production cost of pears in terms of apples. It is the difference in the relative production cost of apples and pears which makes exchange advantageous.

How could an exchange of products between *A* and *B* be made under the cost condition described? We see that *A* produces 1 pear in the time it takes him to produce 3 apples, and that *B* produces 3 pears in the time it takes him to produce 1 apple. The most advantageous exchange for *A* would be to receive 3 of *B*'s pears in exchange for each of his own apples; and the most advantageous exchange for *B* would be to receive 3 of *A*'s apples in exchange for each of his own pears. Both exchanges are possible, but in either case only one of the producers would gain; by an exchange at any level in between *both* producers could gain.

If *A* gives less than 3 apples for each pear he receives, he gains by the exchange, for his production costs are such that he must sacrifice 3 apples for every pear he produces. On the other hand, if *B* receives more than 1 apple for every 3 pears, he also gains by the exchange, for in his own orchard he must sacrifice 1 apple for every 3 pears he produces. The range within which exchange is advantageous for both producer *A* and producer *B* is therefore between $\frac{1}{3}$ and 3 apples per pear, or between 3 and $\frac{1}{3}$ pears per apple.

The actual exchange rate of apples for pears at which the deal will go through depends, in our two-producer economy in which there are no competing parties in the market, upon the respective bargaining ability of *A* and *B*. All that can be stated with certainty is that the rate is bound to be within definite limits, and even that is contingent upon a rational behavior of both producers—meaning that both try to maximize the advantages to be obtained.

Let us assume that the price of pears expressed in apples will be somewhere between the two extremes, say 1 apple for 1 pear. How many apples and pears will *A* and *B* produce and eventually consume? According to Figure 4 producer *A* obtained his 5 pears by sacrificing 15 apples. The possibility of exchange with *B,* whose production cost of pears in terms of apple production time is lower, makes it advantageous for *A* to obtain his 5 pears by exchange with *B* rather than to produce them himself. He will produce only apples—50 as before. Of these he exchanges 5 for 5 of *B's* pears. Besides his 5 pears he will now have 45 apples, instead of 35 as before. He is better off by 10 apples.

Producer *B* got his 28 pears, according to Figure 4, by sacrificing just over 9 apples. He now exchanges 5 of his pears for 5 apples. He has 23 pears and 46 apples, instead of 28 pears and 41 apples. He, too, gains by the exchange because he could have produced the additional 5 apples himself only by sacrificing 15 pears—instead of 5 as he now does.

Some effects of exchange become immediately evident:

(1) Producer *A* now produces only apples and gets all his pears through exchange with *B;* division of labor is complete as far as he is concerned. Producer *B* still produces 41 apples himself, even though his productivity is much greater for pears than for apples. The reason is that *A* offers him no more apples at a price of 1 : 1. Owing to his lower average productivity *A* is too poor to buy more pears from *B.*

(2) The division of labor resulting from differences of productivity in turn increases differences and degree of productivity by specialization of production and work.

(3) The living standard of both *A* and *B* has risen. This is due to the fact that each producer's own more expensive production has been replaced by the other's cheaper production. In the same way international trade raises the living standard when expensive domestic production is replaced by less expensive foreign production. More expensive production of *all* goods, on the other hand, does not lead to increased exchange of goods either in internal or in foreign trade, but merely causes a fall in the living standard.

(4) The reward for the work done by both *A* and *B* has risen as a result of exchange. The labor demand curve (cf. Figure 1) moves up. *Ceteris paribus* the number of work-hours

will be greater. Thus exchange increases the total output not only through increased productivity due to division of labor, but also through an increase in the amount of work done, due to its higher remuneration.

Exchange and Profits

Exchange increases output through division of labor. We defined profit above (p. 6) as a surplus of output over input. We showed that in the case of the single producer an increase in output can never be considered a profit, because his entire output of goods is always the exact result of his input of labor, regardless of the size of the output per unit of input.

We are now dealing, however, with more than one producer, so that the problem of the distribution of the output between them arises. The term profit could now have two meanings: (*a*) it could mean a surplus accruing to the whole two-man community of producers, a profit for their national economy, so to speak; (*b*) it could also mean a surplus accruing to *one* of the producers by an altered distribution of output, a private advantage for one individual producer over the other.

An increase in output as such cannot be considered a profit for the entire national economy, just as an increase in output cannot be considered a profit in the case of a single producer. The economy, as a whole, is nothing but the sum of all individual producers. It does not make any difference whether the increase in output is due to greater productivity of individual producers or to exchange and division of labor. Therefore exchange, too, cannot lead to a profit for the national economy as a whole.

But how about the increases in the income of the individual producer-consumers resulting from a changed distribution of output among them? Such increases do exist, but not all of them are profits. If an individual producer-consumer's share of the total product rises because his own output increases, this cannot be called a profit—at least not if we are to distinguish profits clearly from other forms of income earned by the factors of production. Profit is only that form of income which accrues to one individual because another individual fails to receive, in certain special circumstances, the entire output to which the "demand curve of nature" entitles him, according to his productivity.

Profit is a slice of somebody else's output. We shall often come back to the question of how such profits arise and how they disappear, because this is of fundamental importance for many other problems. We shall see that profits are children of change and uncertainty and that they are temporary in character. Here we only wish to stress that exchange, as such, does not lead to private profits.

It is true that in our example producer A obtains more pears through exchange with B than he could have produced himself at the same expenditure of work-hours. But this only means that his output per unit of input, his productivity, has increased, even though only indirectly. Nothing accrues to him to which he would not be entitled by his work. And nothing is withheld from B, who retains more apples than if he had not entered into exchange with A.

It is furthermore true that A receives more pears for his apples than would be needed to make the exchange worthwhile to him. But this, too, is not profit. It is an advantage comparable to the advantage that accrues to the isolated producer to whom nature yields a greater return for his intramarginal working hours than would have been necessary to overcome his tendency to do nothing. Such an advantage in exchange does not mean that one receives more than one gives. It means only that one receives more than the minimum necessary to make the exchange possible.

The Entrepreneur

We now take a further step toward reality by introducing the most important person within the framework of a free economy: the entrepreneur.

His functions are manifold; we note only the most important at this point:

(1) The entrepreneur is a sort of exchange center. He intercedes in all the exchange activities which we have described so far in our simplified models.

In our isolated single-producer economic model, the worker exchanged his work-hours with nature against the proceeds of his work, the finished products. In the case of a two-producer economy these goods were then exchanged, at least partly, between the workers. A schematic view of this exchange is pictured in Figure 5.

In the real world the workers generally do not exchange their services directly with nature or with other workers. The

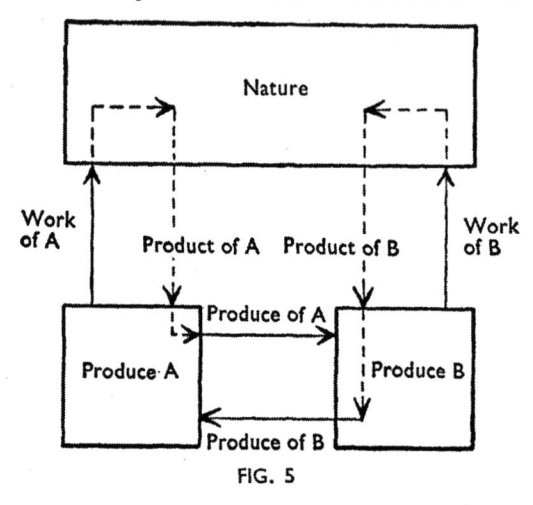

FIG. 5

entrepreneurs intercede in both exchange activities. Our model of an economy of two producers becomes one of an economy of two workers and two entrepreneurs, as schematized in Figures 6a and 6b. In Figure 6a the workers first exchange directly with nature. Entrepreneur *A* then receives the products of the work of worker *A* and exchanges them with entrepreneur *B* for the products of worker *B*. Entrepreneur *B* delivers products of worker *A* to worker *B* in payment for worker *B*'s products, whereas entrepreneur *A* delivers products of worker *B* to worker *A* in payment for worker *A*'s products. In Figure 6b the entrepreneurs have also taken over the workers' exchange with nature. The workers deliver to the entrepreneurs not their products but their work, and it is the entrepreneurs who exchange the workers' work with nature.

THE STATIONARY ECONOMY

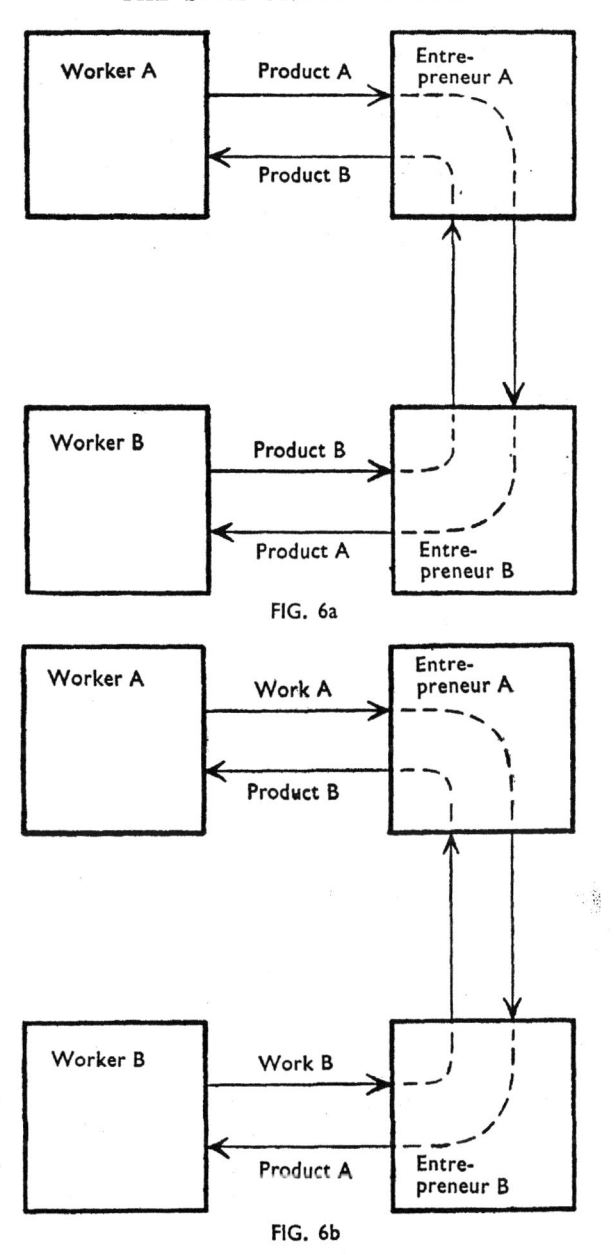

FIG. 6a

FIG. 6b

Each worker, as before, receives for his work the products of the other worker. (Neither model is, as yet, complicated by the existence of money; we are still in a barter economy.)

(2) The entrepreneur is furthermore the beneficiary of production cost differentials. We have assumed above (p. 12) that workers, for various reasons, produce with varying degrees of productivity. To produce the same amount of goods some

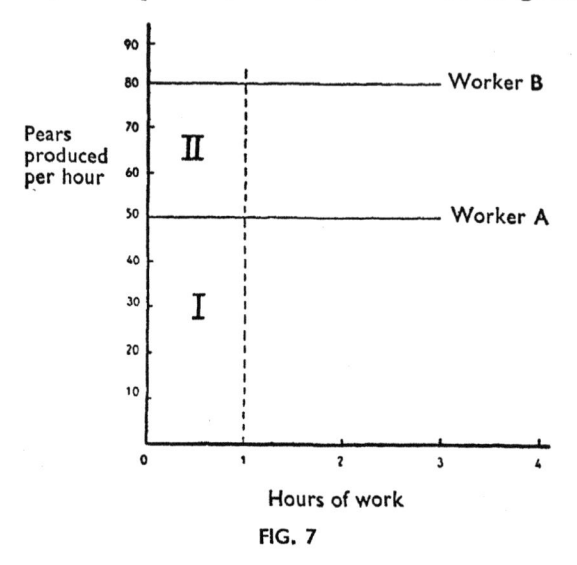

FIG. 7

need a greater, some a smaller, number of work-hours: or, what comes to the same thing, some produce greater and some smaller amounts of goods in the same time. In the real world the greater productivity of the work done is not generally due to some special quality of the worker, but of the enterprise in which he works. It is therefore not the worker but the entrepreneur who reaps the benefits of the higher productivity.

Let Figure 7 represent the hourly output of two workers. Suppose worker *A* produces 50 pears an hour while worker *B* produces 80 pears in the same time. Rectangle I then represents worker *A*'s output per hour, that is 50 pears. Rectangle I and rectangle II together represent worker *B*'s output per hour, that is 80 pears. If it were the difference in the *workers'* efficiency which leads to the differential of 30 pears, the wage of worker *A* would have to be 50 pears, and that of worker *B* 80 pears.

But if not *worker B* but the *enterprise B* in which he works is responsible for the higher output per hour, the owner of this enterprise, entrepreneur *B,* has no reason to pay his workers more than they would produce and receive if they were working in an enterprise of lower productivity—say in enterprise *A,* where 50 pears are produced in an hour. The surplus hourly production of 30 pears, represented in our graph by rectangle II, entrepreneur *B* will keep as a reward for the greater productivity of his enterprise. All workers receive a uniform wage of 50 pears, regardless of the productivity of the enterprise by which they are employed. This is what actually happens in reality. Uniform wage rates are, in principle, paid for the same work.

(3) We have defined profits as income that accrues to some individuals because others do not receive the whole output of their work in special circumstances of a temporary nature. The entrepreneur who keeps as income for himself the additional output of his workers which is due to the higher productivity, not of the workers but of his enterprise, is the profit-maker *par excellence.*

(4) The entrepreneur, however, is also the profit destroyer *par excellence.* If entrepreneur *A* sees that entrepreneur *B* can produce pears at lower cost than he can, he will try—and in the long run he will generally succeed in the attempt—to imitate his competitor's methods of production. As a result entrepreneur *A,* too, will be able to produce 80 pears an hour. The output curve of enterprise *A* in Figure 7 will rise to the level of enterprise *B.* Entrepreneur *A,* too, will make a profit.

This, however, will not be the end of the story. Under the assumption of free competition *A,* as well as *B,* will begin to bid up wages so as to attract workers because any increase in production would enlarge their total profits. The competition for workers will clearly go on until profits are swallowed up by wage increases. Workers will then receive not 50 pears an hour but their whole output, 80 pears an hour. The whole hourly product of labor (rectangle I plus rectangle II) will be paid out as wages. This situation will change only if and when some entrepreneurs succeed in raising the productivity of their enterprises once more.

In a stationary economy, a theoretical model of an economy which goes on each day as it did before, by definition productivity does not change. There can, therefore, be no entrepreneurial profits.

Money

Entrepreneur A can obviously exchange his apples with entrepreneur B, who produces pears, only if he himself needs pears for himself or his workers. If A should prefer butter, he cannot exchange his apples with B because B has produced no butter. Butter may have been produced by C. But if B owns something which is gladly taken by others in exchange for their products, then A can sell his apples to B against this medium and use it in an exchange with C for butter. Nowadays money, mainly paper money, serves as such a medium that is gladly taken by all members of the community in exchange for their products. Money is, therefore, the general medium of exchange.

The chief function of money is to enlarge the number of people between whom exchanges can take place. It is an enlarger of exchange possibilities. It enables any one member of the community to dispose of his goods to any other member, regardless of whether the latter produces anything the first wants; the money received enables him to get the equivalent in goods he wants from a third person.

We have seen above (p. 14) how division of labor increases the productivity of the work done. Division of labor in its turn depends upon the possibility to exchange. Even if B can produce pears at lower cost, this is of no benefit to A so long as B is not prepared to take A's apples in exchange for his pears. It follows that the introduction of money as an enlarger of exchange possibilities must result in increased division of labor and thus in higher output. Since higher output as a rule

THE STATIONARY ECONOMY

increases the amount of hours worked, the introduction of money raises living standards in two ways.

Money works not only as an enlarger of exchange possibilities, but also as an exchange act saver. Before the introduction of money apples wandered from entrepreneur A to entre-

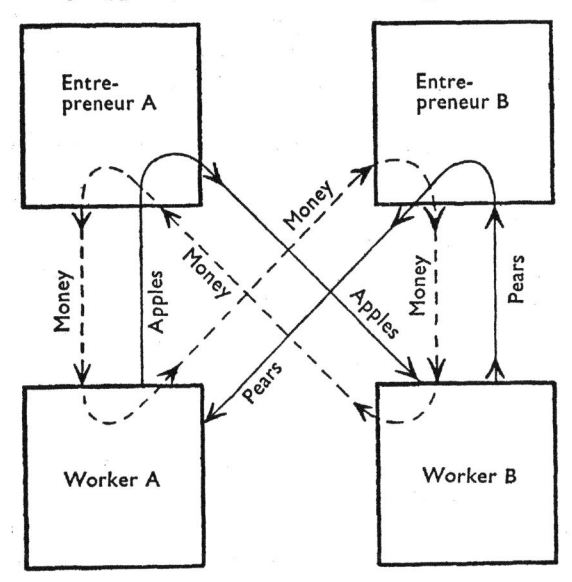

Circulation of money and products
in a two-enterprise two-product economy

FIG. 8

preneur B, who delivered them to his workers, while pears wandered from B to A, who delivered them to his workers—four exchange acts. Now the workers no longer receive the finished goods from their own entrepreneur, who is eliminated as a middleman between them and other entrepreneurs. With the money received from his entrepreneur each worker buys directly from other entrepreneurs—two exchange acts are eliminated.

Figure 8 shows, in very simplified form, the circulation of money in the case of apple production by worker A and pear production by worker B.

Besides being an enlarger of exchange possibilities and an exchange act saver, money has many other important functions. We shall here mention only one of them—that of an indicator of profits, as we can call it.

As we have already seen, there are no profits of the national economy as a whole. In a money economy this is even more obvious than in a barter economy. The same amount of money the entrepreneurs spend on the factors of production—the workers—comes back to them in exchange for their products. Taken as a whole, money received can neither exceed nor be short of money spent—at least so long as the flow of money is not interrupted. This latter assumption applies, by definition, to a stationary economy.

On the other hand, money is clearly the medium in which the private profits of individuals materialize. If an entrepreneur—as described earlier—can manage by his special knowledge and skill to produce 80 pears in one work-hour, instead of 50 as other entrepreneurs do, he spends $37\frac{1}{2}$ per cent less for the production of the same number of pears. The difference will show up as a stock of money not needed for the payment of wages and available for other expenditure. This is the kind of profit we have discussed above; the entrepreneur pays his workers less than the full yield of their work because this yield would be smaller if they worked in another enterprise.

Money is, however, also the indicator of another kind of private profit. It can happen that an entrepreneur makes a profit not, so to speak, at the expense of his workers but at the expense of other entrepreneurs. Entrepreneur A may receive more for his products than corresponds to his input, whereas entrepreneur B receives less. This can obviously not happen in the long run because no entrepreneur will continue spending money on production that he knows he will not get back. But in the short run it might turn out, owing perhaps to a change in tastes, that the consumer-workers spend more money on apples and less on pears than anticipated. The result will be that at the end of the production period the distribution of money among the entrepreneurs will be different from what it was at the beginning. A's stock of money will have grown by the amount that B's has become smaller.

We may, in this connection, add a remark on balance sheets and income statements. These show only the relative prosperity of individual economic subjects, i.e. the extent to which the income and wealth of some entrepreneurs have changed in relation to those of others. They give no information on the absolute wealth of the community because they do not indicate what can be bought with the money amounts shown. A scarcity of goods may lead to fancy prices and hence to higher incomes and capital appreciation for some entrepreneurs. This does not mean that the community's real income or wealth has increased. A community will, on the other hand, have become richer if two-horse carriages have been replaced by 100-horsepower automobiles produced with the same labor effort. But such things cannot be gathered from balance sheets. Simple addition of the balance sheets or income statements of all the members of a community does not, therefore, tell us anything about its real product or income. This should be remembered in appraising some of the usual national income calculations.

The Time Element

Production does not go on in a timeless world. The product is not ready for consumption at the same moment as labor is expended on it. Production takes time.

From this elementary technical fact it follows that the workers cannot consume the products of present labor, but only those of previous labor. In a money economy, the money which the workers receive from their entrepreneurs in wages and spend for their living during any given production period does not buy the products of this same period but those of an earlier period. And by the sale of these products of an earlier period the entrepreneurs receive back the money spent in that earlier period.

All this is unimportant in a stationary economy, where by definition outlays and production do not change from one period to another. But in the real world there are constant changes. Only a model clearly showing the time sequence of events is useful in analysis. It would not be necessary to stress this point were it not for the fact that, under the influence of Keynes' *General Theory of Employment, Interest and Money,* the tendency to use so-called circular analysis, which neglects the time element, has been strengthened.

Circular analysis presupposes that the current income of workers is spent on their current output. This would mean that current production in turn is influenced by current spending. But in reality current spending meets the products of past production which can no longer be influenced by current spending. On the other hand, the fact that a changed demand meets an as yet unchanged supply does lead to price increases and declines and to many other important changes. Only the so-called sequence analysis, as developed especially by Swedish economists, can give a satisfactory picture of these changes. For the analysis of equilibrium situations, for which they are meant in the first place, circular analyses remain permissible but dangerous because they serve very often, consciously or unconsciously, to analyze changes from one equilibrium situation to the other.

As production takes time, and we cannot therefore live from hand to mouth, a certain amount of goods in various stages of production must always be simultaneously present in the economy. Goods ready for consumption are, in the first place, essential for production by enabling the workers to survive during the production period; the other goods, as we shall see later, are essential by enabling the workers to be more productive. We shall call the total stock of these goods the capital of the community, and the individual goods capital goods.

The capital of the community is owned by people commonly called capitalists. For the time being we shall take the ownership situation as historically given. Later we shall inquire into the reasons for capital accumulation and changes in ownership.

In a money economy capitalists do not as a rule actually own the stock of capital goods. They own money and lend it to entrepreneurs, who use the money to pay their workers— who in turn use it to buy goods of a past production period.

As production goes on, new, half finished and finished goods accumulate in the hands of the entrepreneurs. Juridically these goods belong to the entrepreneurs, but economically they belong to the money capitalists because the money used for the production is owned by them. The entrepreneurs are, as it were, the trustees of the money capitalists.

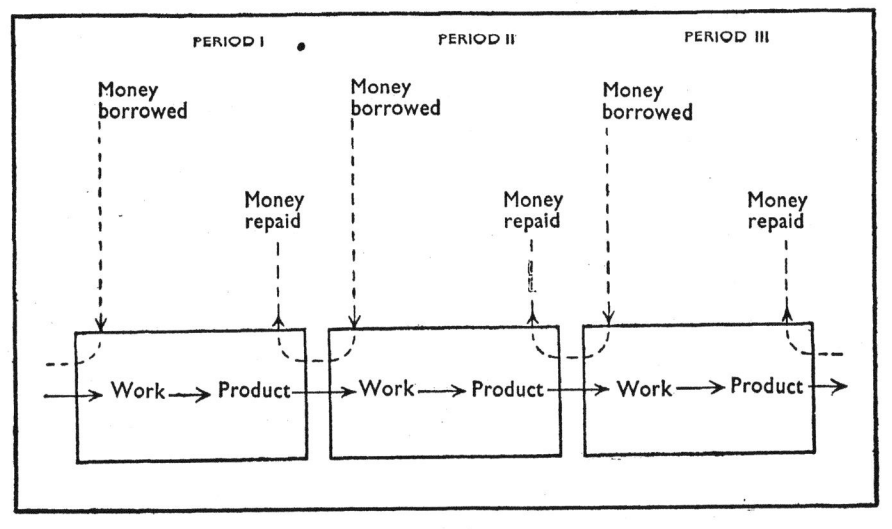

FIG. 9

When the entrepreneurs of the past period sell their products to the workers of the present period, the money they receive enables them to repay their loans and thus to free themselves from their debts to the capitalists.

Figure 9 shows how the money borrowed by an entrepreneur in the current production period is used by his workers to buy the goods produced in a past period, thereby enabling past debts to be repaid.

Expansion of Production Dependent on Capital Accumulation?

Capital is needed to keep the workers alive during the production period. We are therefore faced with the question: to what extent does any increase in employment actually depend upon an increase in capital? We shall deal with this question later in detail. Here we merely wish to make a brief remark on the so-called wage fund theory, which is the classics' answer to this question. This theory assumed that more workers could only be employed if a store of means of subsistence had been accumulated previously by production and abstinence.

This problem—like so many others in economics—is not a real one. The present does not live at all on a store of goods accumulated in the past. The present lives as a rule on goods that flow uninterruptedly from past production into present consumption; stores of goods are neither necessary nor would they be sufficient to enable new workers to be employed. Nor is an increase of production in the past a necessary condition for an increase of the labor force in the present.

What enables an increased labor force to be employed and production to expand is the fact that the entrepreneur obtains money with which to pay new workers. This money may be borrowed from other people who have not consumed all the goods which they were entitled to receive, but have saved some of their income. But even if there are no new savings, employment and production can increase. It is not at all necessary to think of such a thing as a fixed wage fund, as the wage fund theory in its monetary form supposes. The necessary capital can be supplied through savings in other capital needs, or money can simply be created by money-issuing banks, as we shall see in Part III when discussing inflation. Finally, increased employment may not require more capital at all if there is a proportionate fall in wages.

We shall discuss the supply of capital later in detail. Here it suffices to state that neither monetary nor real scarcities need prevent an increase in employment. In whatever way the money with which to pay new workers is made available, its expenditure for labor by the entrepreneurs enforces a redistribution of past products in such a way that the new workers can survive during the current production period.

Amount of Capital Dependent on Volume of Production?

We must sharply distinguish between the question: is the volume of production dependent upon capital accumulation;

and the reverse question: is the amount of capital dependent on the volume of production? The latter question is, of course, to be answered in the affirmative. If more is produced, other things being equal, there is an increase in the amount of capital, i.e. in the amount of goods simultaneously present in the economy—or, better, of goods which reach the future from the present. Such an increase in capital is often spoken of as an increase in the width of the capital structure—just as a river bed becomes wider when the inflow of water increases.

The flow of goods over time has indeed often been compared with the flow of water in a river. It is a useful comparison, and we shall use it to explain many problems in connection with capital.

Amount of Capital and Roundabout Ways of Production

Increase in production is not the only thing which causes the quantity of goods simultaneously present in an economy, the capital of the economy, to increase.

Capital can also increase when production methods become more capitalistic, more roundabout. We can illustrate our argument by returning to our comparison of the flow of goods over time with the flow of water in a river bed. If the river bed becomes wider it can contain more water than before. But the same happens also if the length of two successive river beds increases. The two streams will then overlap, as it were; the first will still be flowing when the second emerges. More water will be present simultaneously. In the same way, the goods simultaneously present in an economy must increase if production takes more time. Figure 10 illustrates this. If production takes twice as long as before, the goods previously ready for consumption at the end of Period I will now not be consumed until the end of Period II, and will therefore still be present in the economy during Period II when a new production process has already started.

The classical roundabout method of production is production by machines: a worker no longer works by hand or with a few tools, but with the help of a machine.

When a worker changes over to machine production, a new

factor of production appears to have been introduced. This, however, is not the case. In the first place the machine itself consists of labor—in so far as it does not consist of raw material, which we disregard for the moment. In the second place, the machine does not really transform the worker's work. What happens is that his present work is added to the work already incorporated in the machine.

The labor incorporated in the machine differs, however, from the labor added in the current production period in that

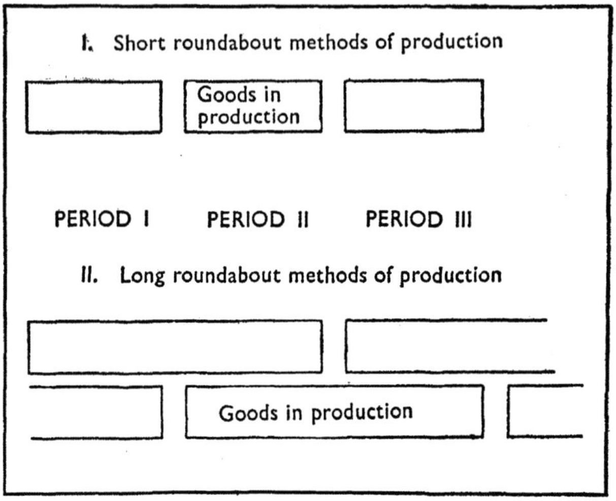

I. Short roundabout methods of production

Goods in production

PERIOD I PERIOD II PERIOD III

II. Long roundabout methods of production

Goods in production

FIG. 10

it is work done long before the current period, and that its result is normally not consumed during the immediately following production period but in a later one. On the average, the machine remains in the production process much longer. It is consumed only over long periods. During these periods the labor incorporated in the machines, together with the labor added in running the machines, goes over into the finished goods. Even if the worker can thus produce more quickly with the help of the machine than he could without it the entire production process lasts much longer. It starts not with the current work of the worker using the machine but with the production of the machine itself, and it ends not with the goods completed currently with the help of the machine but with the last goods which the machine is still able to turn out. Only when the machine ceases to be usable at all has the last of the original labor incorporated in it gone over into finished products. This is why production with more capital, with a strengthened—or, as is sometimes said, a deepened—capital structure, takes more time.

How does an economy change from a less into a more capitalistic one; how does its capital structure deepen? If all the money the entrepreneurs borrow is spent by their workers on consumer goods there is, on our assumptions about their replacement needs, obviously no possibility for entrepreneurs to buy machines. But suppose the workers, or other factors of production who would in the ordinary course of events spend their income on consumption, decide to save and to put the savings at the disposal of the entrepreneurs: then the entrepreneurs would be able to buy capital goods with the money otherwise spent on consumption.

Once the economy has changed over to roundabout methods of production, no further additional saving is needed for their maintenance. The capital structure is deepened once and for all. For the finished goods into which the capital goods are ultimately converted are sold against money. And with this money the entrepreneurs are again able to repay their debts to the capitalists, who can then lend it to them again without recourse to new savings. Figure 11 shows this flow of money.

Needless to say, different goods require production detours of entirely different lengths. Productions taking detours of quite different lengths are therefore always present in an economy. The production detour of domestic help is very short. For the building of houses and skyscrapers the production detour is very long. But if the capital structure is deepened, every production detour lengthens, although not in the same proportion. The new vacuum cleaner used by domestic help, too, means a longer production detour.

The deepening of the capital structure, the lengthening of

FIG. 11

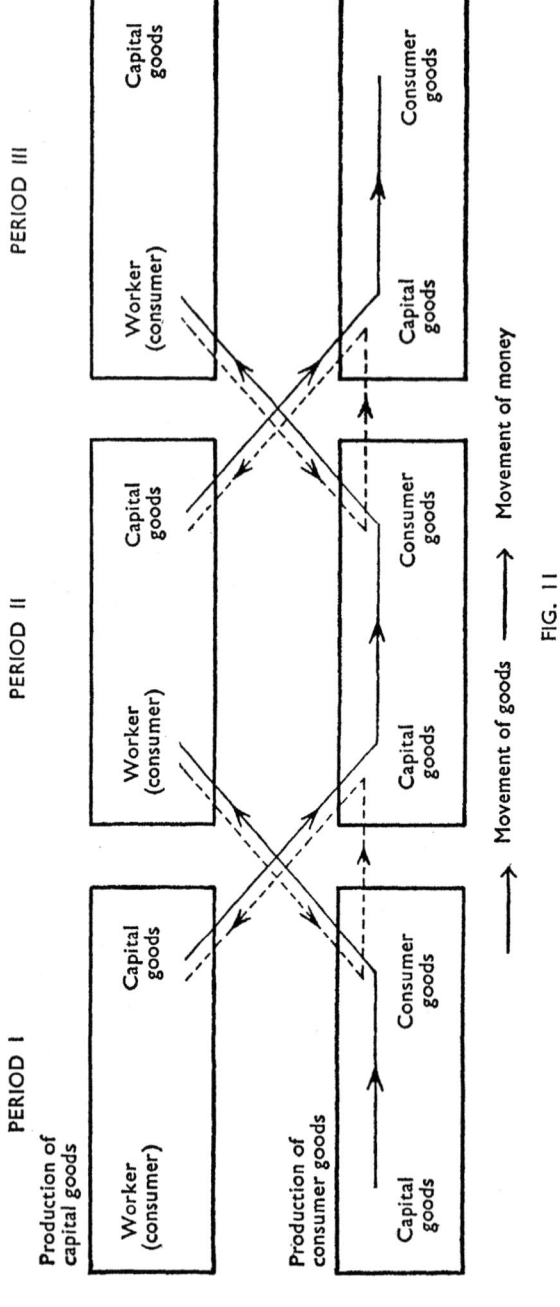

production detours, lead to increased production not by the employment of more workers but by an increase in the productivity of the single worker. Work spent on building and then on using a machine yields technically higher results than work applied immediately to the production of the end product. It is more productive.

But the reason for this increased productivity is not that the services of a machine are essentially different from those of a worker. If the machines really performed different work, if they were a different factor of production, it would be impossible for the price of machines to coincide in the long run, as it does, with their cost price. They would sell at a premium. The reason for the increased productivity is that the results of the work embedded in the machine need be available for consumption only after a longer period, that production—or consumption—is allowed to take more time. *This "being allowed to take more time" is really the second factor of production, capital—if labor is considered the first.*

The entrepreneur who works with machines can repay the money he borrowed from capitalists for the purpose of production only after the amortization of the machines. Per unit of product he thus needs more credits than before the extension of production detours (cf. Figures 10 and 11). For the right to use credits, and thereby to be allowed to take more time —and not for the individual capital good—he has to pay a certain compensation calculated in percentage of the amount of the credits and according to their duration. It is called interest.

What is a Stationary Economy?

This whole first part of our exposition is concerned with the working of a stationary economy. It may be useful to say a few words here on the meaning of this term, in order that the reader may follow the subsequent discussions.

When we speak of a stationary economy, we do not mean an economy in which production and consumption come to a stop. In a stationary economy production and consumption always repeat themselves in the same manner because there are no forces at work which could change them. It is an economy whose course is always exactly repeated. Such an economy does not exist in reality. But it is important to examine how such a fictitious economy would work, so as to be better able to analyze the effects of changes in important data.

The stationary economy is also often referred to as an economy in equilibrium, meaning an economy which has adjusted itself to all past and is not exposed to any further changes.

Production Exchange and Consumption Exchange

We began our economic analysis with the examination of the extremely simplified model of an economy of one isolated worker-producer. Here one single exchange act took place. The worker supplied his work to nature against products and nature demanded his work for them. We have since introduced three important features into this simple world: the entrepreneur, money and the time element.

Through their introduction the single-exchange economy is essentially changed. It becomes a two-exchange economy. Here exchange for production and for consumption are separated into two acts. The worker supplies his work no longer to nature for her products, but to the entrepreneur who demands the work against money. In a second exchange, some time later, the entrepreneur supplies the finished product to the worker who demands it against money. Money thereby serves as a sort of general representative of *utility*. Both the workers and the entrepreneurs value money according to the utility of the goods and services it buys on the market at current prices.

The separation of the production exchange from the consumption exchange does not, however, change the fundamental fact that in a stationary economy production and consumption are always equal. During every production period all factors of production together consume what they produce, or rather what they have produced in the past production period. And during every period the factors of production produce what they consume, or rather what they are going to consume in the subsequent period.

The Fundamental Problems of Economics

The fundamental problems with which economics is concerned can be summarized in two sets of questions. First, what goods and how many of them are produced; by what methods and by whom are they produced? And second, what goods and how many of them are consumed; by what methods and by whom are they consumed?

In a capitalist and competitive economy production and consumption are dependent on each other. Production creates income for the factors of production, and the spending of this income leads to consumption. The size and distribution of income of individuals as well as of whole groups depend on the size of total production, on what each contributes to production, and on the remuneration for this contribution. Consumption, in its turn, depends on the size and distribution of income from production. Production again depends on consumption, because the consumer by his demand determines what is to be produced. Production influences consumption, and consumption influences production.

The fact that the elements of the system are interdependent does not, however, make the system undetermined. Given certain supply schedules for the factors of production and certain demand schedules for finished products, the quantity and nature of the goods to be produced and consumed are perfectly determined. A logical chain leads from production to consumption and back. To determine the beginning of that chain is just as impossible as to establish the priority of the chicken or the egg. Every phase presupposes a preceding phase—which, however, can only be described subsequently. Since a beginning has to be made with some link of the chain, we shall for convenience sake begin by describing the production exchange. We shall inquire first what and how much is produced, by whom and by what methods production is carried on, and how the factors of production are remunerated.

Production Exchange: Production by Labor Alone

If goods were produced by labor alone there would be no problems of capitalist methods of production or of income distribution among groups of different factors of production, particularly between labor and capitalists. There would be only the problem of what and how much is produced. This problem depends, of course, on what the factors of production wish to consume, or better on how they wish to distribute their income on the purchase of various goods. But this is a problem of consumption with which we shall deal later.

Here we have only to state how much, in terms of work-hours, will be produced. The question is easily answered according to what we have already explained above. If labor were the only factor of production, work would be put into production up to the point where the money received for the work is no longer considered equivalent to the sacrifice of leisure. Money is valued here, we must remember, not for its own utility but for the utility of the goods that can be bought with it on the market according to the prevailing prices. Thus more work will be done, and production will increase either when higher rewards are offered for work—for instance, when the productivity of labor has risen—or when the workers are prepared to accept lower wages. We shall discuss this later in more detail. Here we shall but briefly anticipate: in a simple diagram like that of Figure 1 or 4 higher wage offers would mean an upward shift in the demand curve for labor, whereas willingness to work for less money would be expressed by a downward shift in the labor supply curve. It will readily be seen that both movements would result in an increase of the volume of production.

Hourly wages, i.e. the remuneration per work-hour, will —in case of a downward shift of the labor supply curve— remain unchanged so long as the demand curve for labor is horizontal. But as soon as other factors contribute to production, the demand curve for labor (for reasons to be discussed later) will run down to the right, indicating that entrepreneurs are prepared to employ additional labor only at lower wages. In this case—we shall return to it later—a lowering of the

THE STATIONARY ECONOMY

labor supply curve leads to a fall in wages. At the same time, as we shall see, the income accruing to other factors of production increases. The individual worker receives a smaller *share* of the community's whole cake. But the whole cake has grown because more bakers are at work, which in turn is due to the fact that the individual bakers are content with smaller *slices* of cake. The total *amount* of cake received by *all* the bakers now employed, however, and even their share of it, will have become larger.

We are thus led to the important conclusion that, given an unchanged demand situation, a reduction in the individual worker's share in the result of production is accompanied by an increase of the total product, whereas an increase in his share would entail a reduction of the total product—except under quite unrealistic assumptions concerning the elasticity of demand for labor and the elasticity of supply of other production factors.

We shall see again and again the working of this peculiar law, according to which changes in the remuneration of *one* factor of production lead to opposite changes in the volume of the total product.

We shall examine later on, in Part III, whether changes in wages can in certain special conditions influence the aggregate demand for goods, and whether, for instance, wage increases need not have the expected production-curtailing effects. Notwithstanding the possibility of influencing the volume of production by influencing demand, the fundamental fact remains that wage increases *curtail* production. This is a fact often overlooked nowadays by those who overrate the possible secondary effects of wage changes.

There is in a money economy a certain difficulty not existing in a pure barter economy: an increased product cannot be exchanged through the medium of the same amount of money unless the price level declines. We shall, for the time being, evade this difficulty by assuming that enough new money is always introduced into the system to prevent a decline in the price level. The price stability so ensured does not, however, imply wage stability. If labor becomes more modest in its wage demands, the wage level falls relative to the price level. The difference between the amount of money spent on wages and the amount of money received from sales accrues to other factors of production as income.

Production by Labor and Capital

Goods are not in the real world produced by labor alone. Capital is another factor of production. We have described above the nature and significance of capital. Production can require more or less capital. Even in the most primitive circumstances some capital is needed for the survival of the workers during the production period. Modern production, with its very roundabout methods, needs much more capital. As production detours lengthen—say double—a double amount of capital must be in the hands of entrepreneurs. In a modern economy work is directed into roundabout methods of production by entrepreneurs, who borrow money in the form of credits from banks or in various forms from other money owners and spend that money on capital goods. If entrepreneurs should wish to double the length of the production detours, they would need to borrow a double amount of investable funds. The length of production detours depends, therefore, on the supply of and demand for investable funds.

Investable funds are directly or indirectly supplied by people who save money instead of spending it on consumption. How large is the *supply* of investable funds by savers? In a stationary economy, where changes are excluded by definition, we have to ask: how large is the total stock of savings? We do not ask how large is any addition to the stock by new saving. New savings are not necessary to uphold the *status quo* of production detours. The money received from the sale of finished products enables the entrepreneurs always again to acquire the capital goods or semi-finished products they need.

The amount of saving offered is, like every supply in a free economy, a function of the price, i.e. the interest rate. The question of how the supply curve for savings runs in general is controversial. Some people deny that the supply curve runs in the usual way upward to the right, which would indicate that more is saved and more savings offered at a higher interest rate. These authors assume that the curve runs vertically, meaning that the amount of savings is independent of the interest rate. This may or may not be the case. The important point here is that the curve never runs horizontally, i.e. that the supply is never unlimited.

Note that we are here dealing with the question of how much will be saved out of a given income. The further question, how changes in income call forth changes in savings, will be treated later when dealing with the changing economy. The latter question should never detract attention from the former.

What, on the other hand, will be the shape and level of the *demand* curve for credits, i.e. how much capital will be demanded at the various interest rates? In other words, how much interest will the entrepreneurs be prepared to pay for various amounts of capital?

Capital increases the productivity of the labor used in production. Suppose the length of detours of x years of a production in which y dollars are simultaneously invested is increased by 10 per cent of x years. They then obviously need simultaneously 110 per cent of y credits. Suppose that by such an increase of length the annual product increases by an amount equivalent to the output of three workers. Then, obviously, the entrepreneurs would be prepared to pay for the additional credit necessary an interest sum *pro anno* corresponding to the wages of three workers. If the next extension of production detours would again increase the product by the same amount, the entrepreneurs would again be prepared to pay interest corresponding to the wages of three workers. The demand curve would run horizontally. For every additional new quantity of capital the same interest would be offered.

But in reality every additional quantity of capital is less valuable than the former. Therefore the demand curve for credits does not run horizontally but downward to the right. So if the supply of capital increases, the interest rate must decline.

The Law of Diminishing Marginal Returns

This is due to the so-called law of diminishing marginal returns, with which we have to get acquainted now. It is a technical law. It is concerned with the technical productivity of one factor of production used in combination with another.

The law states that, given a certain amount of one factor—labor for instance—the addition of every further unit of the other factor—e.g. capital—increases the productivity of the first factor, but in a decreasing degree. The validity of this law will readily be understood if we consider that an amount of capital applied to labor, for instance in the form of a hammer, is likely to raise the productivity of labor much more than the same amount of capital used for the last refinement of a capitalistic process. This law of diminishing returns, or better diminishing marginal returns, means that the entrepreneurs will be able to pay less interest for every additional amount of capital.

We can now establish how much capital will be used in our stationary economy. Just as on every other market, the quantities borrowed and lent on the credit markets are determined by the intersection point of the demand and the supply curves. Capital will be saved and employed in production up to the point where the higher interest demanded for additional credits can no longer be paid by the entrepreneurs because the additional amounts of capital no longer increase productivity to a corresponding degree. The lending price for capital, the interest rate, is determined by the marginal supply of and the marginal demand for credits.

It should be noted in this connection that the question of combination of capital and labor is not identical with the question of the optimum size of the plant. Nor should either question be confused with the question of the optimum combination of so-called fixed and variable capital. These questions will be treated later on. They do not exist in a stationary economy, where we must assume that adjustments to the optimum size of plants and to the optimum combination of fixed and variable capital have already taken place.

Production Factors are Remunerated according to their Marginal Utility

It is sometimes said that the distribution of the proceeds of production takes place according to the contribution of the factors of production to the total product. Labor receives what is to be imputed to labor; the capitalist receives what is to be imputed to capital. But this is an antiquated and over-simplified way of expression. In reality, the worker, equipped with a certain amount of capital, produces a certain amount of goods —no doubt more than he would have produced without capital equipment. But once labor is so equipped, it is impossible to find out how much of the product is to be imputed to labor and how much to capital. The product is just the result of productive labor. The only thing which can be discovered is how much the product has increased by the addition of the last unit of capital. We can calculate the so-called marginal productivity of capital.

The marginal productivity of capital determines not only the amount of capital used at a given supply of capital; it also determines what part of the total product is branched off and accrues to the capitalists in the form of interest payments. This part is by no means equivalent to the total amount by which production has increased owing to the use of capital. It is less because in accordance with the law of diminishing returns the marginal productivity of capital is less than its intra-marginal productivity. The benefits of the intra-marginal productivity of capital accrue to the workers in the form of higher wages. They cannot be distinguished from the productivity of labor as such.

Production with Land

In addition to labor and capital there is allegedly a third factor of production—land. The production factor labor is always used in conjunction with or on the production factor land. Only the combination of labor and land—plus capital which draws production into detours—leads to the production of goods.

Land is needed in agriculture because we can sow and reap

harvests only on land. Land is also necessary for every other production. The workers have to work somewhere. They cannot work in the clouds.

Economics is usually concerned only with agricultural land or urban landed property. But coal or oil fields are also land. There is no difference of principle between land yielding wheat and land yielding coal, or a river used for navigation or water power. We shall treat as land every part of the surface of our earth that yields space and natural resources, such as coal, minerals and so on. The sea, too, can be considered land in this sense.

Land was formerly defined as the eternal and indestructible basis of all production. This is too narrow and even a wrong definition. If the soil is not conserved, it gets exhausted as do oil wells and coal mines.

As a site for production and consumption land indeed renders eternal services. Its utility to man can, however, vary within wide limits. It can increase, for instance, by the introduction of new means of communication.

The utility of land is identical with the utility of all services rendered by it. If these services are limited, in time the value of land is generally considered as the sum of all these services. In so far as the services are eternal, land is valued as the carrier of recurring annual yields. As we shall presently see, the price of land is equal to the money value of these annuities, capitalized at the prevailing interest rate.

Is Land a Third Production Factor?

It is customary to speak of land and of the products of nature as a third factor of production besides labor and capital. It is equally customary to assume that land and its services can generally be rented for "rent"—as capital is borrowed for interest.

This approach is unrealistic and leads to analytical difficulties. It cannot be denied that land, such as coal and oil fields, is often rented for use or exploitation. Machines, too, are sometimes rented. However, it is far more general for entrepreneurs to buy and not to rent the land where they intend to build their plant, just as they buy their machines rather than hire them.

If we treat land in principle as being rented rather than bought, then we neglect in our analysis the fact that land has to be carried through time just as other capital goods, that it takes credits to do so and that, therefore, an entrepreneur buying land with borrowed money thereby influences interest rates.

Entrepreneurs themselves make no distinction of principle between buying labor, machines or land. Their calculations distinguish only between two totally different kinds of costs: on the one hand the annually recurring interest they pay for the money they borrow, and on the other hand the prices they pay, once only, for labor, capital goods or land bought with the borrowed money. There is for an entrepreneur no difference between a machine in his plant and the land of the site of his plant, just as there is no difference of principle between labor and machines. Machines are labor of previous production periods. Nor can in many cases the land component be distinguished in practice from the labor component.

We shall thus treat land as a sort of capital good, provided by nature rather than by man. We shall consider only two factors of production: first labor, including land as a carrier of services, for which the entrepreneur has to pay a price; and second money capital or credit, for which he has to pay interest.

The Price of the Services of Land

There remains, of course, the question of the pricing of land. Its price will obviously depend on the services land offers to entrepreneurs, including in particular agricultural entrepreneurs, i.e. farmers—just as in a slave society the price of a slave would depend on his services. In a society of free men, of course, only the services have a price and not the man who renders them.

Land, just as capital, is useful to the entrepreneur because it replaces work. This seems paradoxical at first sight, for in raising a crop land does not merely replace labor but is indispensable. It can never be replaced even by the greatest number of workmen. But the absolute absence of land is a limiting case that can be neglected for analytical purposes.

Given a certain area of land and certain amounts of labor, every addition of land for cultivation will increase the productivity of the existing workers and thus replace workers, just as every additional worker will increase the productivity of the existing land and thus replace land.

However, here too we meet the law of diminishing returns, as in the case of the productivity of capital discussed above (p. 40). The productivity of a given number of workers cultivating land of a given quality will increase with the addition of more and more acres, though in a decreasing degree.

Entrepreneurs will obviously be prepared to bid for the service of every additional unit of land an amount as high as the wages of the workers that the addition of this unit can replace. Given a certain supply curve of land services the price of the service is herewith determined.

Land serves not only production but consumption too. A nation's most important durable consumer good is its housing stock. Houses cannot be built on air—they have to be built on land. The value of urban landed property depends on how much of their income consumers are willing to spend for living in certain districts. In essence the problems involved are the same as those we have been discussing earlier in connection with the choice between the consumption of apples and pears.

The Price of Land

In the real world entrepreneurs do not buy the services of land as they do the services of workers. They either rent or buy the land as a carrier of services. It is the usefulness of the services which determines the rent as well as the purchase price of land. The rent for a certain period, say one year, is equal to the value of all the services the land renders during the year. The latter, too, are called rent. But what are the principles which determine the price of land to be bought? One would expect the price of land to be equivalent to the sum of the prices of all the services it renders. But the following has to be considered.

In so far as the services of land are perpetual, the price of land would obviously have to be infinitely high, were it not for the fact that the purchase price is paid in money and that money if lent as credit also yields a perpetual service, namely the interest the lender goes on receiving. Thus the price of land must stabilize at the point where the interest on the purchase price is equal to the price of the service the land renders during a certain period. In other words the price of land is, in principle, the price of its service capitalized at the long-term interest rate for credits. If the service is worth $5 a year, and the interest rate is 3 per cent, then the price of the land is $166, for $\frac{5}{x} = \frac{3}{100}$, therefore $x = \frac{500}{3} = 166$.

If the services of the land—of a coal field for instance—are not perpetual but last only, say, 10 years, the calculation is somewhat more complicated. In this case it is not possible to compare the rent with the interest payments because only the latter are perpetual. One has to compare the present utility of the money on the one hand and that of the annual services of the land on the other. The money is, of course, worth its face value. But if a unit of land annually yields $5 for 10 years, it is worth not 5 × 10, or $50, but less. Since present money yields interest as of today, whereas the annuities yield interest only as of their payment, the annuities can only be valued at a so-called discount. At an interest rate of 3 per cent, land yielding $5 during 10 years and nothing thereafter would be worth about $43.

It may be asked: why is the price of land equal to the capitalization of the services it yields, whereas machines sell at production cost? The answer is that machines can never cost more than their production costs, for their number can be increased at will by payment of these costs. Nor can the productivity advantages of a machine ever be greater than the interest on the cost price calculated for the lifetime of the machine. If the advantages were greater than this amount of interest ever new machines would be constructed. Land, on the other hand, is produced by nature once and for all. It is scarce and cannot be increased by work. Its services are fixed and are not influenced either by production costs or rates of interest. But since in the long run money lent as credit and money invested in land must offer the same yield, the price of land must stabilize at a level where the interest on the purchase price equals the price of the services. Changes in the interest rate must, therefore, entail inverse changes in the price of land. A falling interest rate raises land prices and vice versa.

Differential Rents and Differential Prices

Land is not homogeneous, as we have assumed so far. It differs in quality. One of the chief qualitative differences of land rendering comparable services in other respects is the result of differences in distance from production and consumption centers.

Suppose the last additional unit of what we could call standard land, cultivated by 1,000 workers, increases the productivity of those thousand workers by the product of five workers. There may exist other land of which the last unit, added to an equal area, increases the productivity of the same number of workers by the product of three, two or one worker. There may even exist land of such poor quality that additional amounts do not increase the product at all—marginal land.

Except for this last-mentioned case, entrepreneurs will be prepared to pay money for all land, but obviously less than for standard land. Their bids for various sorts of land will vary according to the work-replacing capacity of the land. Land of which additional quantities add nothing to the productivity of a given number of workers is worthless and generally free, i.e. it is nobody's property.

The classical economists explained all the advantages accruing to the owner of land—they called them rent or ground rent—by the fact that good land yields more than bad land. In a certain sense all ground rent is indeed differential rent. But in this sense all wages, too, are differential rents. They are the difference between what is paid to a worker of high and to a worker of low or zero productivity. But the differential rent theory does not explain the laws according to which land of a given quality cultivated by a given number of workers is to be valued. Nor does this theory explain the point at which land becomes marginal.

The expression rent, and more particularly ground rent, for all the benefits land yields to its owners is none the less still in current use.

Obviously land of very different quality is used simultaneously, but as land of lower quality yields less vast acreages of it are equivalent to small areas of good land.

Differential rents and differential prices caused by quality differences should not be confused with the rents and prices of homogeneous land of a certain quality worked by a given number of workers.

Homogeneous land of a certain quality yields its owner a revenue which corresponds to the additional productivity of the last unit of such land taken into use. The benefit of the higher productivity of preceding units accrues to the workers in the form of wages.

Land of inferior quality yields less revenue according to its lower productivity. Compared with the rent of such inferior land the rent of the better land is indeed a differential rent.

Rent from good land can never be higher than rent from inferior land offered at correspondingly lower prices. Scarcity of land is a relative concept. With correspondingly higher demand inferior or more distant land is taken into use. The "frontier" moves further out.

Land Prices, Wages and Interest Rates

We have so far examined what determines the value of the services of land and its price on the assumption that the number of workers and the amount of investable funds are given. In reality neither is ever given; both are subject to constant change.

We shall examine the effects of changes in the supply of and the demand for capital and labor later on. Here, only a few preliminary remarks.

If the supply price of labor, i.e. the wage demands, declines, more workers can be employed, as explained earlier. Given a certain amount of land, each worker will then have less land to work on. The law of diminishing returns works in the opposite direction. The productivity, i.e. the labor-replacing capacity of the land, becomes greater. The rent from land increases.

If the supply price of capital, i.e. interest, declines, the cost of production declines. But the cost reductions vary according to the length of the production detours. With short production detours costs decline to a lesser degree than they do with long production detours, because capital costs enter into the former less than into the latter. Now the use of land means a long, in fact an infinitely long, production detour. If somebody borrows money to buy land, he has to pay interest on this money in eternity in order to profit from the land's equally eternal and not amortizable benefits.

For this reason a lowering of interest rates must mean a very substantial reduction in the cost of the use of land. This reduction in costs will result in sub-marginal land becoming marginal. This land will now yield a revenue even though its technical productivity has not risen. All land prices will go up until the—now lower—interest on the—now higher—prices is again equal to the rent.

Variable and Fixed Capital

We have already mentioned that the production detours made possible through the use of capital are of different lengths. Labor used for the construction of a machine and labor used in working a machine represent the most important examples of such differences in length. In the former case the product of labor is fully consumed only when the machine is worn out; in the latter case labor—including work for the production of raw materials fed to the machine—is as a rule consumed not long after input. Capital which cannot be consumed or converted to other uses until after protracted time periods, such as machines, industrial plants and so on, is called fixed capital. Capital such as that embodied in the consumption fund for workers or in raw materials, which can quickly be consumed or easily be switched into other forms of capital, is called variable capital. There is, however, no sharp borderline between the two kinds of capital.

It is often contended that fixed and variable capital have to be combined in a certain way for technical reasons. It is assumed that a certain number of workers, a certain amount of raw material, and a certain amount of capital equipment must be combined if optimum results are to be achieved. This view, however, over-simplifies the problem.

There are really two problems involved which have to be clearly distinguished. On the one hand, there is the problem of the combination of variable and fixed capital generally, and, on the other, the combination of variable and fixed capital frozen into certain forms.

As regards the first problem we must remember that work as such can always be applied to simple and relatively inexpensive as well as to complicated and relatively expensive machinery, and that raw materials can be transformed into goods with the help of the former as well as of the latter. In other words the amount of fixed capital is never determined *a priori*. The use of fixed capital is determined by the same laws as is the use of capital in general. It is applied up to the point where the cost of additional fixed capital is still matched by a corresponding increase in productivity.

Now the demand for fixed capital is much more sensitive with respect to interest rates than is the demand for variable capital. Whether credits are available at 3 per cent or at 4 per cent makes hardly any difference if they are used for wage payments, but a great difference if they are used to buy real estate or to build factories. The reason is that in the first case small amounts, and in the second case large amounts, of credit are needed per unit of finished goods. It is, therefore, the height of the interest rate which, at a given marginal productivity of fixed and variable capital, determines the way in which both are combined. There is no *a priori* optimum combination.

The second problem, that of the optimum combination of variable and fixed capital frozen into certain forms, is a short-run problem which does not arise in a stationary economy, where by definition the length of production detours does not alter any more, and where, therefore, it is immaterial whether capital is frozen into certain forms or not.

The second problem is not concerned with the question whether workers should, for instance, work with hand tools or at one huge steam hammer. It is concerned with the question of what happens when there is a change in the combination of variable and fixed capital once the steam hammer is installed —for instance if workers are dismissed or new workers taken on. It is the combination of variable capital with certain existing capital goods rather than with fixed capital as such that is at stake.

Suppose employment is curtailed because wages have gone up or prices gone down, as the latter do in depressions. Then the entrepreneur uses less variable capital. But the use of fixed capital frozen into certain capital goods like machines, plants, etc., cannot be undone retroactively. The fixed capital and the charges payable on it remain the same even when the entrepreneur has curtailed his use of variable capital. This leads, indeed, to combinations of variable and fixed capital which cannot be optimal.

In the long run, however, there cannot be other than optimum combinations between variable and fixed capital; they are determined by the productivity of fixed capital and of variable capital respectively and by the interest rate.

The Size of the Firm

Not to be confused with the problem of the best combination of variable and fixed capital is the problem of the optimum size of the firm, that is of how many units of combinations of fixed and variable capital should be joined together physically and/or financially in one place or under one management.

In practice this is a question difficult to decide. In theory the answer is easy. There is one particular size for each firm at which its costs are lowest. If the firm is smaller, its overhead expenses per unit of product increase. If the firm is larger, bureaucratic methods, for instance, lead to the same result. The task in practice is to determine the exact size at which the cost-increasing forces are at their minimum.

In a stationary economy deviations from the optimum size of firms are excluded by definition. Here it has to be assumed that the adjustment to the best size has taken place and no more changes occur. It is only when the output of an industry suddenly increases or decreases that the size of an enterprise may turn out to be larger or smaller than optimal. Entrepreneurs continue to produce in the existing plant, rather than close down factories or build new ones.

Even if entrepreneurs manage in such cases to combine fixed and variable capital in the optimum way, they will still be faced with the difficulty that the single firm may have become too large or too small. In either case unit costs increase.

Variable and Fixed Costs. Total Costs. Unit Costs and Marginal Costs

The use of fixed and variable capital involves certain expenditures. During a production period—or as we may assume at its beginning—entrepreneurs spend money on variable capital goods, particularly raw materials and labor. These expenditures, which include also interest payments to the capitalists who lend the money so used, are called variable costs of production. Entrepreneurs furthermore have to spend money for those parts of their fixed capital goods that are being consumed during the period. (The main part of the fixed capital is carried over into the next production period as the capital stock.) These expenditures, which include also the interest payments on fixed capital, are called fixed costs. Variable and fixed costs together are called total costs of production.

The combination of fixed and variable costs is, of course, a function of the combination of fixed and variable capital. This means that in the long run there is no special problem of optimum combination of variable and fixed costs. In the short run there is such a problem: variable capital declines or increases—with declining or increasing output—whereas the fixed capital frozen in certain capital goods remains the same. Therefore variable costs fluctuate, whereas fixed costs remain more or less stable. This has certain consequences for the so-called unit costs, i.e. the total costs divided by the number of units produced.

If less is produced than anticipated when the fixed capital goods were installed, the entrepreneurs will have more machinery, land, etc., in hand than they need for the smaller output. Fixed costs do not decline as much as output. As they have to be distributed over a smaller production, unit costs increase.

If more is produced than anticipated variable costs rise—for instance because work can be organized rationally only in a factory which has been appropriately enlarged. This, too, leads to an increase in unit costs.

Unit costs will thus be lowest when production is exactly of the size which long-run plans anticipated it to be. When production is smaller the stability of fixed costs, when it is larger the increase in variable costs, will tend to give an uplift to unit costs.

All this is treated very elaborately, too elaborately perhaps, in the usual textbooks on economics. The development of unit costs is usually represented by a graph, which we reproduce in Figure 12 in a form which though greatly simplified is sufficient for the purposes of our argument. The graph shows three kinds of curve: the marginal cost curve, the unit cost curve and three price lines. The marginal cost curve indicates at what additional cost additional units can be produced. The price lines show the price the product can bring on the market. Production, as we know, expands up to the point at which the price just covers marginal costs, i.e. the cost of the last additional unit produced. The intersection points of the marginal cost curve and the price lines indicate the amounts that can be produced. In our graph the $10 price line cuts the marginal cost curve at an output of 10,000 units (P_1). At a market price of $10, 10,000 units will be produced. Assuming that this is the output for which the plant has been planned, this will be the point of optimum combination of variable and fixed capital. Unit costs will be lowest at this point and will coincide with marginal costs. For any output larger or smaller than 10,000, unit costs will be higher for the reasons explained above. The unit cost curve rises to the right and left of P_1. It is said to be U-shaped.

A change in price causes a shift in the point at which the costs of the last additional units are still covered. Output will change. If the price declines to $5, the price line in our graph cuts the marginal cost curve at 5,000 (P_2), and output will shrink to 5,000. If the price rises to $15 per unit the marginal cost curve and the price line intersect at 15,000 (P_3), and output will rise to 15,000.

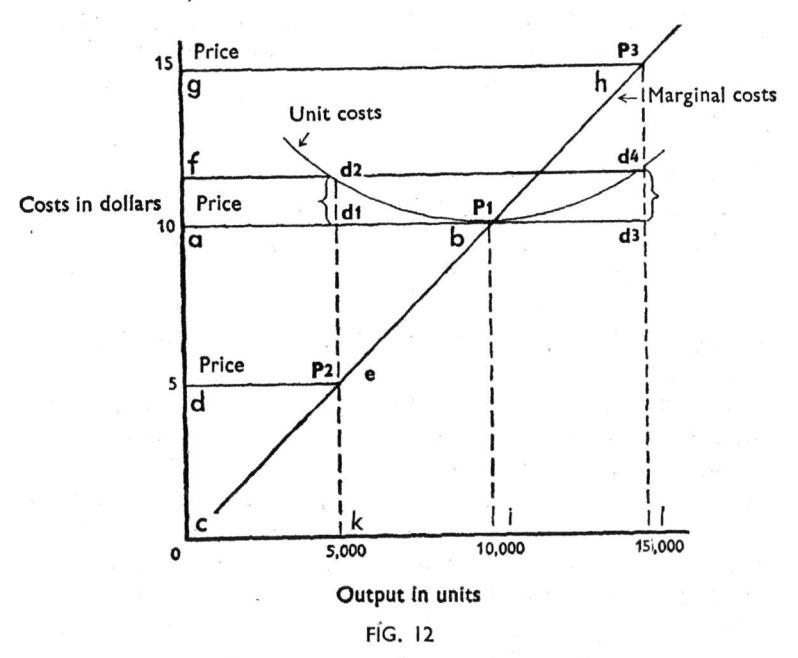

FIG. 12

What will be the effect on the entrepreneur's profit and loss of these changes in output? For simplicity's sake we shall assume an entrepreneur who is able to produce 10,000 units without profit or loss at a sales price of $10. His revenue, as his costs (price and unit costs multiplied by production), correspond to the area a–b–i–c. If the market price drops to $5, his output drops to 5,000 units. His revenue is reduced to an amount which corresponds to the area c–d–e–k whereas his costs are c–f–d_2–k. For, due to unchanging fixed costs, his unit costs have increased by d_1–d_2 to k–d_2. He suffers a loss which corresponds to the area $d-f-d_2-e$, a loss which, however, can never surpass the fixed costs. For if the variable costs are no longer covered by the revenue, production will be stopped.

If the market price rises to $15 and the production to 15,000 units, the revenue of the entrepreneur rises to $c-g-h-l$. But because his unit costs have risen by d_3-d_4, his costs are now $c-f-d_4-l$ and his profits are not $a-g-h-d_3$ but $f-g-h-d_4$.

All this is valid not only for each individual entrepreneur but also when the general price level fluctuates, as in inflation or deflation, for the whole economy, i.e. for all the entrepreneurs together.

The Consumption Exchange

We have so far examined the production exchange, by which the factors of production supply their contributions to production in exchange for money as a sort of general representative of goods. For what goods, for how many of them and by whom, will this money be spent in the consumption exchange to which we now turn?

The first thing to note is that, provided there is no interruption in the flow of money, all the money present in the economy must be spent on all the products coming to the markets. All the money buys all the goods. As a result, a certain price level will be reached at which the supply of goods and monetary demand balance. This is the starting point of the famous so-called quantity theory of money, which deals with the relation between the quantity of circulating money and the price level. We shall return to this later in connection with inflation and deflation.

But what products will be demanded and by whom? The quantity theory does not furnish us with an answer to either question. The two questions are closely related. What goods are demanded for consumption depends essentially on the distribution of income. A wealthy capitalist will generally wish to consume other goods than a low-salaried employee. The distribution of income in turn is dependent upon the contribution to production of each of the production factors

THE STATIONARY ECONOMY

and upon their remuneration. In the long run consumption follows production just as production follows consumption.

Since the distribution of income is of paramount importance for consumption demand, we shall briefly recapitulate the following points.

(1) Labor is rewarded for its contribution to production by the payment of wages on the part of entrepreneurs.

(2) The capitalists, who lend entrepreneurs money for wage payments and the purchase of capital goods, are rewarded by the payment of interest.

(3) The share of the total product which the capitalists receive is determined by the marginal productivity of capital. For each unit of capital they receive a reward corresponding to the productivity increase due to the last unit of capital added. This reward is smaller than would correspond to the productivity increase due to intra-marginal units of capital. The difference accrues to labor in the form of higher wages.

(4) No separate allowance is made in our model for rent as a reward for the owners of land. It is assumed that land is bought in the same manner as capital goods and that its contribution to production is, therefore, rewarded by the interest paid to the capitalists who have lent the money for the purchase. To assume that the landowner receives a rent would be tantamount to counting twice the reward for the use of land. The landowner gets his reward in his capacity of capitalist. He lends the money which he receives for the sale of the land.

The Purchase of Intermediate Goods

The factors of production receiving money in the production exchange for their contributions to production spend this money in the consumption exchange for the goods of the past period in order to consume them and to survive during the current period.

This description of the process is, however, only partially correct. As we explained in connection with roundabout methods of production, entrepreneurs buy not only labor of the current period (using the machines) but also labor of past periods (building the machines). The purchase of intermediate goods is again mentioned here because in a certain way it, too, belongs to the consumption exchange category and occupies an intermediary position between production exchange and consumption exchange. Just as in the case of consumption goods the products of past labor are purchased. And again the receipts from the sales enable the sellers to continue production in a new period.

On the other hand the purchase of intermediate goods belongs to the category of the production exchange inasmuch as the products of past labor are not consumed immediately but directed into the longer production detours, so that their consumption does not take place in the current period but together with that of the labor of the current period in a later period.

Equality of Production and Consumption

The goods supplied during a production period for consumption or as intermediate and capital goods and the goods actually consumed or used as intermediate and capital goods are necessarily the same. This is a truism in a stationary economy which is, by definition, in equilibrium. In an economy in equilibrium all goods produced are also consumed, for otherwise they would not have been produced. This is the substance of a law known as J. B. Say's Law of Markets. In a changing economy, such as it exists in reality, this law is not always valid. We shall later return in detail to the questions connected herewith.

Equality of Costs and Revenue

Input and output comparisons in real terms are either truistic—because labor produces neither more nor less than it actually produces—or nonsensical—because labor and product cannot be reduced to a common denominator. But how about comparisons between the money spent for production —the money costs of firms—and the money received for products—the money revenue of firms? The statement that money costs equal money revenue is, as such, not at all nonsensical, for sums of money can be compared with each other.

But it is again a truism to say that costs equal revenues when the costs and the revenue of the whole economy are meant. Clearly, in a stationary economy all the money spent must be recovered as revenue.

The statement that costs equal revenues for the whole economy has to be sharply distinguished from the statement that costs equal revenues for a single entrepreneur. This latter statement is no truism but, in a stationary economy, is necessarily always correct. It implies that the money spent by an entrepreneur on factors of production and the money received by him for products must balance in the long run. For a deficit would restrict, and a surplus would expand, the production of any entrepreneur until costs and revenues again balance.

Labor and goods cannot be compared for lack of a common denominator. But each entrepreneur's contribution to the total production expenditure of an economy can be compared with his share in the total product. Since, in an economy in equilibrium, entrepreneurs' monetary receipts exactly match their expenditure, each individual entrepreneur's percentage share of total input equals his percentage share of total output. For the money paid by each entrepreneur to the factors of production represents a certain percentage of the total money stock of the economy and thus attracts the same percentage of productive forces into his enterprise. The money received, too, represents the same percentage of the money stock. This proves that the entrepreneur's percentage share in the total product of the economy is the same.

In a stationary economy an entrepreneur is certain of the demand for his products and of the resulting price conditions. But in a changing world he might make mistakes because the future is uncertain. In a changing world costs and revenues might not balance in each case. The demand for pears and their price may rise, those for apples fall. The producers of apples will then receive less than they spent, the producers of pears more. Profits and losses will result.

The Profits of Entrepreneurs

We are now in a position to add some precision to our earlier remarks about entrepreneurial profits.

(1) Profits in the sense we use the word—in accordance with the definition of Schumpeter and Knight but contrary to the business man's notion—does not include the return on the capital used and the compensation for managerial services.

(2) If profits cannot exist in a stationary economy, then they can, in a non-stationary competitive economy, only be of a transitory nature.

If, due to a change in taste, more of one product and less of another is wanted on the markets, the price of the first product will go up, the price of the second will go down. The producer of the first product will make a profit, the producer of the second a loss. But after a certain time profits as well as losses will disappear. The firm which makes a profit will expand, that making a loss will restrict production until prices and costs again reach balance through the changed supply position.

Profits may, however, be the result not only of higher prices but also of lower costs. Technical progress is one of the chief reasons for declining costs. The dynamic entrepreneur who is the first to make use of new inventions or of new methods of production makes profits. But as time goes on, other entrepreneurs follow his example. All entrepreneurs are then able, and through competition among themselves forced, to pay higher prices for the factors of production: profits disappear.

If, however, the new invention or method of production is protected against imitation by patents or secrecy, the profits remain—they become "frozen". Monopoly profits, too, are essentially such frozen profits.

(3) Profits are not really, as often stated, a reward for bearing a risk. The entrepreneur reaps a profit not because he has taken a risk but because he has been correct in his anticipations. If he has not been correct, he suffers a loss and does not gain a profit. The profits arising from the changes are the counterpart of and not the reward for the risk.

(4) Profits can be made only by individual entrepreneurs and not by the economy as a whole.

In the case of profits through change of taste this is quite obvious. If the total amount of purchasing power in the hands of the population is limited, the prices of certain products can rise only if those of others fall.

But the statement is also correct in the case of profits through cost saving. From the point of view of the whole economy, cost savings represent increased productivity of the factors of production, particularly labor, but not profits.

Thus a sharp distinction must be made between the resulting stationary benefits and the temporary profits made by individual entrepreneurs who deprive the production factors of the benefits of the productivity increase and keep these profits for themselves. Profits are interpersonal shifts of income; they are private in character and do not concern the national economy as such.

(5) The so-called losses of the national economy through misdirection of production or through faulty investments are not losses of the national economy either. Suppose a luxury hotel is built and later goes bankrupt for lack of clients able to pay luxury prices. This does not mean that the labor spent on its construction is lost for the whole economy. The rooms may later be rented to more modest clients at reduced prices. From the standpoint of the community it does not make any difference what class of people enjoy the luxury of the hotel. What the misdirection of production has accomplished is only that the final distribution of the total product of the economy does not coincide with the initial distribution of wealth. The owners of the hotel have lost to others their claim to the products of a certain amount of work because they overestimated the demand for the product of their investment. Misdirection of investment can lead to national losses only if entrepreneurs, through lack of further finance, have to abandon a construction project before it is able to render any services— say a half-built railway. But in such cases other entrepreneurs will usually acquire the assets cheaply through forced sale. These other entrepreneurs will complete the project. The

latter may even become profitable for them since their fixed costs are much smaller. In any case the losses here, too, are private and not national ones.

(6) This economic misdirection by misjudgment of demand has to be distinguished from what could be called technical misdirection. If an entrepreneur uses methods which are inferior to those that can be used or are being used by others, the productivity of the whole economy is affected. In this case one speaks frequently of a loss to the whole economy. A lowered productivity of an economy which results in a lower aggregate output is, however, not a loss in the sense of the counterpart of a profit as defined.

Profits, Interests, Rents

Profits and interests should always be sharply distinguished from each other. The latter do not disappear through adjustment to changes. Capital is remunerated by interest payments in a stationary as well as in a changing world, at least so long as capital supply is not unlimited.

The so-called rents, too, are not in principle transitory in character. Linguistic usage is somewhat vague in these matters. What is meant by rents in the first place is the additional income accruing to certain entrepreneurs due to inventions or production methods protected by law, or due to a monopolistic position. These are the frozen profits of which we spoke earlier. Frequently rents are also understood to mean all the monetary receipts or advantages of a more or less durable character which accrue to the owners of certain property, such as land (ground rent) or claims and titles (annuities, perpetual rents from non-redeemable securities, etc.).

Rent, in the sense of what is paid for a lease, is also of durable nature. Rent in this sense is normally the money paid for the use of land, houses, certain machines, patents, or other carriers of services. This money is paid to the owners of these carriers by people who need the services for production or consumption, but who are not willing or able to buy the carriers.

The rent paid for the use of land is, in principle, always

equal to the value of the services of the land. In case of divergences the land would be bought rather than rented, or vice versa. The rents for land and for all goods which are not freely reproducible lead, as it were, a separate existence of their own; they are independent of the rate of interest and of any production costs.

Things are different in the case of rent for property which, like built-up land, is partly, or like machines wholly, reproducible. These rents are dependent upon interest rates. Rent for machines must always equal the interest on their purchase or cost price. If the rent rises beyond that interest it will become profitable to build more machines for the purpose of renting them out. If the rent falls below the interest, the production of machines falls.

If interest rates fall, machines requiring a higher capital outlay can be taken into use. The productivity of those machines is greater, but the marginal productivity of the capital incorporated in them is smaller. The rent for those machines, calculated on the cost price, will fall accordingly.

The rent for plants installed previously at higher interest rates will fall even more. The owners of the old machines save less labor per unit of output than do those of the new machines, yet they have to compete with the latter for labor. The return on the old machines is smaller than the return on the new ones, and the rent for old machines falls below the rent of new ones.

If the machines are not leased but sold, then their owner incurs a corresponding loss by selling below his cost price. For the buyer of the old machines can compete with the owners of new machines only if his higher production costs are matched by a saving of interest on his purchase price.

Security Prices

We do not wish to conclude our description of the fictitious stationary economy without drawing some preliminary conclusions concerning stock price formation. In doing so we have to bear in mind that we are dealing with an economy in equilibrium: the economy is not subject to changes—in particular the demand for and supply of capital, and therefore the interest rate, are constant. This stationary economy is also a riskless one. The future is like the present, and the present of course is known to all.

In such an economy in equilibrium all loans are always worth exactly the original sum lent. No matter how long the duration of the credit, all credits are always worth "par."

For short-term credits the above statement is obvious. So long as the debtor is solvent—and in a stationary economy he is so by definition—the claim is worth 100 per cent.

Capital is made available to entrepreneurs mainly against common shares, preferred shares or bonds. Such capital does not become due for repayment for long periods, or indeed at all.

In a stationary economy the price of common shares would always equal the original issue price. Dividends would equal interest on the issue price at the prevailing interest rate. Entrepreneurs would be able and willing to pay in dividends on the shares exactly as much as they would have had to pay in interest for a loan equalling the issue price of the shares. At an interest rate of 5 per cent dividends of $5 would be paid on each share issued at $100. The share would always be worth exactly $100.

For preferred shares bearing fixed dividends and for fixed-interest bonds the proposition is even more obvious. They would always be worth par provided the preferred dividends and interests are fixed in accordance with the prevailing interest rate, as they must be in a riskless economy in equilibrium.

The fact that long-term investments are worth par and that their yields, i.e. their interest payments as a percentage of their price, are always equal to the interest rate paid for credits, is important for the understanding of the price formation of securities. Naturally, significant qualifications have to be made in the real, changing and uncertain world. We may anticipate two essential points.

(1) There is always a risk that the expected earnings might not materialize, and even that losses will be incurred. If the

risk is considered high, a common share paying a dividend of $5, at an interest rate of 5 per cent, might not be worth $100 but only $50 and thus yield 10 per cent.

(2) There is always a risk of future changes in the interest rate. If people are "bearish" regarding the interest rate, i.e. fear that it will fall, then the price of long-term investments will be above par and their yield below the prevailing short-term interest rate. On the other hand, the price of long-term investments may be lower than par and their yield above the prevailing short-term interest rate if people are "bullish" regarding the interest rate, i.e. expect it to rise. While both cases happen in practice, the latter seems to be more frequent. Long-term investments as a rule yield a higher return than short-term investments. This proves that generally debtors fear and creditors hope that funding operations, i.e. transformation of short-term into long-term investments, will in future only be possible at higher interest rates. The liquidity factor, which is often considered the reason for the higher long-term interest rates, is of no importance as far as investments in negotiable bonds are concerned. Bonds are not less liquid than short-term credits but are more price sensitive. It is the expectation of sinking prices, not illiquidity, which keeps their yield up.

Both these risks are, as it were, the final expression of a whole series of other risks. The risk of losses or diminished profits arises from the risk of changing demand for and supply of goods. The risk of changing interest rates arises from the risks of changing productivity of capital and of a changing rate of savings.

All these changes influence security prices. We shall be able to discuss these influences better when we have examined the direct effect of the changes.

Part II

THE CHANGING ECONOMY

J. B. Say's Law

In the real world the economy changes continuously. Neither what is produced, and by whom and by what methods, nor what is consumed, and by whom and by what methods, remains the same.

What are the causes and effects of the more important changes? These questions will be examined in this section under a specific assumption, namely that the quantity of money present in the economy and the velocity of its turnover do not change.

On the assumption of constant circulation of money, all the money paid out during a production period to the factors of production must be spent on the resulting products. Total monetary demand remains constant. To the extent to which demand for consumer goods falls owing to saving there will be a rise in the demand for capital goods and intermediate goods on the part of entrepreneurs, who get as credits such amounts as have been saved.

Our assumption coincides roughly with that of the famous Law of Markets of J. B. Say. This law states that all that is produced is also consumed because the factors of production spend all the money they get on the results of their production.

We shall see later that the assumption of Say's law is by no means correct in every case. The circulation of money can increase and decrease. In other words, there can be inflation and deflation of money. One can even go so far as to say that stability of money circulation is the exception.

It remains nevertheless important to examine the changing economy under the assumption of an inelastic money circulation. Inflations and deflations are in most cases short-term, reversible phenomena. They carry within themselves the seeds of self-destruction. Prosperity follows depression. But the fate of an economy in the long run, in the aggregate over time, must be the concern of the economist at least as much as short-run situations. Only an analysis which abstracts from inflation and deflation can explain by what forces the economy is influenced in the long run. Only such an analysis can show how the economy would develop if the traditional mistakes in monetary and credit policy were avoided—a possibility which many contemporary economists, accustomed as they are to completely elastic supply of money, no longer seem to envisage at all. Even where inflation is not reversible—as it fails to be in the case of governmental mismanagement of the currency, particularly during war-time—analysis on the assumption of inelastic money supply remains of interest. It shows what happens when, in the further course of an inflation, all members of the community have become fully aware of what is going on and have adjusted their supply and demand for goods and services to the diminishing value of money.

Twenty years ago it would not have been necessary to stress the importance of a non-inflation–non-deflation analysis. Every economics textbook started with the analysis of an economy exposed to no changes from the money side. Money was considered only a veil, behind which were hidden real economic processes, but which did not cause these processes. This has changed radically under the influence of Keynes' *General Theory of Employment, Interest and Money*. Newer textbooks seem no longer to know a world in which money is inelastic. In their world inflation increases and deflation decreases not only the nominal, but also the real income of nations in the long run, as well as in the short run. As a result a whole generation of economists seems to believe that the wealth of nations is dependent upon the willingness to develop effective demand, rather than upon the willingness to work. And it can be said without exaggeration that no single fact has done modern economic analysis so much harm as the assumption of a very elastic money supply.

A description of an economy without inflation or deflation therefore appears indeed timely. None of Keynes' thesis is appropriate to such an economy. This proves—as cannot be stressed too often—that Keynes' theory belongs to the realm of inflation and deflation and business cycle theory and not to that of a general theory.

We shall begin by examining changes in production and consumption. Our results immediately proceed from, and in part repeat, the findings of our examination of the stationary economy in Part I.

Changes in Consumption

If all the money earned by the factors of production is spent on consumption goods, total consumption remains constant. It can never change autonomously. Only if production expands or contracts can total consumption expand or contract. The consumption of individual products can, of course, fluctuate. The consumption of apples may increase, but only if the consumption of other goods—say pears—declines.

Changes in the composition of consumption goods are in the first place due to changes in the taste of consumers. They can also be due to changes in the distribution of income among the factors of production. If income shifts to higher brackets the consumption of luxury goods, if it shifts to lower brackets the consumption of mass consumer goods, will increase relatively.

As in the case of all changes short-run effects have to be distinguished from long-run effects. In the short run an increase in demand causes prices to rise substantially above production costs. But after some time the productive resources of the economy are again directed toward the production of various goods according to the new wishes of the consumers. A new equilibrium is established. Prices again stabilize at the marginal cost level. The production of all goods expands up to the point at which the consumers are prepared to pay a price covering the cost of the last unit produced.

Changes in consumption can also be due to changes in production costs and resulting changes in prices. If production of apples becomes cheaper, whereas the production of pears becomes more expensive, the consumption of apples will increase while the consumption of pears will decline.

Changes in Production

In contrast to consumption, there can be changes in production not only of a qualitative but also of a quantitative nature. In other words, the total amount of goods available for direct or indirect consumption, or the gross national product as it is called somewhat equivocally, may change.

Given a certain productivity of, and the resulting demand for labor, and given a certain supply of capital, the volume of total production is a function of the supply of labor. This means that the volume of production depends on the extent to which people are willing to work. This fact has to be emphasized over and over again. Our view is in flat contradiction to the prevailing demand theory of employment and production, according to which it is the demand for, rather than the supply of, labor that fundamentally determines employment and production. In an economy without inflation and deflation the changes from the side of the supply of labor are obviously more important than those from the demand side. This implies that this is also the case in reality in the long run, and in the aggregate over time. So-called structural unemployment—as distinct from cyclical and frictional unemployment—is always due to excessive wages, i.e. to an over-expensive labor supply.

Unemployment, a Vague Concept[1]

Labor is not offered at any price except under very special conditions. The quantities offered vary with the wages demanded. Against a high compensation more labor is offered as a rule than against a low compensation, exactly as in the case of the isolated producer which we examined at the outset. The elasticity of labor supply will, of course, be different in various countries and at various times. But according to all experience it is safe to say that labor supply is never entirely inelastic, that it always depends to some extent on the wage level.

Therefore the concept of full employment, as used in political discussions and also in various full-employment laws

---

[1] For this and the following special reference is made to Chapters 6 and 11 of my *Economics of Illusion*.

all over the world, is a somewhat vague one. Those who consider the product of their work insufficient compensation for sacrificing their rest or recreation will remain unemployed even in a boom.

Unemployment is thus not an absolute but a relative concept. One can only speak of unemployment at a certain—say at the prevailing—wage level. From the point of view of policy, employment should be guaranteed only to those who are willing to work at wages fixed by the government. Those not willing to work at these wages should be considered as voluntary unemployed, and excluded from any unemployment benefits.

But must the prevailing wage level always be maintained in all circumstances? And at what level should a government, obliged by law to maintain full employment, fix wages? Some say wages should be fair, obviously meaning sufficient for a decent standard of living. This is a purely political and not a scientific point of view. In a free economy there is in the long run and after adjustment to all disturbances only *one* fair level of wages—the level at which the labor supply is absorbed by the demand for labor. In practice this is the wage level which corresponds to the product of the marginal worker, i.e. the least productive worker still employed at given demand.

The Basic Law of Employment

Given a certain demand for labor, the degree of employment is a function of the supply price of labor, of wage demands. This is true in spite of the fact that labor unions, which minimize the importance of the wage level for the level of unemployment, generally do not admit it and in spite of the fact that this importance, unbelievable as it may appear, was hardly ever mentioned in the vast literature on post-war unemployment. It is true even where the elasticity of the demand for labor is small. There must always be a wage level that is sufficiently low to guarantee the absorption of supply by demand. The wage level would be indifferent for employment only under the unrealistic assumption that the demand for labor was entirely inelastic, i.e. that labor could be employed regardless of its price. This is in contradiction not only to practical experience but also to the laws governing all markets. On the labor market, as on every other market, supply can never exceed demand provided no obstacles are put in the way of price formation.

Growth, as well as cheapening, of labor supply expands the total production of the country. This is often forgotten, notably by those who oppose immigration of labor. Whether such an expansion of total production benefits or damages the community as a whole is another question to be discussed later.

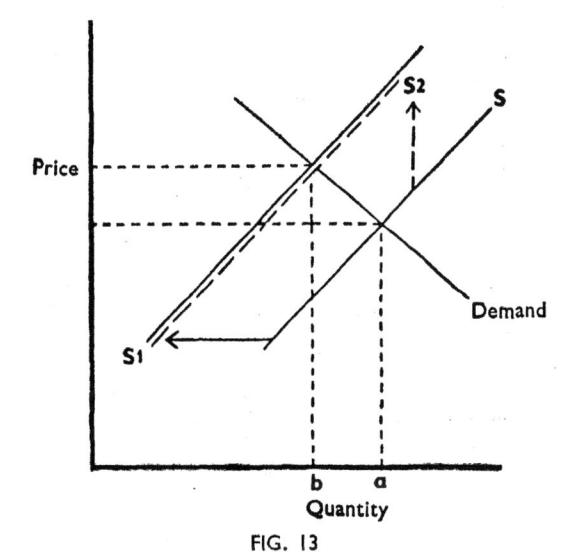

FIG. 13

Changes in the Supply of Labor

Changes in the supply of labor, as of all other goods, can take either of two forms: either the price for the same quantity changes, or the quantity offered for the same price.

Both changes operate in the same direction, as is evident from Figure 13. Whether the labor supply curve (S) moves to the left to S_1, indicating that smaller quantities are offered at given price levels, or whether the supply curve moves up to S_2, indicating that the given quantities are offered at higher prices, the quantity of labor actually done is reduced by *ab*.

70 COMMON SENSE ECONOMICS

There remains, however, the question whether, for instance, a 10 per cent rise in wage demands always has the same restricting effect as a 10 per cent reduction of work-hours offered. This depends on the slope of the supply curve. A steep supply curve indicates that price has a relatively small influence on the

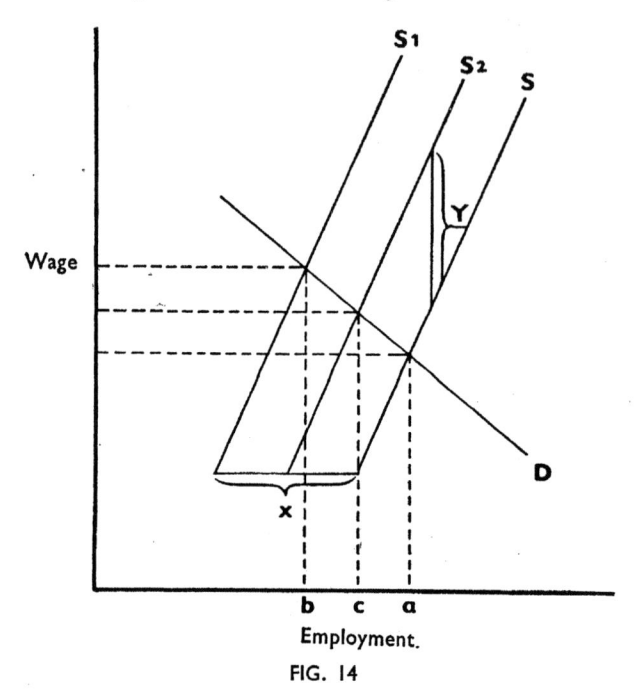

FIG. 14

amount of supply. If, therefore, the labor supply curve is steep, as in Figure 14, the demand of a wage rise of 10 per cent will restrict employment less than a 10 per cent reduction in the work-hours offered at various wage levels. The rise in wage demands, expressed by an upward shift of the supply curve to S_2, will restrict employment only by *ac;* an equivalent reduction in work offered, expressed by a shift to the left of the supply curve to S_1, will restrict employment by the much larger amount *ab*.

Changes in the supply of labor may, but need not, lead to changes in the number of workers employed. A smaller or costlier supply of labor causes less work to be done per unit of time—say per week. This can happen through all workers working fewer hours each week, or through some workers not working at all. Whether the higher cost or the reduction of the supply of labor will actually lead to unemployment or not depends on the manner in which either the offer of weekly work-hours at prevailing wages is reduced or the wage demands raised. The weekly work-hours offered may be reduced (*a*) by all workers being unwilling to work more than a certain time each week, or (*b*) by some workers being unwilling to work at all. The supply price of labor may rise (*c*) by wage demands being raised for all weekly work-hours, or (*d*) by wage demands being raised only for the later hours of weekly work, i.e. by demands for earlier operation of overtime pay. There may also be various combinations. In particular, it is not unusual for a claim for shorter weekly work to be combined with a demand for unchanged weekly wages (combination of *a* and *c*), which means higher hourly wages. The labor supply curve then moves upwards as well as to the left, and the curtailing effect on production is cumulative.

The effect on employment of each of cases (*a*) to (*d*) will be different. A reduction of the working week for all workers (case *a*) while reducing the total of hours worked creates no unemployment. The reduced work is spread among the existing number of workers. If the demand for labor is inelastic it may even happen that the total of hours worked declines less than the hours worked each week by the individual workers. In this case employment increases.

A reduction of weekly work-hours, through some workers being entirely unwilling to work at the prevailing wage level (case *b*), creates voluntary unemployment.

A raising of wage demands for all hours (case *c*) will reduce the number of workers employed. Entrepreneurs, having to curtail production, will generally prefer to dismiss workers rather than curtail weekly working hours.

A raising of wage demands for the later daily or weekly hours, i.e. the claim for earlier overtime pay (case *d*), reduces the weekly work done by those employed. To make up for the reduced working time entrepreneurs may employ new workers. In this case the work is spread among more workers, the number of workers employed increases.

Reasons for Scarcer and Costlier Labor Supply

The supply of labor becomes scarcer or costlier when the workers' valuation of the wages offered decreases in relation to their valuation of leisure.

A priori it is to be expected that such a change in relative valuation should find expression both in higher wage claims and in a diminution of labor supply, whether through certain parts of the population not working at all or through a shortening of the working week. Indeed, economic history shows examples both of higher wages and of reductions in the weekly working time, as well as of curtailment of the degree of activity of the population (elimination of child labor, to a large extent of women's labor).

It is to be noted, however, that the workers' claims for shorter working time are apt to meet with obstacles of tradition. An eight-hour day introduced in a certain factory or in the whole country generally remains unaltered until strong forces of a technical or social character enforce changes.

It is hard to predict whether the workers' claims will in the future concentrate more on higher wages or on shorter working time. All that can perhaps be said is that with a rising standard of living labor will prefer more extended leisure to increased consumption. Technical progress and increased capital equipment may one day lead to a state of affairs where men will be willing to work only a very few hours each week. A very few hours, spent in supervising highly productive machines, may guarantee such a high standard of living that its further improvement is of little interest. An ever-growing increase in leisure, rather than, as some fear, over-production of consumption of goods no longer in demand, may turn out to be the end of a development which would leave a rational use of leisure as the only problem.

Note that a withdrawal from the labor market may, in our time of labor monopolies, not be caused at all by a changed valuation of leisure or of compensation for work. Labor may strike not because workers wish to be unemployed rather than work at the prevailing wage rate, but because they try by means of the strike to obtain wages which they believe entrepreneurs could pay without resulting unemployment.

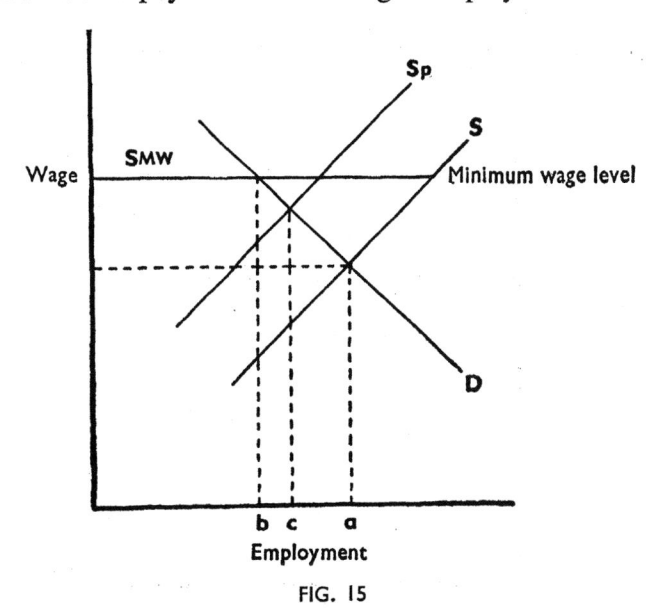

FIG. 15

Minimum Wage Laws. Laws Limiting Labor Supply. Union Action

The effects of minimum wage laws and of laws limiting the supply of labor, such as laws forbidding the occupation of minors, are demonstrated in Figure 15.

Minimum wage laws create, as it were, an artificial labor supply curve running horizontally at the minimum wage level. The supply curve S is replaced by the line S_{MW}. All those whose services are no longer demanded at this wage level become unemployed; the amount of unemployment so created is *ab*. Laws prohibiting the employment of minors create a new supply curve (S_p) to the left of the original supply curve. The interval *ac* represents the production-curtailing effect.

This does not, of course, imply that minimum wage laws or laws against the work of minors are not warranted. It only shows the curtailing effect of such laws on production, against which have to be weighed the favorable effects on the health and the general well-being of those remaining in employment and of those now unemployed.

Apart from the case where labor is faced with monopolies, it

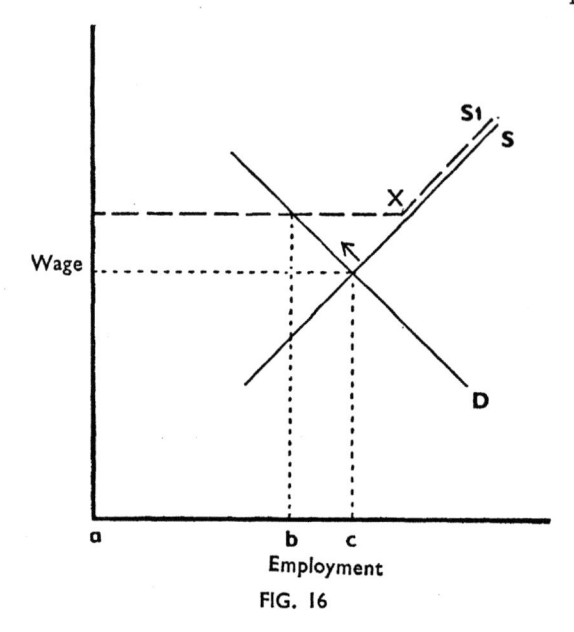

FIG. 16

is the task and the justification of labor unions to fight, on behalf of their members, for wages higher than those that would come about on a free market. The effect of union action is highly complicated. In principle, its effect is a general increase in the price of too cheap labor, and therefore an upward bending of the left side of the supply curve (*S*) in Figure 16 to, say, a point *X* which is higher than the free market price of labor. The result is a raising of the wage level, i.e. an improvement in the situation of those employed (*ab*) to the detriment of those who become unemployed (*bc*) because their services are no longer demanded at the new, higher, wage level. The least skilled and least productive workers are the chief sufferers.

The Demand Curve for Labor

The effects of changes in labor supply are, of course, largely dependent upon how much of the labor offered at various prices entrepreneurs are able to employ, or, in the language of curve analysis, on the shape of the demand curve for labor.

The question is a complicated one. We have in principle to start from the fact mentioned in Part I that, according to the law of diminishing marginal returns, the productivity of the individual worker—given a certain amount of capital—is reduced through the employment of new workers, because the capital equipment per worker becomes scantier. It follows that entrepreneurs disposing of a given amount of credit will, in principle, employ new workers only at lower wages corresponding to their lower productivity. The demand curve for labor will thus in fact run downward to the right.

Whether its slope will be more or less steep depends, of course, on the degree to which a diminution of capital equipment per worker reduces the productivity of labor. We must assume that the reduction in productivity is a significant one, i.e. that the demand curve has a steep slope. Under modern conditions a newly employed worker can have the same productivity as those already employed only if an equal amount of capital is invested for him. Where this is impossible, because the amount of capital is given, the productivity per worker must fall sharply when the number of workers grows.

All this rests on the assumption that entrepreneurs neither do nor need to reckon with changes in the price level for finished goods. We shall see later that this assumption, which we make here for purposes of exposition, is not entirely correct.

Effects of Changes in Labor Supply

Assuming, then, a demand curve running steeply downward to the right, what will be the effects of changes in labor supply? The answer can be found in Figure 17.

In the first instance it will be seen that if the labor supply curve S moves downward to S_1, employment increases by ab.

The increase in employment causes an increase in the product, but this increase in the product is smaller than the one resulting from the preceding additions to employment because the new workers, as explained above, have a lower productivity. The increase in the product is represented by the area $AabB$; the total product is now $efBb$, as against $efAa$ before.

Hourly wages fall by AC. If the demand curve D had a horizontal course, total wages would not fall. The decreased wage demands would spend themselves in an increase of employment. If the demand curve were vertical, i.e. if no capital at all were available for the purpose of employing additional workers, total wages would fall by the whole amount of the reduction in wage demands (AE). That wages fall by less than AE is due to the fact that the demand curve is not completely inelastic.

Where does the capital come from which entrepreneurs need for the employment of new workers, since we have assumed that the total amount of available credit is given? The answer is this: employment of new workers not only leads to a fall in the marginal productivity of labor; it leads at the same time to an increase in the marginal productivity of capital, since the demand for capital per worker becomes more urgent. As a result, capital will be withdrawn from the most labor-saving enterprises. The credits saved in long production detours can, by widening the capital structure, be used in shorter production detours. This saving of credits in the longer production detours is the reversal of the phenomenon discussed in Part I in connection with the need for larger credits for longer production detours.

If the supply of labor becomes scarcer or costlier, an opposite effect will take place. Employment will fall, the volume of production will shrink and wages will rise. Capital will be re-directed from the shortest to the longest production detours. This is an expression of the fact that capital no longer needed for the payment of the marginal workers and their equipment with capital can now be used to increase the productivity of the workers still employed, by transition to more capitalistic methods of production.

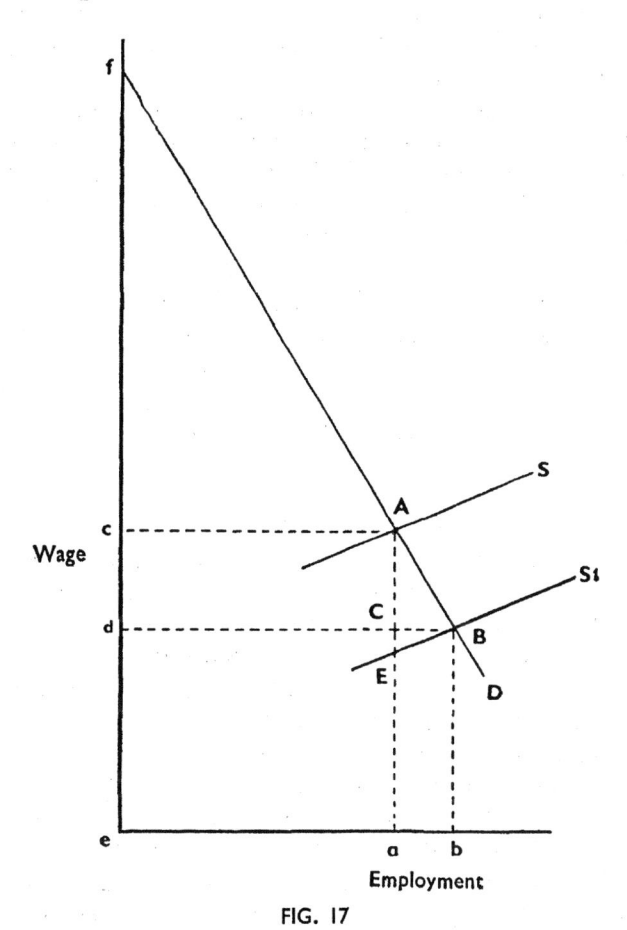

FIG. 17

Reaction on Profits and Interest

Figure 17 shows that a reduction in wage demands decreases the wages of *all* workers to the level of productivity of the "new" marginal worker. Owing to this general fall in wages entrepreneurs make extra profits. A share in the total product corresponding to the area *cABd* accrues to them. These extra profits will induce entrepreneurs to compete for the given amount of capital and to bid up interest rates. As a result, capitalists will receive higher interest, an expression of the fact that the productivity of capital has risen through the increase in labor employment.

But this is not the end of the story. When the factors of production later spend their income, they will realize that interest rates have risen. They will tend to spend less and to save more. Their savings may go to entrepreneurs in the form of larger credits. Entrepreneurs will thus be enabled to increase the capital equipment per worker, and the productivity of labor will rise. The demand curve *D* in Figure 17 will become less steep. The product increases, wages rise and interest per unit of capital remains lower than assumed above.

If labor supply becomes dearer, the effects will be opposite to those described.

Changes in the Demand for Labor

We have so far examined the effects of changes in the *supply* of labor at a given demand for labor. We shall now examine the effects of changes in the *demand* for labor. The demand for labor may change for a variety of reasons.

One reason is to be found in the changes of capital supply, to be discussed later. The main reason, however, is a change in the productivity of labor.

An important distinction has to be made here. A change in the productivity of labor is not identical with a change in the productivity of capital applied to labor, although this is assumed in most wage negotiations. The productivity of labor increases when technical improvements enable savings of labor in proportion to the amount of labor applied; the productivity of capital increases when such improvements enable savings of labor in proportion to the amount of capital applied. When the productivity of capital is increased labor saving will therefore be negligible in industries using little capital, but very important in industries with large capital investments per unit of product.

Changes in the Productivity of Labor

A change in the productivity of labor creates a whole chain of reactions. Workers are set free in those enterprises in which the increase in the productivity of labor makes workers

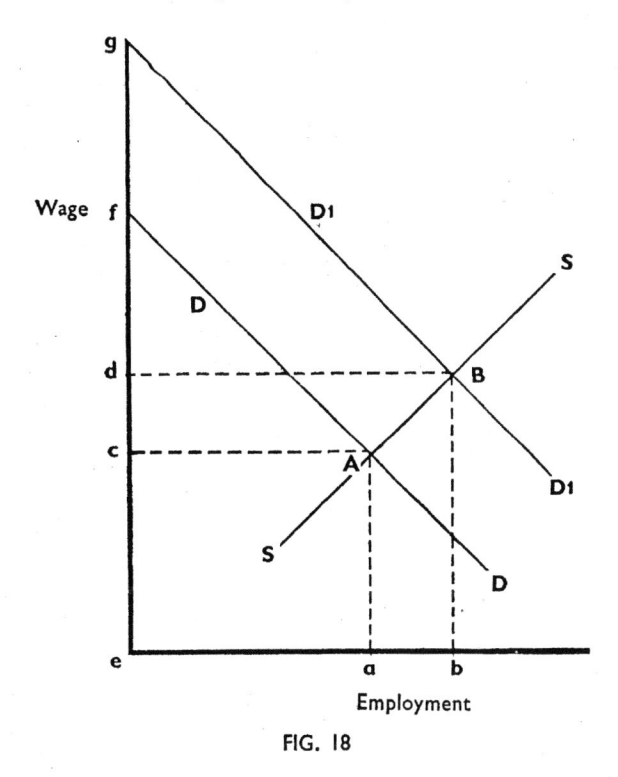

FIG. 18

redundant. On the other hand, in other enterprises hitherto unemployable labor can be set to work, because the higher output per work-hour allows the employment of labor previously too expensive or of too low productivity.

After completion of all the transition stages a new equilibrium will emerge. Since the productivity of the individual worker has increased, entrepreneurs will be prepared to pay higher wages according to the higher productivity. Figure 18 shows the resulting changes. The demand curve D will move up to D_1. This has, in the first place, the result that employment increases by *ab*. The increase in employment causes an increase in output. Since, at the same time, the productivity of the workers has risen, the increase is this time greater than that due to cheaper labor supply. The increase corresponds to the area *aAfgBb*. The total product is represented by the area *egBb*. Wages increase by *cd*. This increase is smaller than would correspond to the increase in productivity because the wages of *all* workers are in accordance with the productivity of the marginal worker. Entrepreneurs make an extra profit, represented by the difference between the triangle *dgB* and the triangle *cAf*. These extra profits induce entrepreneurs to compete for the given amount of capital. The interest rate rises.

Again we are faced with the question of how entrepreneurs pay the more numerous and more costly labor. Again the answer is that they pay their workers with capital hitherto used in the longest production detours. The higher productivity of labor makes it profitable to withdraw capital from the longest production detours and to use it for paying labor, even though the latter has become more expensive.

A decrease in the productivity of labor has opposite effects. Employment contracts, total output diminishes, wages fall. The marginal productivity of the capital distributed among fewer and less productive workers falls, and with it the interest rate.

In our days, with free market conditions, except in time of war or other catastrophes, it is hardly likely that the productivity of labor will fall. New methods of production are permanently at work to raise, not to lower, the productivity of labor. However, the productivity of labor is sometimes lowered artificially. So-called feather bedding, as practised in the American railway industry, and similar restrictive devices are examples.

Changes in the Productivity of Capital

As we have stated earlier, changes in the productivity of capital are not to be confused with changes in the productivity of labor. Increased productivity of capital normally causes entrepreneurs to raise their offers of interest and thereby leads to higher income for the capitalists. In a free competitive economy the workers can benefit from an increase in the productivity of capital only when the supply of capital grows at the same rate as the demand for capital and when, therefore, interest rates do not change. In this case, competition among the entrepreneurs leads them to bid up wages according to their own higher profits.

Trade unions often consciously or unconsciously claim for their members wage increases corresponding to the increased productivity of capital. Unless the supply of capital has risen to the extent of the increased demand for capital, the enforcement of higher wages is bound to give rise to unemployment. But even when interest rates do not go up, because capital supply has increased and entrepreneurs are therefore in a position to grant wage increases—even then higher wages must lead to temporary unemployment in some enterprises. The benefits of increased productivity of capital are obviously much higher in enterprises needing much capital than in those needing less capital. Given a more or less uniform wage level, labor will have to shift from less capitalistic to more capitalistic enterprises, so that the latter can absorb the workers dismissed by the former.

It is often maintained that the productivity of labor as well as that of capital increases when wages are forced up by trade unions. In fact, this argument is used in favor of wages increasing ahead of an increase in the productivity of labor and capital. The truth is, however, that entrepreneurs are permanently at work to lower costs by new production methods and thus to maximize profits. Wage increases ahead of productivity increases as such do not accelerate this process. What wage increases are doing is to increase the productivity of labor, because they make labor scarce and cause capital equipment per remaining worker to increase. In the last resort this means substitution of capital for labor. Under our assumption of a given capital supply (in fact always except under the assumption of a very elastic capital supply—a very unrealistic assumption in a non-inflation economy) the substituting capital will never be sufficient to replace all workers dismissed. Nor will the new capital installations provide employment opportunities for the workers dismissed as too expensive. The capital structure has deepened but also narrowed, with the result that the total product of the economy does not grow but diminishes.

Changes in Production Coupled to Changes in Income Distribution

We can now formulate a law that we have already briefly mentioned. Every change in the supply of or the demand for one factor of production, e.g. labor, does more than just lead to a change in the employment of that factor and thus to a change in the total product. Unless other factors, e.g. capital, change to the same extent, any such change in the total product is always accompanied by a change in the distribution of the product among the factors of production. Production and income distribution are linked in such a way that an increase in output by the increased employment of one factor goes along with a decrease in the share of the total product accruing to this factor per unit of contribution. And every decrease in output by decreased employment of one factor goes along with an increase of his share per unit of contribution. If, for instance, total output increases because labor supply has grown, wages go down and interest rates up. If the increase in total output is due to an increase in the productivity of labor, wages go up, but less than would correspond to the increase in productivity.

This result follows, of course, from the law of diminishing returns. If more labor is combined with the same amount of capital, the marginal productivity of labor and the wage level decrease. Since to apply more labor to the same amount of capital means, by implication, less capital in relation to the previous amount of labor, the marginal productivity of capital and the interest rate increase. If the greater employment of labor is due to an increase in the productivity of labor, the wage level does not fall absolutely, but only in relation to the higher productivity.

Changes in the wages of individual workers per unit of their contribution, say one work-hour, have to be distinguished strictly from changes in the total wage bill accruing to labor as a whole. If more work is done and the total product thereby increased, the total income of the working class as a whole, i.e. the workers formerly employed and those newly employed, will increase both absolutely and relatively. The total wage bill paid out to the increased labor force always increases more than the interest paid to the capitalists for the same capital. Yet the share of the individual worker in the proceeds of one hour's work will have decreased. If, on the contrary, less work is done and the total product thereby decreased, the working class as a whole will be hurt. Yet the hourly wage of the individual worker will have increased. The question whether a decrease in total product is not too high a price to pay for a higher wage level is a political one. The answer depends on many considerations. The elasticity of the demand for labor is of decisive importance here, because it determines the extent to which higher wages are accompanied by a large or small decline of the total product.

Changes in Supply of Capital

The supply of capital can change in two ways. Either the savers—the people who refrain from consumption—offer the same amounts of capital at higher or lower interest rates, or they offer bigger or smaller amounts at given interest rates. Normally both cases have the same result: the amount of capital used in the economy increases or decreases.

This increase or decrease comes about as described in Part I. If the factors of production save part of their income and put it at the disposal of entrepreneurs, purchases of products for more or less rapid consumption are replaced by entrepreneurs' purchases of capital goods or intermediate products. After a transition period, which we shall describe later, this will result in a lengthening of the production detours by adding, as it were, a lengthening piece to all production detours. Whereas formerly, for instance, hammers were produced to be consumed ultimately in the form of nails produced with their help, now a steam hammer may be produced. It may not actually cost more than the former hand tools, but its installation requires more credit, since the capital invested does not reach the consumption stage until much later and the credits, therefore, cannot be repaid until then.

If former savings are withdrawn in order to be consumed the contrary happens. The production detours are shortened. And instead of machinery, to be consumed only later, consumption goods to be consumed immediately are delivered to the markets. Hammers are replaced by nails.

Increase of capital results, of course, in higher productivity of the labor now used in more capitalistic production methods. More finished goods can be produced with the same amount of labor. Decrease of capital, on the other hand, results in lower productivity of labor. The same amount of labor produces fewer finished goods.

The Reasons for Saving

The amount saved at various interest rates depends primarily on the savings habits of the community. On this there seems to be general agreement.

But is more saved at higher interest rates than at lower ones —in other words, is the supply of savings elastic or inelastic? This question has already been touched on in Part I; we must now discuss it in more detail. It is an axiom of classical economics that on every market the supply increases with higher prices, except under very special conditions. As regards the supply of capital, it has been pointed out that those wishing to provide for old age through saving might save less, rather than more, when the interest rate is higher because the accumulated interest would then contribute more to the sum desired as provision for old age. This kind of reaction is certainly possible, but will be limited to only a very small part of the saving public. The overwhelming part of savers do not have in mind some fixed amount which they would wish to provide for their old age. They simply compare the utility of present consumption with the utility of future consumption. And as higher interest rates increase the sum available for future consumption, because the accumulation of interest at the future date becomes greater, the propensity to save will, other things being equal, increase as interest rates rise. Although the matter is highly complicated, as will be evident later on, we can start from the assumption that as a rule the supply of capital is a positive function of the interest rate. If interest rates rise, for instance, because of higher demand for capital, more will be saved per unit of time.

This is true even in times of slow inflation, when a further decline of purchasing power is not generally expected. Therefore a rise in interest rates will in such times, too, induce people to shift their present consumption to the future. If inflation progresses quickly or over long periods, the population becomes inflation-conscious and apprehensive of further inflation. In this case interest rates lose their power to check present consumption.

What amounts are people prepared to save at given interest rates?

Here, under the influence of Keynes, a whole set of opinions has developed which has no foundation in reality. Savings are supposed to depend on the size of incomes in such a way that higher incomes lead not only to absolutely but also to relatively higher savings, i.e. the rate of saving increases. A so-called psychological law allegedly induces people to set aside a higher percentage of their income for future consumption, the more the necessities of the present are covered. This assertion often leads to far-reaching conclusions, especially to the so-called stagnation theory to which we shall return later.

We encounter here one of the half-truths so frequent in Keynes' teachings. No distinction is made between increases in the income of individuals compared to the income of other individuals, and increases in the income of the whole community; nor is one made in the latter between short-run, especially cyclical, and long-run changes.

It has long been established that the rich save more than the poor. When an individual's income increases, his savings rate will as a rule increase. But so long as the income of the whole community remains the same, the incomes of other individuals must obviously decline, as must their savings rates. Unless, then, the whole community becomes richer, the average savings rate, and thus aggregate saving per unit of time, cannot increase through some individuals becoming richer.

If, on the other hand, a whole community's income increases —and the only way this can happen in real terms is through increased work or increased productivity of labor—the total amount of saving generally grows, but the savings rates do not increase. They remain stable over time. At least for many modern industrial countries this is a statistically established fact. It is quite easy to understand. An individual becoming rich acquires the traditional consumption habits of the higher income brackets, where indeed larger parts of income are saved. If, on the other hand, a whole community becomes richer all people, including those of higher incomes, adjust their spending habits to this increased income. There is no reason why their propensity for future spending should increase more than their propensity for present spending. The community's traditional standard of living, which puts a brake on the present consumption of the newly rich, does not operate when the standard of living and, with it, consumption habits of the whole community change. Newer developments in the United States seem to suggest that with increasing wealth the savings rate even declines. A sort of inverse psychological law seems to induce at least Americans of today to spend more in the present, once a certain provision for the future has been secured.

In the short run, especially during a business cycle, savings rates indeed do fluctuate with income. If incomes increase during the upswing, saving increases over-proportionally, at least at the beginning and in the middle of the phase. But this has nothing to do with the psychological law establishing a growing preference for future consumption. Something quite different is at work: during an upswing prices rise because of credit and monetary expansion; people, not accustomed to the new prices, decide to wait with spending until prices come down again. For this reason savings increase more than incomes. We shall examine such prosperity saving later on in detail.

There is no doubt that total savings increase absolutely when total income increases. But this again does not follow from any psychological law but from the simple arithmetical fact that if the savings rate is stable, higher total income brings about correspondingly higher total savings. But as higher real incomes are chiefly the result of higher productivity through increased use of capital, such higher incomes will not change the relative strength of demand for and supply of capital. The higher savings are the result as well as the prerequisite of higher income. The fears of the so-called stagnation school, which since the publication of Keynes' *General Theory* has been alarming the world with the assertion that savings will outrun investment opportunities, are obviously unfounded both when based on an increase in the savings rate and on an absolute increase in savings.

Changes in Demand for Capital

We have seen that increased *supply* of capital leads to a lengthening, and a decreased supply leads to a shortening of the roundabout methods of production.

Increased *demand* for capital leads to exactly the same result as increased supply, namely to an increased use of capital and thus to a lengthening of the roundabout ways. Decreased demand for capital leads to the same result as decreased supply, namely to decreased use of capital and a shortening of production detours.

The effects of changes in demand for capital on interest rates, however, are opposite to those resulting from changes in supply. Whereas increased supply leads to lower interest rates, increased demand leads to higher ones. And whereas decreased supply leads to higher interest rates, decreased demand leads to lower ones.

The effects of changes in supply of and demand for capital on the amounts of capital used and on interest rates are demonstrated in Figure 19.

When supply of capital moves from S to S_1 (representing a decline in supply) the amount of capital used declines by *de*, just as it does if demand moves from D to D_1 (representing a decline in demand). Interest rates, however, rise by *ab* in the first case, but fall by *ac* in the latter case.

When the supply of capital moves from *S* to *S*₂ (indicating an increase in supply), the amount of capital used increases by *df*,

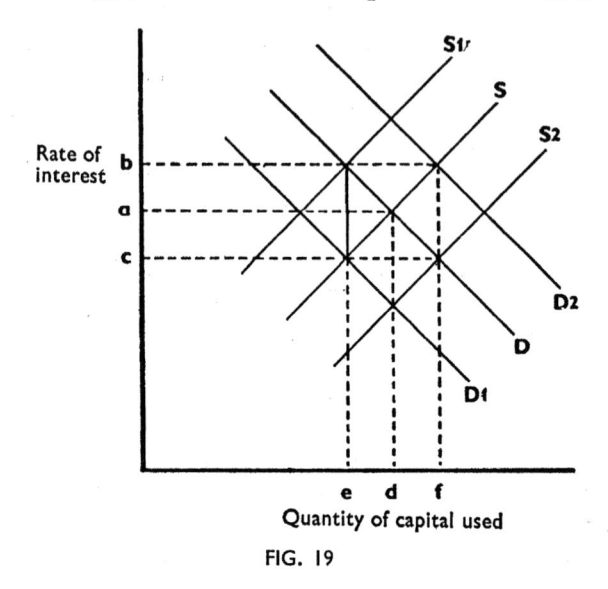

FIG. 19

just at it does when demand moves from *D* to *D*₂ (indicating an increase in demand). Interest rates fall by *ac* in the first case, but rise by *ab* in the latter.

We have already mentioned one of the reasons for increase and decrease in the demand for capital. We have described how an increase or decrease in the number of workers alters the marginal productivity of capital and thus causes demand for capital to increase or decrease. We have seen that, for instance, an enlarged labor supply as a rule increases the demand for capital because it encourages entrepreneurs to compete for the existing capital and to bid up interest rates.

Besides such induced increases and decreases in demand for capital, there are also autonomous increases and decreases. The chief reason for autonomous increase is to be found in new inventions enhancing productivity, i.e. the labor-saving effect of capital. If, by applying x units of capital, one can save not y but $2y$ workers, one will be able to pay $2z$ instead of only z as interest on these capital units. Autonomous decreases in the demand for capital never happen for economic reasons, since technical development always progresses and never regresses. But such decreases can happen for political reasons. Any threats—such as political unrest or widespread strikes—to the continued use of the plant to be built, or the machines to be installed, lower the demand for capital.

Changes in Capital Supply and Demand Influence Demand for Labor

We have described above how changes in the demand for and supply of labor give rise to induced changes in the demand for capital. We have seen that when, for instance, the supply of or the demand for labor grows, the latter because of an increase in the productivity of labor, the demand for capital rises. The same is true for the converse case. If the supply of or the demand for capital rises, the latter because the productivity of capital has gone up, there is an induced demand for labor. Through the use of cheaper or more productive capital the entrepreneurs reap extra profits, enabling them to compete for the existing labor and to bid up wages. Workers who have hitherto been too expensive or not productive enough to be employed can now be set to work. This is the explanation of the well-known fact—which, however, cannot be stressed too often—that, other things being equal, higher savings raise employment as well as the wage level. Should the supply of or the demand for capital fall, which is unlikely to happen in the long run, the result would be a reduction in employment and a fall in wages.

Personal and Corporation Taxes Influence Capital Supply and Demand

Taxes exercise a decisive influence on the demand for and the supply of capital and thus on the volume of production. This is a fact often mentioned but seldom sufficiently heeded in political discussions. Without going in detail into the complicated questions arising in this connection, we wish to present a few basic considerations.

Income taxes affect the borrowers as well as the lenders of capital. Borrowers of capital—in the wider sense comprising financing through the issue of shares, etc.—include in the first place corporations but also single entrepreneurs working with other people's money. The lenders include the capitalists proper but also the entrepreneur-capitalists, i.e. entrepreneurs substantially working with their own capital. In so far as the income of the first group is derived from the use of capital, an income tax is bound to reduce the demand for capital. If, for instance, a corporation has to pay taxes in the amount of 50 per cent of its revenue from capital, it will obviously be able to offer only half the compensation for the use of capital—at least against common and preferred shares—that it could offer without the tax. Higher income taxes for the second group, the capitalists and entrepreneur-capitalists, on the other hand, result in a reduction of supply. In the case of a 50 per cent income tax the capitalist will, in principle, offer the entrepreneur the same amount of capital, and the entrepreneur-capitalist will employ his own capital, only at twice the interest. It is always the net amount to be earned which counts for those who demand, and the net amount received which counts for those who supply capital.

It follows that in so far as the supply of capital is not completely inelastic, i.e. in so far as capitalists are unwilling to supply the same amounts of capital at lower interest rates, both corporation taxes and personal taxes are bound to have a restricting effect on the use of capital. This effect, in turn, can lead to the shifting of such taxes on to the workers or consumers. To the extent to which wages fall as a result of smaller capital equipment, or fail to rise as much as they would have done otherwise, the burden of the tax is shifted on to the workers. To the extent to which smaller capital equipment causes production costs to rise, the burden may be shifted on to the consumers. There are good reasons for believing that such shifts have, indeed, taken place in the past. For the gross earnings of corporations have, on the average, risen to such an extent that their net earnings after deduction of tax have not fallen but risen in spite of continuous tax increases. By pressing, in all countries, for ever higher corporation taxes labor appears therefore somewhat shortsighted.

It should also be mentioned that a strongly progressive income tax not only tends to reduce the supply of capital in general but brings about a relative scarcity of venture capital, i.e. capital prepared to take risks. For the capitalists' profits are taxed away to a greater or lesser degree, while they are left with the losses. A relative scarcity of risk capital is bound to reinforce the tendency towards curtailment of production. It follows that the view, upheld chiefly by labor leaders, that there are no limits to height and progressivity of income taxes is not correct. Very high income taxes must have serious consequences for production and employment, unless the State were to take over the role of the private investor, in one form or another, in accordance with the predictions of Keynes and the wishes of socialists and communists.

Changes in Use of Capital Coupled to Changes in Income Distribution

We again encounter the law mentioned above, according to which the use of a factor of production—and thus the total output—and the distribution of income are linked to each other. If more capital is used (capital being in cheaper supply or more productive), the whole output increases, but the compensation of the capitalist per unit of capital employed decreases. When the use of capital increases owing to cheaper or increased supply of capital this is self-evident, because in this case the interest rate falls. When the use of capital increases owing to higher productivity of, and hence higher demand for, capital the interest rate rises, but the compensation per unit of capital nevertheless decreases relatively to the compensation of labor because for a given labor force wages rise more than interest per unit of capital. If less capital is used, the opposite development takes place. The compensation of the capitalist per unit of capital increases. The amount saved per unit of capital, because of lower interest rates, accrues to labor in the form of higher wages. This is why labor is so interested in strong capital formation.

Whereas the compensation of the capitalist per unit of capital employed declines with greater use of capital, the compensation for the whole of the, now, larger capital employed nevertheless increases, although not proportionally to the increase in the capital employed. Therefore the share of the total product going to the capitalists as a class also increases both absolutely and relatively. But the increase in the share of capital is smaller than the increase in the use of capital. The margin accrues to labor.

Changes in Consumption and Investment do not Affect Aggregate Demand

Our argument so far has been based on the assumption that everything saved is invested by entrepreneurs, and that everything invested by entrepreneurs must be saved. On this assumption total demand cannot be affected by fluctuations either in consumption or in investment. When more is consumed, for instance, less will be invested, and when more is invested less will be consumed.

This statement differs substantially from the currently prevailing view of the situation. It is now held by most economists that if the population consumes more, i.e. saves less, aggregate demand increases because investment does not fall off. This increase in demand is even said to be cumulative, because, according to the so-called acceleration principle, increased consumption causes increased investment expenditure.

On the other hand, it is also said that aggregate demand rises when more is invested. This increase, too, is said to be cumulative, because, according to the so-called multiplier theory, increased investment causes increased consumption expenditure.

Our assertions are diametrically opposed to this view. To a certain extent, of course, they simply follow from the assumption underlying this part of our analysis, namely that inflation and deflation of purchasing power are absent from the economy. On this assumption investment and saving must always balance without the aid of the phenomena resulting from inflation or deflation. Any minus or plus in purchasing power spent by consumers must, in this case, be counterbalanced by a plus or minus in purchasing power spent by entrepreneurs on investment. There can be neither a deficit nor a surplus of savings.

Our assumption of an economy without inflation and deflation is in contrast with the method of exposition prevailing today, which makes the opposite assumption—namely that inflationary and deflationary gaps continuously develop in the economy. In such an economy saving and investment are, of course, never in equilibrium without the aid of inflation and deflation. Surpluses can push money out of circulation and deficits can draw money into circulation. When examining the phenomena of inflation and deflation we shall, later, have to deal extensively with the disappearance of money into "death traps," as this process has been called, and its reappearance from them. Here it suffices to state that except under special conditions involving certain rigidities money does not *in the long run* disappear in death traps. Hence there can, in the long run, be neither too much nor too little saving and investment. If this is true, then the volume of production does not, in principle, depend upon fluctuations in expenditure but upon the people's willingness to work. The description of an economy without inflation and deflation shows this with complete clarity, and this is why such a description is of great importance.

Under-employment as such does not Invalidate this Statement

The description is also important for the following reason. Keynesians generally concede that increased investment implies decreased consumption and increased consumption implies decreased investment in a fully employed economy, but maintain that as long as unemployment prevails increased consumption leads indeed to increased investment and increased investment to increased consumption. Our description puts this under-employment argument—with which, incidentally, the most paradoxical statements are sometimes justified—in its right place. First, no degree of under-employment whatever—accepting for once this vague notion—can have the result that more investment creates more consumption, or more consumption more investment as long as inflation is prevented. In an economy exposed to inflation, the latter can produce additional investment and additional consumption. But these additions, the result not of consumption or investment but of inflation, will as a rule be only nominal, not real. In real terms what is more consumed under inflation is less invested, and what is more invested is less consumed.

Nor does the presence of unemployment as such change the situation. It does not protect money inflation from resulting in pure price inflation, contrary to what is so often assumed. It will lead to increased production—and thus to increased real investment or real consumption—only under one of the two conditions: Either the labor supply curve must remain stable in spite of rising prices—for any length of time an entirely unrealistic assumption of Keynes who maintains that the supply of labor is not a function of real wages (*General Theory*, p. 8); or labor supply must be perfectly elastic for a certain time, as in the special situation of the recovery phase of the business cycle. We will treat these matters when dealing with effects of inflation (pp. 117 and 176) and the business cycle (pp. 177 and 178). To treat business cycle phenomena as general cases and to build on them a general theory can only lead to general confusion.

Deflationary Effect of Increased Employment

Our analysis so far was implicitly based on the assumption that, so long as the circulation of money is inelastic, the general level of prices and wages is not subject to any changes. Any purchasing power not spent by consumers, for instance, would go to the entrepreneurs, who would replace the savers as buyers on the markets. As a result, the general price level would not change.

The assumption of an unchanging price level needs to be qualified when more labor is employed owing to an increased supply of labor or capital, i.e. when the stream of goods in the economy is widened. Whether the money needed for the payment of the workers is withdrawn from longer production detours, or whether it is made available by new saving, the fact remains that this money now has to be turned over twice during the same period. It is now no longer spent by the consumer or entrepreneur himself for the products of the past period, but is in the first place used for wage payments. It is only the wage earners who then perform the "saved" act of purchase.

Unless, then, the money simultaneously present in the economy is increased, or unless its velocity of circulation increases, the money will not be sufficient to pay out all the credits which ought to be available according to the savings situation. The resulting situation will be exactly the same as if a Central Bank reduced the circulating issue. We shall discuss in Part III the consequences of such monetary deflation on prices, wages, and possibly employment.

It is often said that a growing economy, which means in essence one in which employment rises, requires money circulation to be increased. This is a justified claim, but it is justified not because the economy could not otherwise grow, but because its wage and price system would be subject to considerable deflationary pressure even if enough new savings to pay the new workers were forthcoming.[2]

Wage and Price Level and Increase in Productivity

Further difficulties are involved when there is an increase of the productivity of labor, which we discussed above. Here an additional need for money arises from the increase in wages due to higher productivity of labor. At a given circulation of money this increased need for money must again lead to a deflationary situation such as that described above.

In this connection, too, an increase of money is often demanded; the volume of money should be adjusted to the increase in the volume of goods due to the higher productivity.

We are here faced with a dilemma: to satisfy this claim would mean withholding the benefits of the higher productivity

[2] See, however, p. 123.

from the general public, in particular from those employed at fixed rates, instead of channeling those benefits to them by means of a general fall in prices. The other alternative, namely deflation of the price level at constant wages, meets with the resistance particularly of the debtor class, which incurs losses if the prices of its inventories fall while its monetary debts remain the same. We shall deal with other aspects of this dilemma below.[3]

Changes in Consumption and Investment do not Change Employment

Unless changes in consumption and investment lead to inflation or deflation, they cannot have any influence on aggregate employment. If less is consumed, for instance—which means that more is saved—more will be invested, there will be more employment in capital goods industries and less in consumption goods industries. The aggregate demand for labor remains unchanged. There is only a shift in demand as between industries.

But even where changes in saving or investment do lead to inflation or deflation, because money disappears in death traps or reappears from them, they can lead to fluctuations in employment only under the special conditions already mentioned. Employment never fluctuates if labor demands higher money wages when prices rise through inflation and is content with lower money wages when prices fall through deflation.

We shall later come back again to the problem of non-adjustment of nominal wage demands to a rising price level. Here it suffices to state that as long as wage demands are fully adjusted to changes in the value of money inflation and deflation simply lead to, or are identical with, changes in the level of wages *and* prices but do not alter the employment level.

If unemployment prevails in an economy which is not deflationary but even inflationary this cannot be due to a deflation effect, but the reason can be only a decision by labor to restrict its supply or make it more expensive. At the peak of the boom in 1937 about nine million were still unemployed in the

[3] See pp. 127–128.

United States, in contrast to the countries of Europe which enjoyed full employment. The prevailing unemployment can only have been voluntary unemployment, i.e. caused by the autonomous decisions of labor, supported by the government, to maintain a wage level which prevented employment of the unemployed. Unemployment had nothing to do with deficient demand, whether due to excessive saving, low investment or any other reasons. This is denied by New Dealers and trade unions. They maintain that many other reasons could have been causal—for instance the pessimistic expectations of business men, the scarcities in construction credits, and so on. These factors, however, could have created unemployment only via a reduction in aggregate demand, i.e. deflation. But a look at the charts of the pertinent data (investments, money circulation, bank credits, etc.) shows clearly that the economy was by no means deflationary. Credits were ample, and expectations in spite of the New Deal atmosphere not such that deflation followed. What happened was simply that labor had priced itself out of employment by autonomous decision favored by the New Deal administration. It was replaced by capital that had become cheaper. Exactly the same happened in Germany during the years 1926 and 1929, when in an inflationary environment—created by cheap foreign loans—many millions became unemployed as much as two years before the deflation of 1929.[4]

Many New Dealers and Keynesians believe, in accordance with certain theses in Keynes' *General Theory,* that too high wages not only do not prevent full employment but actually raise the level of employment by increasing demand for goods and thus for labor. We shall deal with the fallacies of this so-called purchasing power theory later on.

Facts and Expectations

At this point we must, at least briefly, touch upon a problem that is widely and extensively discussed among economists just now—the problem of how far actual changes, and how far the

[4] I described these phenomena as early as 1930 in my study, *Ist Arbeitslosigkeit unvermeidlich?*, Berlin, 1930.

correct or incorrect expectation or anticipation of future changes determine the decisions of the economic subjects.

Everything we have said so far was based on the assumption that demand and supply decisions of factors of production, and more particularly of entrepreneurs, are influenced by the changes actually taking place. This is the assumption regularly made by the classical economists.

But this way of presentation does not take into account that entrepreneurs cannot sell at once what is produced in the current production period, for the simple reason that production takes time. Therefore, entrepreneurs must always try to visualize what changes may take place in the future. Knowledge of the present is of little help to them, since every economy is subject to continuous change.

Unfortunately the future can never be anticipated with certainty. It is open to only probability judgments. Were this otherwise, were the future recognizable with certainty by everyone, all future changes would be discounted in advance as if the future were the present. No price changes could happen any more between the present and the future.

In fact, it is a prerequisite of market changes that future changes in data are not, or not sufficiently, recognized by all the parties on the market, i.e. that at least some believe, wrongly, in the continuation of the *status quo*. In a certain sense the prices of the present always rest on errors.

These errors have far-reaching consequences for the structure of the economy as a whole, as well as for the profit and loss situation of individual entrepreneurs.

Often errors in one direction will be compensated by errors in another. This suggests that the classical procedure of bagatellizing in general the problems of anticipations remains correct within wide limits.

Maladjustments to Future Changes

Most entrepreneurs make their decisions on the basis of the data of the present. Misdirection of production must ensue. If consumer tastes change, for instance, it may happen that too many apples and not enough pears will be produced. This is misdirection of production within the group of consumption goods. More important is the misdirection of production in respect of whole groups of goods. When savings increase, the demand for capital goods rises while the demand for consumption goods contracts. For a time too much of the latter and too little of the former will be produced.

Most entrepreneurs adjust their production to changed demand only when the change in the latter has actually taken place. In many cases adjustment to the new demand pattern takes place even later, when the machines serving only the production of goods now in reduced demand have been used up. Only then can entrepreneurs recover the capital they need for starting up new production. In the meantime a complicated pattern of intermediate situations will develop which cannot be described here in detail. The prices of some goods fall, and the prices of others rise. But these price changes normally do not exceed certain limits. Price increases above production cost will be considered as temporary by buyers, price declines below production cost as temporary by sellers. Apart from exceptional cases the former prefer to wait with their purchases and the latter with their sales, until production has adjusted itself to the new demand pattern.

Profits Result from Correct Anticipations

Without errors about the future there could be no profits. Profits, as defined by us, disappear as soon as the supply and demand of all producers have been adjusted to changes. In fact, however, entrepreneurs do not at once bid up the prices of the factors of production to the point where future price rises can no longer yield profits. The reason is that not all entrepreneurs anticipate higher prices. Some entrepreneurs do, while others expect prices to remain stable or even to decline. Those entrepreneurs who have anticipated higher prices and have therefore enlisted factors of production at the ruling, lower, prices make profits; those who have not anticipated higher prices and have wholly or partly abstained from enlisting factors of production fail to make profits or even suffer losses.

Do Profits Disappear in the Long Run?

As the future approaches and becomes the present, everybody recognizes the changes. More and more entrepreneurs raise their bids for factors of production—when there is a rise in the price of goods. Finally, there is no further possibility of making profits through correct anticipation of this particular segment of the future. At the same time, however, a new segment of the future appears on the horizon of time. Again, guesses about the future have to be made; again there are possibilities of error, and again possibilities of making profits by avoiding errors.

Each new segment of the future is as uncertain as the one before. The changes taking place in one period can never do more than indicate a tendency of price movements—they can never definitely determine future prices, since, as the future approaches, prices begin to feel the influence of the expectations of a more distant future.

In statistical works on the distribution of income the statement is often found that profits are stable in the long run, in the sense that the percentage of national income distributed as profits does not change over long periods. These statements are, however, not concerned with profits as defined by us above, but rather with the incomes of corporations and individual business men from interest and rents of all kinds.

Security Prices and Changes in Demand for and Supply of Capital

Let us briefly examine some consequences of what we have said for the stock markets.

If interest rates decline owing to declining demand for or rising supply of capital, or if interest rates rise for the opposite reasons, this must have decisive effects on the prices of shares and bonds.

These effects are of a somewhat complex nature. Shares, common as well as preferred, and bonds represent capital invested in an enterprise. We may start from the simplest case that, as time goes on, this capital is always set to work again—reinvested—by the enterprise. The earnings on these investments must obviously be identical with the benefits derived from the marginal unit of capital to be used, i.e. with the general interest rate.

If now these benefits decline, e.g. because of labor becoming more demanding, then the earnings of the companies will decline and so will interest rates. It follows that, in this case, the price of common shares will on the average remain unchanged. For earnings decline neither more nor less than the interest rates at which these earnings are capitalized. But where the securities bear fixed dividends or interests, as in the case of preferred shares and bonds, their prices must go up. For the payments received remain the same—whereas the capitalization factor, the interest rate, has declined. The prices of common shares of companies with bond or preferred issues ahead must decline, because the earnings of these companies have to cover fixed bond interests and preferred dividends

If, on the other hand, capital invested in enterprises yields more than previously, for instance because the productivity of capital has increased, then the earnings of the companies will rise and so will the interest rate. Therefore there will again be no changes in the prices for shares with variable dividend rates because the higher dividends are now capitalized at a higher interest rate. But where the dividends or interests are fixed for long periods, as with preferred shares and bonds, prices will decline. For the fixed dividends or interests are now capitalized at a higher interest rate. Prices of common shares of companies with preferred shares and bonds ahead will rise.

All this supposes, however, that all the capital invested in an enterprise can, in fact, always be reinvested whenever a change occurs. This is, however, only correct from the moment when capital, frozen in production detours of a certain length, can be replaced. Until then, the old capital may yield less than the new capital.

If, for instance, interest rates decline under the impact of increased savings, enterprises beginning at that moment to build their plant can invest in a more capitalistic way. They save labor and can therefore pay higher wages. The old enterprises will be forced through competition to pay the same higher wages, but can profit from the advantages of the longer production detours only after the old plant is amortized and replaced. The earnings of enterprises with old plants will, therefore, be lower than the earnings of those with new ones. The prices of shares of the former enterprises will for a certain time remain below the prices of shares of the latter.

If, on the other hand, interest rates rise under the impact of contracting savings, enterprises then beginning to build their plant can invest in a less capitalistic manner. They need less capital and thereby save interest. The old enterprises will be able to save interest only after the old plant is amortized and replaced. The earnings of such enterprises will be lower than earnings of enterprises with new plants. The prices of shares of the former enterprises will for a certain time remain below the prices of shares of the latter, except if they have covered their long term capital needs at the previous, lower, rates of interest.

Rents and monopoly profits are, in general, not affected by changes in demand for and supply of capital. Therefore, a fall in interest rates will raise the prices of shares with earnings coming largely from rents and monopoly profits, and a rise in interest rates will depress the prices of such shares. The fact that the revenues of most enterprises include strong elements of rents and monopoly profits explains why, in contrast to what we said above, lower interest rates generally lead to higher, and higher interest rates to lower, stock prices.

Corporation Taxes and Share Prices

Corporation taxes are taxes on the earnings of corporations. They tend, as demonstrated above (p. 90), to lower the demand for capital.

The effects on share prices of such a reduction in demand for capital will, however, be somewhat different from those of declining demand for capital in general. For corporation taxes lower the earnings only of corporations, not of other entrepreneurs whose business is not incorporated. Therefore, earnings of corporations will decline more than the interest rates. Investors, however, will compare the reduced earnings of corporations with other, not reduced, earnings on capital. They will buy shares only at prices taking the lower net yield of corporations into account. For it is only the net earnings—earnings after taxes—not the gross earnings that count for the investors.

A capitalist who newly invests in shares does not suffer through the introduction or raising of a corporation tax. He buys the reduced earnings at a correspondingly lower price, so that the net yield of his capital is not impaired. The old shareholders, however, suffer through the introduction or increase of corporation taxes. They had invested at prices corresponding to earnings not reduced by the tax. The introduction of the tax depresses share prices to a level corresponding to the new net earnings. The introduction of a 50 per cent corporation tax threatens the old shareholders theoretically with a loss of 50 per cent of their capital.

Personal Income Taxes and Share Prices

Personal income taxes on earnings from capital reduce the supply of capital, as explained above.

The effects on share prices of such a reduction in the supply of capital will, again, be somewhat different from those of a reduction in the supply of capital in general. Progressive income taxes, such as are usual nowadays, do not affect all kinds of investment in the same manner. An investor has the choice of investing in bonds involving low yields and lower risks or in shares involving high yields and higher risks. If the yield of shares exceeds bond yields by a certain amount, he will choose investment in shares in spite of the higher risk. Under a system of highly progressive income taxes the lower income on bonds is less affected than the higher income on shares. The investor might decide that the net earnings of common shares, which are significantly reduced by the progressive taxes, are no longer a sufficient compensation for the higher risk. For, again, it is only the net earnings, the earnings remaining after payment of taxes, that enter into his calculations. He will invest in shares only at a higher gross yield, i.e. at lower prices.

A capitalist who newly invests in shares after the introduction or raising of a progressive income tax will not be affected by the fall in share prices. He buys the shares at a price which already reflects the reduction of its net earnings as compared with the yield of bonds. The old investor, however, again suffers losses.

It is a well-known fact that during the 1940s the yields of common stocks in the U.S. increased on the average, whereas the yields on bonds declined: the margin between bond and share yields widened substantially. It can be assumed that the progressivity of the income tax was largely responsible for this development. Investment in common shares with its much greater risk seems to have appealed to capitalists in high income brackets only at yields compensating at least partly for the higher income taxes. During the last years the spread has narrowed considerably. The experiences of the war and post-war inflation seem to have resulted in investors becoming less income conscious and more substance conscious. It is, however, too early to judge whether a structural change in the attitude of investors has taken place or whether only the well-known phenomenon of boom periods is repeating itself.

Part III

THE ECONOMY IN INFLATION AND DEFLATION

The Preconditions of Inflation and Deflation

So far we have examined the working of an economy in which the volume of money and its velocity of circulation remain unchanged. In the real world both change continuously. They increase in the case of inflation and decrease in the case of deflation. This is why the study of preconditions and the effects of inflation and deflation are of such paramount importance. Many, one can almost say most, seemingly very complicated questions—also in the field of the theory of foreign trade, as for instance regarding the foreign trade multiplier—become easily solvable when analyzed in terms of inflation and deflation theory.

Much has been written about the circumstances in which inflation and deflation of the circulation of money should be tolerated or avoided. It is generally held that the circulation of money should be neutral, i.e. should be regulated in such a manner that the price level is not influenced from the "money side." But what if there are influences tending to change the value of money, originating on the "goods side"? Should such influences be compensated from the money side? If, for instance, productivity of labor rises, as discussed earlier, should a deflation of the price level be tolerated or prevented? If in the latter case monetary circulation is inflated, the general price level, however defined, does indeed remain stable and to this extent inflation is neutral. But it is neutral only to this extent because other effects of inflation—such as inflation profits due to price support in spite of lower costs and a resulting inducement to expand production—are by no means ruled out. Such inflation would not be entirely neutral. We need only recall the undoubtedly inflationary boom of the twenties, when the price level had, if any, a falling tendency. Whereas the question of "inflation without inflation," i.e. without inflation of the price level, is highly controversial it seems to be generally agreed that inflation and deflation *involving* changes in the price level represent a degree of unneutrality that should, in principle, be avoided.

It is generally assumed nowadays that a stronger propensity to save or a weaker propensity to invest leads to deflation, and that a weaker propensity to save or a stronger propensity to invest leads to inflation. But obviously neither inflation nor deflation can occur unless money is somehow able to disappear from circulation into death traps. Otherwise higher savings, for instance, would lead not to deflation but, via lowered interest rates, to higher investment; and lower savings would lead not to inflation but via higher interest rates to lower investment. The question of which conditions lead to inflation and deflation is, therefore, identical with the question of which conditions force money out of or into these death traps.

Two sorts of death traps have to be distinguished in a modern economy—the cash hoards of private individuals and the cash reserves of the Central Banks. The first we shall call the small, the latter the big death traps.

The role played by money substitutes, chiefly demand deposits with banks, will be discussed later.

The Myth of the Small Death Traps

The appearance and disappearance of money out of and into private hoards can also be regarded as a change in the velocity of money turnover.

The reason for private hoarding—or for a decrease in the velocity of monetary circulation—is nowadays mostly explained in terms of the liquidity preference theory, as developed by Keynes. According to Keynes, people have a tendency to hoard cash. This tendency decreases when interest rates rise. Interest is, indeed, regarded as compensation for parting with cash, i.e. with liquidity, rather than as compensation for abstaining from consumption and thereby making credits available. Money disappears into hoards with falling and reappears with rising interest rates.

The factual assumptions underlying this reasoning are, like so many others in modern theory, entirely unrealistic.[1] Interest rates on the one hand, and investment and consumption decisions on the other, influence each other, but they by no means determine the amount of cash the business community and private individuals keep in their office safes or at home. Decisive are the payment habits of the community, and as long as these do not change, cash holdings can be regarded as stable. Changes in these payment habits occur from time to time—for instance when black markets develop. For obvious reasons many people will then increase their cash holdings rather than pay them into the banks, whence they could re-enter circulation.

Nor do cash holdings increase if interest rates fall to zero or near zero because of very low credit demand. Very low interest rates, or even no interest at all, do not seem to induce people to keep their money at home. For reasons of convenience and security, they continue to pay their excess cash into the banks so that private hoards do not increase. Some people, of course, have no bank accounts, and others may, in special circumstances, prefer to keep some of their unspent and uninvested money in their own pockets or desk drawers. To this extent private hoards can increase. Such an increase can, in fact, be observed in times of depression.

As a rule, however, there is no such thing as a *general* tendency to hoard cash. Any theory of inflationary and deflationary gaps, if resting on the existence of the small death traps, is therefore untenable. And interest is not a compensation for not hoarding but for saving and lending—according to the pre-Keynesian view which, while less original, remains correct.

The Large Death Traps

Much more important nowadays than the small death traps are the large death traps: the Central Banks into which money

[1] See Chapter 13 of my *Economics of Illusion*, to which the reader is especially referred.

disappears and out of which it reappears, and which have the power to destroy and to create money.

These death traps open whenever there is a significant difference between interest rates prevailing on the money and capital markets on the one hand; and on the other hand the Central Banks' discount rate for commercial bills—the bank rate—which also determines the price at which Central Banks buy and sell government bonds by so-called open market operations. When, for instance, the interest rates on the credit markets are higher than the bank rate, individuals and banks will sell bills and bonds to the Central Banks. The cash paid out by the latter for the bills and bonds swells the circulation of money and thereby creates money inflation. In the contrary case when the bank rate is higher than the market rate, individuals and banks will redeem bills and bonds from the Central Banks. Cash will flow from circulation into the Central Banks' cash reserves, and money deflation will ensue.

In a world with changing rates the large death traps are, therefore, opened by the unwillingness or inability of the Central Banks to adjust their rates to the market rates so quickly that neither purchases from nor sales to the Central Banks are made. The relative stability and rigidity of the bank rate is, therefore, in the last instance the cause of the instability and flexibility of the monetary system.

Involuntary Rigidities

Failure to adjust the bank rate to the rates of the free credit markets may be due to deliberate policy or happen, as it were, by mistake.

The latter sort of non-adjustment is a typical feature of business cycles. During the upswing the demand for credit increases. Interest rates have a rising tendency. If the bank rate moved up accordingly, the large death traps would remain closed because, however strong the demand for credits, there is always an interest rate high enough to prevent a further expansion of the circulation—even without applying such crude means as credit restrictions. During a depression, on the other hand, the demand for credit declines and interest rates have a falling tendency. If bank rates were lowered accordingly, no deflation would occur, provided the demand for credit did not become so abnormally low as to force interest rates on the market down to, or nearly down to, zero. This is a special case which we shall discuss presently, and which accounts for the asymmetry in the power of Central Banks in booms and depressions. A boom can always be broken by purely monetary means; a depression might need other measures.

As a rule Central Banks follow the changes in the market rates only with a substantial lag. This lag is mainly caused by the inability of Central Banks to recognize the inflationary or deflationary character of the economic situation in time, and —in the case of inflation—also by the unpopularity of restrictive monetary policies.

This, by the way, is in essence the idea underlying the business cycle theory of the great Swedish economist, K. Wicksell. His "natural" interest rate was, basically, the rate at which demand for and supply of credit are in balance without any interference from money-creating or money-destroying Central Banks. According to his view, boom and inflation, depression and deflation, are caused—or at least made possible—by time lags in the adjustment of market rates to rising or declining natural rates. The adjustment lag of market rates in its turn is due to the adjustment lag of the bank rate. Wicksell took it for granted that differences between market rates and natural rates were pathological exceptions to be avoided. He never went so far as to maintain that credit demand and credit supply balance only by chance without money deflation or inflation. In short, Wicksell considered the so-called deflationary gaps, the interruption of the money flow from saver to borrower, as altogether abnormal. To Wicksell, in contrast to Keynes, Say's law appeared valid in the general case and not only by accident.

Deliberate Maladjustments

In some cases Central Banks deliberately fail to adjust the bank rate to the natural interest rate.

Most important nowadays is the case of the permanent

cheap money policy, such as was practiced until very recently in the United States and Great Britain. This policy is advocated for various reasons. One such reason is the erroneous, Keynesian, belief that low interest rates are a sort of insurance against unemployment; another, the equally erroneous belief that they reduce the cost of government debts to the taxpayer. However, the cheap money policy as practiced for the last two decades was, if not the cause, then certainly the necessary condition for the strong inflations during that period, and thus much more costly than higher interest rates—at least for all those taxpayers who did not make inflation profits.

Budgetary Deficits and Surpluses, as such, do not Create Inflation or Deflation

Many people believe that budget deficits lead to inflation, budget surpluses to deflation. This view, however, is correct only in certain circumstances. A budget deficit creates credit demand on the part of the government, and thereby raises interest rates. But inflation follows only if the Central Banks fail to raise the bank rate accordingly. Thus, whether a budget deficit creates inflation or not depends entirely on the supply price for credits determined by the Central Banks, which, it is true, is often dictated by the governments wishing to raise funds.

Likewise, a budget surplus need not necessarily lead to deflation. If the government uses the surplus to repay its debts, supply on the credit markets increases and interest rates fall. But deflation need follow only if the bank rate is not reduced correspondingly. It may, of course, be technically impossible to reduce the bank rate—namely when it is already very near zero. Otherwise the increased credit supply is absorbed by credit demand without deflationary consequences.

Budget surpluses may even coincide with inflation, when the increase in credit demand from the private sector of the economy exceeds the increase in credit supply due to the repayment of government debts. Unless the Central Bank then raises its discount rate and lowers the price at which it is prepared to buy government bonds inflation will ensue. This is why, in the United States, 1947 with its budget surplus was not a year of deflation but of inflation.

Death Traps Open when the Credit Demand is Extremely Weak

Even if the Central Banks do keep the discount rates adjusted to the market rate, the large death traps will open whenever credit demand declines to such an extent that even at extremely low interest rates part of the credit supply is no longer absorbed by demand. If credit cannot be cheapened any further, it is clearly impossible to bring about inflation, or, as it is often said, reflation, by means of discount policy. All that can be done then is to unbalance the budget and thereby create credit demand by the government. This process is known as deficit spending.

Cyclical Deflation

Deflation due to deficient credit demand is characteristic of the depression phase of the business cycle. This kind of deflation alternates with the inflation of the prosperity phase.

The cause of excess supply on credit markets during depressions is a combination of strongly declining demand for investable funds, due to entrepreneurs' reluctance to invest, and of strongly increasing supply of such funds, due to consumers' reluctance to spend. This is why Keynesians—and many economists before them—try to explain crises and depressions by over-saving. But this explanation cannot be satisfactory, at least not when saving is understood in the usual sense of the word as the expression of the wish to provide for the future by curtailing present consumption. If it were true that saving in this sense is responsible for depressions, interest rates would begin to fall slowly at the end of the boom, for saving habits do not change suddenly at the upper turning point of the business cycle. In fact, interest rates do not fall at all during a crisis; on the contrary, as we shall see, they even rise. They decline only later on, and then abruptly.

What creates excess supply and deficient demand on credit markets is something else: it is the more or less simultaneous reluctance of consumers to consume and of entrepreneurs to invest. This double reluctance is essentially due to waning confidence in the demand and price structure. Keynes and many of his followers lump both kinds of abstinence from consumption together under the expression "lacking propensity to consume." They fail to distinguish between a long-run, on the one hand, and on the other a short-run cyclical phenomenon. This is the main reason why I cannot share the opinion, held also by many non-Keynesians, that Keynes' abstract conceptual apparatus represents significant progress.

We shall deal with the phenomenon of cycles later in detail. It suffices here to emphasize that the existence of cyclical depressions does not invalidate our basic proposition that changes in the propensity to save do not lead to inflation or deflation, to the appearance and disappearance of money in and out of circulation.

Secular Deflation (Stagnation)

Our proposition that in the long run a disproportion between credit supply and credit demand leading to deflation is impossible, is contrary to the so-called stagnation theory of Keynes and certain of his followers. According to that theory permanent, non-reversible, deflation is not only possible but indeed probable in the not too distant future. The argument runs roughly along these lines: while the communities become richer, both the amount of annual saving and the saturation of the economy with capital are bound to reach a point where there is no further investment opportunity for additional savings. From this point on it is said, a so-called investment gap will lead to permanent and even progressive deflation.

We do not know what will happen in a hundred years. For the present the whole approach of the "stagnationists" appears highly unrealistic. Every entrepreneur knows that he would be able to improve the productivity of his enterprise by using ever more capital. Most entrepreneurs have plans for such improvements, and abstain from carrying them out only because the great majority of them cannot obtain the required credits for sufficiently long terms or on profitable conditions.

During the past few years it has, incidentally, become quiet on the stagnation front—perhaps owing to developments in the atomic and related fields. Stagnation theorists seem even to have switched to the idea that we are living in an age of permanent inflation—an idea that will not fail, in its turn, to be discredited by events. So far as Europe with its lack of capital is concerned, the idea that unemployment should essentially be due to investment lagging behind saving seems—in Professor Adolf Weber's words—just a bad joke. This idea is simply the typical product of the Great Depression which has misled some authors to regard as secular a phenomenon which was no more than cyclical. Like bad stock exchange speculators they could not grasp the reversibility of a trend.

This does not mean that credit demand can never be deficient in the long run. Wages and taxes may be raised to such a high level that additional investment might, indeed, appear unprofitable. Then the demand curve may reach such a low point that part of the supply of credit is no longer absorbed. Many Keynesians advocate ever higher wages and ever more progressive income taxes with a view of redistributing income to the advantage of those with a higher propensity to consume. To the extent that this advice is followed, stagnation may indeed take place—but only because Keynesians have themselves created the conditions in which their theory, as such incorrect, would become valid.

Checking Accounts and Cash

So far, we have dealt only with money, in the sense mainly of banknotes and currency. We now turn to the so-called money substitutes—mainly demand deposits with banks, from which payments are ordinarily made by check. Undoubtedly the overwhelming part of all payments in a modern economy are made by check or other transfers. Nevertheless it is, for analytical purposes, correct to describe and examine in the first place the inflation and deflation of the circulating cash.

Checking accounts may simply be created because the owners of funds consider an account more convenient than cash and, therefore, pay their money into checking accounts.

Checking or other deposit accounts may also be created by banks through crediting the amounts to their clients.

Such granting of credits is inflationary, i.e. increases the quantity of money, unless other checking or deposit accounts are simultaneously immobilized—consolidated—by repayment of credits or by abstinence from spending, i.e. saving. The granting of credits in cash, too, is inflationary to the extent that corresponding amounts are not paid into the banks as repayment of credits or saving.

In all these cases the creation of bank money for the purpose of granting credits obviously involves inflation just as does the issue of money by the Central Banks; inversely, the destruction of bank money through repayment of credits involves deflation just as does the retirement of banknotes by the Central Banks.

Economic literature has extensively dealt with the question whether, for these reasons, the power of Central Banks in preventing inflation and deflation is not a very limited one. Are not, in reality, the private banks responsible for inflation and deflation? Some writers have answered this question in the affirmative. They advocate, therefore, a hundred per cent coverage of demand deposits with the banks by deposits of the bank with Central Banks, in order to strengthen the control of the Central Banks over the money circulation. Notwithstanding the propaganda made in its favor by enemies of banks this claim is not justified. Whether payments are made by check, banknotes or paper money, the responsibility of Central Banks for the volume of money circulation remains the same. This is undeniable for the simple reason that some—even if only a small—part of the aggregate payments in the economy is always made by cash. By supplying the necessary amounts of cash the Central Banks govern, so to speak, the whole pyramid of credit erected by the banks. In order that the banks can grant credits in the amount of x, Central Banks have to issue a certain fraction of x in banknotes. Nor are the Central Banks powerless with respect to an increase in the velocity of the circulation of bank money following changes in the spending policy of consumers, described later, pp. 130–131.

In order that the velocity of circulation of bank money can increase by x per cent, Central Banks have to issue a certain fraction of x in new banknotes, to allow for a greater turnover per unit of time. It is true that this does not hold when the velocity of circulation of banknotes, too, increases. But the protection against this contingency is not a full coverage of bank money through deposits with Central Banks, but a reduction of the note issue.

In these circumstances we can state that so long as the payment habits of the community, i.e. the ratio of cash payments to non-cash payments, do not change—and they normally change only very slowly—the credit policy of private banks is rigidly tied to the credit policy of the Central Banks. Only in times of transition—when, for instance, cash payments decline as against non-cash payments—are banks and owners of checking accounts independent of the Central Banks in their credit and spending policy.

This situation may be compared with the situation of a dog which is kept on a leash. Whether the leash is long or short, he cannot get away. Only when the leash is loosened can the dog move freely—and then only within certain limits.

Where, as in the United States, commercial banks have to cover a certain percentage of their demand deposits by accounts with the Central Banks, these have—by raising the so-called reserve requirements and hardening the conditions under which they can be acquired—a direct and immediate influence on the creation of bank money.

Circular Flow and Sequence Analysis of the Effects of Inflation and Deflation

The effects of inflation and deflation are not easily described. Not only are they manifold, interdependent and different according to various causes—they also change over time. A single dose of inflation has effects in the current production period quite different from those in more distant periods. Its as it were, retroactive effects on the products of past periods, namely on their prices, are again quite different.

This is why the so-called circular analysis, preferred nowadays by many economists under the influence of Keynes' *General Theory* which mostly uses this method, can only lead to unrealistic results. If we assume that everything in an economy happens at the same time, a complete confusion of cause and effect must ensue. What happens on Saturday—for instance saving—must indeed then be considered to have influenced retroactively what has happened the previous Monday in the sphere of production and employment. As a result, neither the real causes of unemployment nor the real effects of insufficient consumption are correctly described or explained and one forgets that, in order to spend, one has first to earn.

Only the so-called sequence or chain analysis, which clearly distinguishes what happens in the past, in the present and in later acts of the drama of inflation, can correctly describe and explain the causal connections.

Effects of Inflation and Deflation on the Capital Structure

The effects of inflationary credits are, in many respects, different from those of non-inflationary credits. But the consequences on the capital structure are the same. What is decisive for the effects on the capital structure is not the nature of the supply, but the nature of the demand for credits.

If the additional purchasing power created by inflationary credits is directed towards consumption goods, as happens in war-time, production or consumption detours become shorter on the average. If, on the other hand, the additional credits are used for purposes of production—as they are in times of normal cyclical prosperity—all those effects will be created which have been described in Part II as the effects of increased use of capital. Production will be directed into longer production detours, the capitalistic structure of the economy will be deepened. It makes no difference whether the credits are granted with money created *ad hoc* by Central Banks or private banks, or with money reaching the banks through genuine saving.

THE ECONOMY IN INFLATION AND DEFLATION 117

Effects of Inflation and Deflation on Employment

The effects of inflationary credits are not limited to lengthening production detours. Since the additional supply of inflationary credits lowers interest rates not only more capital but also more labor can be used. Employment increases because the lower loan costs of capital allow the employment of submarginal workers. As the supply curve of capital moves downward, so the demand curve for labor moves upward. And higher employment means *ceteris paribus* a greater product.

Inflationary credit expansion, as well as credit expansion due to higher genuine saving, indeed increases employment. Deflationary credit contraction, as well as credit contraction due to lower genuine saving, decreases employment. And lower employment means *ceteris paribus* a smaller product.

Are these Effects Lasting?

It is important to note that if—but only if—no changes in the supply price of factors of production, especially labor and capital, occur simultaneously with credit inflation the latter's effects on capital structure as well as on employment are lasting. The inflationary credit expansion can then, in fact, have results which seem quite miraculous. Nor need the situation deteriorate again in the next production period, always assuming the supply prices of production factors remain unchanged. But, as we shall see, this can never be the case for any length of time. Generally, by the next production period, the factors of production will react to the higher price level—which is the main consequence of inflation—by raising their supply prices. This is the chief reason why the Keynesian demand theory of employment, according to which employment is a function of monetary demand, is unacceptable to neo-classical economists.

Does Saving Equal Investment?

If entrepreneurs borrow money, there must be people who save money. Savings must therefore equal investments, as surely as a liability in the balance sheet of one member of the economy must correspond to an asset in the balance sheet of another. On the other hand, we have seen that saving and investment may not balance at "unnatural" interest rates, so that inflationary and deflationary gaps develop.

The problem of how saving and investment can at the same time balance and not balance has been discussed at great length in literature. The problem, like so many in modern economics, is, however, only an apparent one. The real problem is not whether but in which way—with or without inflation and deflation—they balance.

Obviously saving and investment are not equal in so far as they balance only if and when the banks have expanded or contracted their credits by inflation or deflation. But once this is done, saving equals investment. When the banks grant credits having no counterpart in simultaneous saving, they simply create new savings, as surely as the new debtors in the balance sheets of banks must be matched by new creditors, and the new bills in the balance sheet of Central Banks by new banknote liabilities.

The Banks and the Central Banks are the Savers

Who are the new savers? If the banknotes issued by the Central Banks and the checking accounts created by the private banks were real liabilities, the answer would be somewhat complicated. But they are not. As long as the banknotes circulate and the checking accounts are used for payments, they are liabilities of the banks only in a formal sense, but in reality capital the banks created, so to speak, out of nothing. They could figure on the right-hand side of the banks' balance sheets as capital rather than as debts, as long as the above conditions are fulfilled. If this is correct, then the money-creating institutions themselves can be considered as the savers of the money that has been lent to entrepreneurs.

Inflation is often supposed to cause or work through forced saving. By this is meant that the consumption of the holders of old money is curtailed through rising prices, in favor of those competing on the markets with new money. While such a curtailment of consumption by holders of old money happens, indeed, it is entirely misleading to describe this process as forced saving. It would be more correctly described as forced restriction of consumption, for the holders of old money do not emerge with more money or other assets, as they should do if they had saved.

If saving exceeds investment, entrepreneurs are able to satisfy their need for credits on the open markets in one way or another and to repay bank loans. Money in the wider sense will disappear from circulation, but at the same time the quasi-capital of the banks and of the Central Banks, which was created by the earlier granting of credits, will be destroyed.

Forced restrictions of consumption are the reasons why inflation can have a lasting effect on the capital structure. But it is a regrettable and undeniable fact that inflations generally lead to the dynamic processes which we shall examine later and not to stable equilibria situations.

Inflation and Deflation and the General Price Level

The increased purchasing power created by credit expansion never buys the goods produced in the same period. It is important to keep in mind that it buys the products of a former period, when production cannot yet have been influenced by inflation and when output can, therefore, not yet have increased. Production cannot yet have caught up with the new, greater, purchasing power. The result is an increase in the prices of the products of the past period. A further result is the general expectation that this new price level will remain or even rise. This expectation, in turn, is responsible for most dynamic phenomena of inflation.

Why the general price level rises when new money is introduced into the economy is easy to understand. Entrepreneurs use this money either directly for the purchase of capital goods and intermediate products, or to pay workers' wages. In the latter case the money increases the demand on the markets for consumption goods. In both cases the average demand curve for goods shifts to the right and cuts the supply curve at a higher point.

The function of the higher price level is, of course, to curtail the demand until supply again equals demand. The demand of the buyers owning the new, additional, money can only be satisfied at the expense of the old buyers' demand. To use a simile often quoted in this connection: if, unexpectedly, fifteen guests sit down to dinner at a table prepared for only ten, then obviously "old" guests can eat only two-thirds of the meal originally intended for them.

This is a correct description of the effects of money and credit inflation of the current period (Period II) on the prices of goods produced in the past production period (Period I), in which inflation could not yet influence the volume of output.

In practice, under certain exceptional circumstances, the current period's new money does not raise the price level of both capital and consumer goods produced in the past period. When inventories have accumulated during a depression because of the sellers' unwillingness to sell at the market (at any price), the higher demand can for some time be met out of stock. To this extent the higher demand leads to increased sales rather than to higher prices. We shall deal with such cases of price rigidity later, when describing the mechanism of the business cycle. For the moment we are dealing with a perfectly competitive economy, with no interruption of the continuous flow of goods from producer to consumer.

The Demand for Products of the Current Production Period

The effect of inflation on the prices of goods produced in the current production period (Period II) is much more complicated, because now not only the demand for, but also the supply of goods increases.

Demand is obviously dependent on the amounts entrepreneurs will be prepared to spend on production in the next, the future, production period (Period III)—just as the demand for the goods produced in the past period (Period I) was dependent on the amounts entrepreneurs were prepared to spend in the current production period (Period II). The demand for the goods produced in the present thus depends on how much entrepreneurs decide to spend in the future on capital goods, intermediate goods and wages.

These decisions are to a large extent determined by the prices entrepreneurs expect to get for the products of

Period III. By and large we can assume as a first approximation that entrepreneurs will expect prices to remain as they developed when the inflation of Period II met the goods produced in Period I. Some entrepreneurs will, of course, assume that prices will rise still higher, some that they will fall again. But, on the average, the price expectations of entrepreneurs will be higher than at the time of the production decisions for Period II. As long as entrepreneurs have to pay only the former wages and interest, the margin between outlays and expected revenues—and thereby their profit expectations—will increase.

This, again, means that the demand for credits with which to pay for capital goods, intermediate goods and wages rises in Period III, just as in the case of an increase in the productivity of capital for reasons of new inventions (treated above on p. 81). Unless the additional credit demand is checked at this stage by a rise in discount and interest rates, there will be a second inflation in Period III. The demand for the products of the current Period (II) during Period III will therefore be higher than the demand for the products of Period I during Period II.

The Supply of Products of the Current Period

However, the supply of goods produced in the current Period (II), too, is higher than it was at the end of Period I. Supply adjusts to demand even though with a time lag, provided the supply schedule of labor remains stable, as we assume as a first approximation to reality.

The mechanism through which a first dose of inflation increases supplies works as follows. Greater supply of credit at the old rates, or the same supply at lower interest rates, improves profit expectations of entrepreneurs. They will decide to expand their enterprises. To do so they will compete for labor with the result that wages go up. The higher wages draw more workers into production. Production increases. The extent of the increase clearly depends on how many additional workers are available at higher wages—in other words, on the elasticity of the labor supply. If the labor supply is elastic, the increase in employment and production is substantial. If it is inelastic, meaning that hardly any additional workers are available at the higher wage level, the increase in employment and production will be negligible. This happens regularly when the economy is anywhere near what is traditionally felt to be full employment. In this case the additional credits will increase only the use of capital but no longer the employment of labor.

The Price Level for Products of the Current Period

The price level for products of the current Period (II) is determined by the demand emanating from the purchasing power created in Period III, and by the supply of goods produced in the current Period (II). Both have increased: the future demand through the second injection of inflationary money, and the supply—with a time lag—because depending on the elasticity of the labor supply entrepreneurs produce more in the current Period (II) than they did in Period I.

At the end of the current period the price level will receive a further lift through the inflation of Period III. However, the lift will not be as great as the one resulting from the first inflation. For meanwhile the lagging effects of the first inflation on the production of Period II are felt—the more so the more elastic the labor supply has proved. If, and as long as, labor supply is perfectly elastic the lift will be negligible, because the additional increase in demand will be matched by higher supply; if it is quite inelastic the lift will be strong, because supply fails to increase. If the elasticity of labor supply is somewhere in between, the new money will—as is often said—be spent partly on higher prices and partly on a larger product.

Production can be increased in the current period only when it starts from scratch in that period. A steam hammer cannot be produced in the current period to be sold at its end, because it takes many periods to build it. This does not mean, however, that the prices of capital goods taking time to construct must at the end of the current period rise far above their production costs. Plans for the use of such capital goods reckon generally with long construction periods. Therefore, people will not, generally, be prepared to pay more for those immediately available. This fact slows the effect of inflation on prices. The immediate adjustment of the economy to inflation is also often prevented by the fact that the amount of fixed capital cannot be increased as quickly as the amount of variable capital. For this reason the optimum combination of fixed and variable capital can only be restored after some time. In the transition period the amount of variable capital, especially the capital used for payment of wages and thus leading to increased employment, will only be increased to the extent to which the production advantages due to inflation outweigh the disadvantages caused by the unfavorable combination of fixed and variable capital.

It is often said that inflation has no effect on the price level as long as there is a reserve of unemployed labor. But, as already mentioned, what mitigates the inflationary effects in this case is not the prevailing unemployment as such; it is the fact that in such a situation additional labor is generally, though not necessarily, available at the old wage level, i.e. that the supply curve of labor runs horizontally at this wage level for a certain time.

Must or Should Growth be Financed by Inflation?

Most of the so-called growth theories, so popular nowadays, try to demonstrate—with the help of innumerable and mostly entirely speculative models—that a population growth, if not accompanied by a proportionate increase in the capital supply, is bound to lead to all sorts of difficulties in the economic development, both short and long run. In general, an increase of the capital supply by the banks is, therefore, considered a necessary and innoxious condition for unhampered growth, for no general price rises are anticipated from such an increase.

To prevent misunderstanding we wish first to emphasize that the problem of providing an adequate capital supply by inflationary credit expansion must not be confused with the question dealt with earlier (pp. 94–95). There we dealt with capital—also capital supplied by genuine saving—that is newly used for paying the wages of an increased labor force. Here new money must indeed be introduced into the system in order to avoid deflation of the whole price and wage structure. In this case—which corresponds somewhat to the case of changing payment habits—an increase of the quantity of money by inflationary credit expansion has no influence on the general price level since the quantity of money appearing on the markets for goods in a certain period is not increased. The satisfaction of a genuine "need for money"—to employ this so-often misused term—is at stake.

Growth theories, however, are not—at least not in the first place—concerned with this more or less technical problem. They are concerned with the lack—or sometimes abundance—of capital necessary to absorb the new labor force into the productive process, the problem of need for capital as distinct from the problem of need for money from which it has to be—but seldom is—clearly distinguished.

Without penetrating too far into the thicket of the growth theories the following might be remarked:

Growth theories, mostly concerned with the consequences of a lack of capital offered, are the exact counterpart of the stagnation theories, concerned with the consequences of an excess of capital offered. The former theories are nowadays, during the boom, as eagerly discussed as the latter were in the 1930s, after the great depression—a new proof of how quickly fashions in economics change and how economists are prone to overestimate the importance, in the long run, of a momentary situation. Growth theories may turn out to be just as devoid of practical significance as the stagnation theories.

Most growth theories suffer from the fact that they assume certain data, for example wages, as fixed, whereas they should, for the purpose of analysis, be considered as flexible. The assumption of inflexibility of wages diverts attention from the fact that the supply of labor is, via the price mechanism, adjustable to every capital supply situation, at least for the longer run. It misleads furthermore to the idea of so to speak "natural" or "warranted" relationships between capital and labor, assumptions which render the resulting theories useless for economic theory and policies in a world in which most data of an objective as well as of a psychological nature are exposed to permanent changes. We shall have to raise the same objection when dealing with multiplicator and accelerator theories and their mechanistic assumptions.

As soon as one concedes that the rigidity of wages is not godsent, one recognizes that inflationary credit expansion is not the necessary and indisputable remedy for discrepancies between labor and capital supply, but that one is dealing with a genuine dilemma: the pros and cons of an entirely inelastic money supply—and therefore the absence of any inflationary credit expansion—have to be set against the pros and cons of filling the alleged capital gap by inflationary credit expansion.

In order to come to a decision in this dilemma no special growth theories are needed. The principles developed in Part II, in which an economy with an inelastic money supply, and in the present one, in which an economy in inflation and deflation is examined, are completely sufficient.

We have shown earlier (pp. 75–77) that, given a certain capital, the effects of an increased labor supply are: increased production as a result of increased employment, declining wages and increasing interest rates as a result of the distribution of the given capital to equip an increased number of workers, and the consequent increased marginal productivity of capital. The general price level remains stable, provided the deflationary effects of increased employment are counteracted through satisfying the money need just described.

The difficulties of overcoming in this way the discrepancies between growth of population and a fixed capital supply arise of course, in practice, from the rigidity of wages on the downside that is enforced by unions and is now already traditional. If wages are not allowed to decline under the impact of increased labor supply, the increment in population will remain unemployed instead of being absorbed in the productive process.

If one wishes to avoid these consequences, wages must be

supported by applying more capital, and this can *ceteris paribus* be achieved only by inflationary credit expansion (going beyond the satisfaction of the technical money need mentioned).

In defense of such credit expansion, use is often made of the argument that it would have no inflationary effects on prices. More workers being employed, the increased amount of money would meet an increased quantity of products so that the new money, while not neutral in absolute terms, would at least be price neutral.

This argumentation is the result partly of confusing the problem of capital need with the problem of money need, and partly of thinking along the lines of a very rough form of quantity theory. It contains a circular analytical error in that it forgets that the new money does not buy what will be produced by the newly engaged workers, but the products of the smaller labor force of a past period. It forgets, furthermore, that to maintain the economy in its previous equilibrium not only the consumer goods for the newly employed but also all the equipment necessary to produce them have to be provided by an increased credit supply.

This can, of course, be achieved by preventing the rise of the interest rates in spite of the increased demand for capital, i.e. by supplying the needed capital at the old rates by inflationary credit expansion. But the result, as described above (pp. 119–121) must inevitably be a rise of the price level with all its dynamic and cumulative consequences. Thus the wage level is, in the last analysis, held up by those sections of the population who are forced by inflation to curtail their expenditures in real terms. They supply the capital needed to pay and equip the increased labor force and maintain its marginal productivity.

Economic policy has thus, obviously, to choose between the advantages of stabilizing wages and thus preventing unemployment, and stabilizing prices, thus preventing a rising price level and the originating of cumulative processes. According to the economic and political situation of the moment, a middle-of-the-road policy may be advisable which tries to keep unemployment as well as price rises within limits. It is, in any case, entirely erroneous to assume, as is so often done, that a credit expansion sufficient to employ the growing labor force at the prevailing wage level is always warranted and innoxious.

Should Increased Productivity be Met by Inflationary Credit Expansion?

We have already touched this question (*see*: Wage and Price Level and Increase in Productivity—pp. 95 and 96) and would add here the following:

If productivity increases—following technical progress or increased capital investments—within the framework of a totally inelastic money circulation, as presupposed in Part II, prices will of course sink because an increased production meets an unchanged monetary demand. Wages remain stable. In this case the advantages of increased productivity are shared by all sections of the population, including recipients of rents and fixed salaries, and owners of monetary claims.

This method of coping with the problem of increased productivity has the disadvantage, as already mentioned, of inflicting losses on those who hold inventories and durable capital goods. The consequences of such losses on the anticipations of entrepreneurs should not be overrated, however. Entrepreneurs are influenced in their decisions less by losses in the past than by anticipation of profits in the future. As prices have not fallen more than costs they won't curtail production, except if they assume that productivity increase—and thus falling prices—are a permanently repeating phenomenon.

A much more important difficulty follows from the fact that labor leaders prefer to fight for a raising of money wages in accordance with increased productivity rather than for a lowering of consumer prices. This is quite understandable, first, because when money wages are raised the increased productivity benefits only labor; second, because the success of unions appears much more impressive if wages are raised in monetary rather than in real terms.

If entrepreneurs are induced to pay higher wages in accordance with increased productivity, the prices of the increased products have to be prevented from sinking, for if wages are pushed up in the face of sinking prices, unemployment must ensue.

The only way of supporting the price level is by increasing monetary demand through inflationary credit expansion. This inflationary credit expansion, while supporting the price level, will, however, not raise it because the increased money circulation meets a supply of goods that has been increased through the higher productivity.

Such an "inflation without inflation"—which, incidentally, should not be confused with the "volume prosperity" which develops in the first phase of a business cycle, as described later (pp. 177–178)—is in general considered harmless in every respect. The question whether this is correct is of the highest importance at present.[2]

Those who consider an "inflation without inflation" to be harmless overlook the fact that productivity increases mean profit increases for the entrepreneurs as long as costs—for labor as well as for capital—are not fully raised accordingly. It does not make any difference whether profits rise because prices rise or because costs decline by increase of productivity. The result is, or can be, in both cases the beginning of a cumulative process. Cumulative processes to the upside break down sooner or later and are followed by depressions—as we shall see later when the business cycle is described—if only because every stimulus finally exhausts itself. Through an energetic raising of discount rates such cumulative processes can be prevented. But by preventing them one will meet all the difficulties connected with a sinking price level and the drive for higher wages mentioned above.

Again the decision on the policy to be followed must take into account all the pros and cons of both possibilities. In any case, the usual attitude which, relying on its price neutrality, overlooks entirely the dangers of credit expansion is not warranted.

[2] See Foreword and Appendix I, p. 223.

THE ECONOMY IN INFLATION AND DEFLATION 129

Cumulative Effect of the Original Inflation

The second money inflation (in Period III) is caused, as we have seen, by the fact that the first inflation (in the current Period II) lifted the prices of goods produced in the past (Period I). Now the second inflation, in turn, lifts the prices for the goods produced in the current period, except in the case of completely elastic labor supply. This new price level again induces entrepreneurs to expand production in Period IV and to seek additional credits for this purpose, provided the supply schedules of the production factors remain unchanged as we assume for the time being. Thus inflation leads to higher prices, and higher prices lead again to new inflation. Therefore, inflation does not lead to new equilibrium but to a dynamic upward movement.

This cumulative effect of inflation often results in what may be characterized as an accelerated cumulative effect. Entrepreneurs, experiencing for a protracted time that prices are higher at the end of each production period than they were at its beginning, will expect prices to rise again during the current period and will base their production decisions on these expectations. Thereby the cumulative process started by inflation will be reinforced or accelerated.

The process comes to a stop only when either the credit supply is curtailed or the confidence in the permanency or further rise of the price level is shattered. In the latter case credit demand collapses, as we shall describe later in detail.

Inflation Profits are Mostly Apparent Profits

Entrepreneurs selling at prices increased through inflation reap profits, so-called inflation profits. These profits are generally unexpected and thus windfall profits. Had these profits been expected by all entrepreneurs, the effects of future inflation would already show up in the current period. Prices could no longer rise between the present and the future. The future inflation would be discounted in present markets.

Inflation profits need not be real profits. They usually are apparent profits—*Scheingewinne,* as they were called during the great German inflation. The entrepreneur receives a greater amount of money for his products than he expected and than he spent on factors of production. But he usually needs this greater amount if he wants to re-purchase the same quantity of goods or services. In fact he may need even more, namely if inflation has made further progress between the receipt and the spending of the money. The fact that most inflation profits are not real but only apparent is usually not recognized by tax and other laws until the depreciation of money has gone very far.

If the supply of labor is extremely elastic, it can happen that inflation profits do increase the wealth of the entrepreneur class not only in nominal but also in real terms. In such a case it may be possible to buy an even greater amount of labor with the higher receipts. This can happen particularly at the beginning of the recovery phase of a typical business cycle.

Prices and Production in Deflation

We need not describe in detail the effects of deflation on prices, employment and production, as they are exactly opposite to the effects of inflation. It suffices to recall that deflation, too, is cumulative. The deflated purchasing power of the current production period meets the, as yet, undiminished product of the past period. The prices decline. The lower prices induce the entrepreneurs to curtail their credit demands, with the result that the prices for the products of the current period drop still lower. These low prices, in turn, influence the decisions of entrepreneurs in the next period, and so on.

Waiting and Hurrying

A human factor tends to complicate the effects of money and credit inflation on the price level even more. The effects of money inflation on the price level are generally mild at the beginning, even if the labor supply is not very elastic, but become much stronger as inflation proceeds. At the beginning of a war, for instance, governments spend huge amounts of money newly created by banks and Central Banks, yet prices remain fairly stable for quite a while.

There are good reasons for this peculiar behavior of prices.

Human beings have a natural inclination to consider the purchasing power of money as stable until they finally awaken from this money illusion, as it has been called, and then consider rising prices (or falling prices, in the case of deflation) as normal. When prices begin to rise under the impact of credits granted to some groups of entrepreneurs—or in wartime to the government—other buyers will for the time being withdraw from the markets for consumer as well as capital goods. They will wait with their purchases, hoping that they will be able to buy again at the old prices later on. This happened regularly at the beginning of all the great European inflations. The strong American inflation after the outbreak of the Korean war in 1951 constitutes an exception to the rule. This exception was due to the inflation-consciousness of the public that had just experienced the inflation of the second world war.

As the entrepreneurs base their price expectations for the groups slowly realize that their hopes of the old prices returning are futile. Now the pent-up demand of those who have waited will come to the markets and lift prices substantially. This price rise will convince more and more people that it is better to buy now than later. The markets experience what has been called anticipatory buying. People now hurry, in contrast to their former waiting. The result will, of course, be that prices go up more than if only the current and the pent-up demand had to be satisfied.

As the entrepreneurs base their price expectations for the future in general on the prices of the products of the past, such hurrying must render them even more optimistic. Their demand for credits will become still stronger. This stronger demand will result in still higher prices, and these, in turn, in still higher credit demand. In other words, the phenomenon of hurrying reinforces the cumulative effects of inflation. The stage is set for a so-called runaway inflation.

Unless checked in time by counter-measures, runaway inflation must end in the total destruction of the function of money to serve as means of payment. Once people begin to understand the vicious circle of inflation, they will anticipate infinitely high prices for the future. Nobody will any longer sell goods or services against money. Money loses its function as general means of payment. Exchange stops or has recourse to foreign currencies.

Credit Supply in Inflation is Enhanced by Waiting and Curtailed by Hurrying of Buyers

Inflationary credits are, as we have seen, financed by the banks and the Central Banks, with newly created checking accounts and banknotes. Waiting, in its turn, increases non-inflationary credit supply; hurrying diminishes it. When consumers and producers hoping for lower prices delay the purchase of consumer goods and capital goods, they deposit the money earmarked for these purposes with their banks, thus creating an additional, if usually only temporary, supply on the credit markets. This quasi-saving, as we might call it, explains a well-known feature of the early phases of most inflations: the abundant supply on the free capital markets, which although itself due to inflation in turn curbs inflation.

Figure 20 shows what happens. If the credit supply curve is $S(_n)$ and the demand curve D, supply and demand for credits balance at an interest rate of 5 per cent without the help of inflationary credits. The amount of credits granted and used will be *ox*. Suppose now the banks lower their interest rates to 3 per cent, i.e. are prepared to satisfy all credit demand at 3 per cent. The supply curve for credits will no longer be $S(_n)$ but will run horizontally as $S(_i)$. The amount of credits granted increases by *xa,* and is now altogether *oa*. Since, with the original supply curve $S(_n)$, the amount of non-inflationary credit offered at 3 per cent would be only *od*, *da* would be inflationary credits. However, as we have seen, inflation creates quasi-savings, and these increase the supply of non-inflationary credit. The supply curve $S(_n)$ moves to the right to $S(_{n1})$. The result is that only the amount of credit *da* minus *db*, i.e. *ba,* is inflationary. The inflationary credit supply has created a non-inflationary credit supply.

The same happens if the inflation is not due to greater or cheaper supply of credits by banks, but to a stronger demand

THE ECONOMY IN INFLATION AND DEFLATION 133

for credits. Suppose entrepreneurs are expecting higher productivity of capital, or governments with unbalanced budgets require credits. The higher demand is satisfied by inflationary credits, unless banks raise their discount rates with increasing demand. But as the inflation again creates new quasi-savings, the higher demand is ultimately at least partly satisfied by the public's quasi-savings rather than by inflationary bank credits.

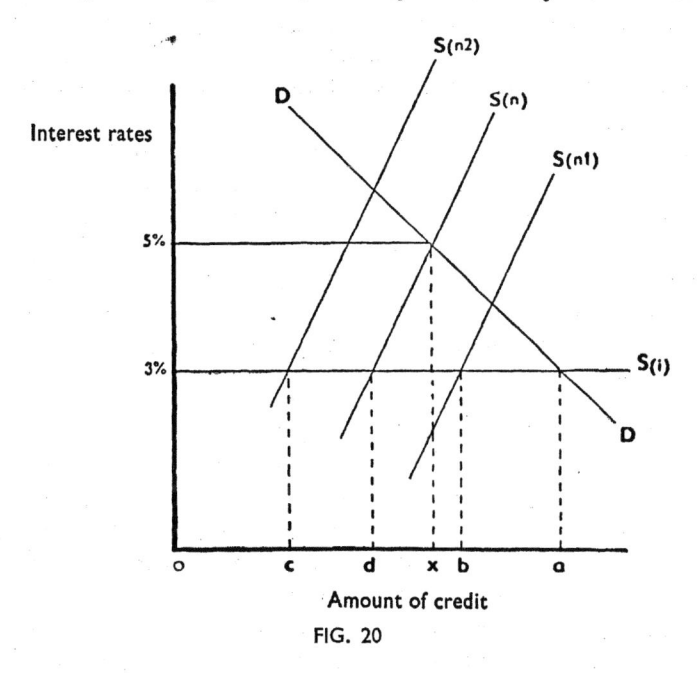

FIG. 20

As the result of the formation of such quasi-savings, huge amounts of bonds and other securities can regularly be placed with the public. As another result, the interest rates for some kinds of credit tend to fall below the discount rates. These phenomena never fail to amaze financial writers who, particularly when a war is financed by inflationary means, are apt to praise the strength of the national economy. In reality the phenomenon is simply the result of the power of inflation to create savings, because of people's inability to grasp quickly the full implications of inflation.

Incidentally, quasi-savings will in the main not be accomplished by depositing new cash with banks, but through the immobilization of checking accounts, which later are used to pay for the securities.

When waiting turns into hurrying, the opposite phenomena take place. People now mobilize checking accounts or withdraw from the banks cash formerly deposited. They spend their quasi-savings, once hope for lower prices has given way to fear of higher prices. Graphically, curve $S(_{n1})$ moves to the left to $S(_{n2})$. As a result, the inflationary credits are increased by *ca,* instead of by only *ab.*

Following such quasi-dissaving, by which funds are withdrawn from capital and money markets, interest rates go up—as can indeed be observed in the latter phases of inflation, particularly of inflationary booms. The end of a boom is therefore not marked by over-saving, which would necessarily be accompanied by low interest rates. Contrary to Keynesian views, over-saving can therefore not explain why prosperity turns into depression.

Velocity of Money Turnover during Inflation

The initial waiting and later hurrying of buyers are reflected in people's bank accounts by the later or earlier withdrawal of cash and the later or earlier disposal by check. The resulting monetary changes are often referred to as changes in the velocity of the money turnover. Many controversies created by this interpretation could be avoided by speaking—much more realistically—of changes in the quantity of money rather than in its velocity of turnover. If people withdraw cash from bank accounts in January which formerly was withdrawn only in February, then the quantity of money in the hands of the public in January is increased, but the individual banknote need not change hands more often than previously—say once a month. If, in January, people draw checks on accounts which formerly were immobilized until February as quasi-savings, the quantity of bank money is increased in January and that of quasi-savings accounts diminished; the checking accounts as such need not necessarily be turned over any quicker than previously. We can therefore interpret a premature turnover of cash or checking accounts as an increase, and a delayed turnover as a decrease, in the volume of money.

As mentioned earlier (p. 107), some people do not deposit with their banks the money not needed for the time being. If these people begin to wait, or indeed to save genuinely, the quantity of money in the hands of the public does not decrease, though it is temporarily withdrawn from circulation. Money does not disappear into the big death traps, the banks, but goes into the small death traps, the private hoards. And if these people hurry or dissave, the quantity of money in the hands of the public does not increase. It simply comes out of the private hoards. In these cases, therefore, one is justified in speaking of an increase and decrease in the velocity of money turnover. The single banknote if spent after one month instead of, as previously, two months, indeed changes hands twice as quickly as before. At the same time, the quantity of money remains the same. Inflation is as it were unofficial.

While the effects of unofficial and official inflation on the price level are the same, the effects on the supply of credit are quite different. If money is paid into the banks or checking accounts immobilized through quasi-saving, the lending capacity of the banks is increased, at least temporarily. If the money disappears into private hoards, no such effect follows. In the opposite case, if money is withdrawn from the banks through quasi-dissaving, the credit supply is curtailed. No such effect follows the reappearance of money out of private hoards.

In so far as waiting and hurrying alter the velocity of money turnover, they also account for a further well-known phenomenon observed during all great inflations: at first the price level increases more slowly than the quantity of money issued by the Central Banks—the official money inflation; in the later phases the price level increases more quickly.

Whereas money is in general dishoarded—and the velocity of money turnover thereby increased—in the later stages of inflation, the contrary may happen in the special cases of money and credit crises. If people begin to lose confidence in the banks, they fail to deposit the money temporarily not needed and keep it in their own safe instead. The creation of such private hoards has in the past often led to deflation. But this kind of deflation is most unlikely to occur again in the future. Governments, anxious to avoid money crises, are sure to replace the hoarded money in one way or the other.

Inventories during Waiting and Hurrying

Another feature of waiting is the decrease of inventories in the hands of consumers and some entrepreneurs. Consumers waiting with further buying must obviously continue to live, and to this end draw on their stocks. Some entrepreneurs waiting to replenish their inventories of raw materials and semi-finished goods may nevertheless continue to produce if they expect to sell their products; in order to do so, they must draw upon their inventories. Deposits with banks, shares and particularly government bonds will replace the former inventories among the assets of consumers and entrepreneurs.

In the subsequent hurrying period of inflation, the inventory situation is, of course, reversed. Inventories increase with the expectation of higher prices, until finally they are so swollen that they alone can account for the ensuing slump.

Credit Demand in Deflation is Enhanced by Waiting and Curtailed by Hurrying of Sellers

We speak of money deflation if banks and Central Banks restrict their lending so that bank money and currency are destroyed or withdrawn from circulation.

Deflation can be due either to reduced credit demand of entrepreneurs, or to a reduced or dearer credit supply by banks. In both cases demand and supply on the credit markets will balance with less than—or altogether without—the credits formerly created by banks.

The first stages of deflation may be characterized by a peculiar behavior of sellers—the counterpart to the behavior of many buyers observed during the early stages of inflation. Whereas, at the beginning of inflation, many buyers wait because they do not as yet believe in the permanency of the price rise, many sellers now wait because they are as yet not convinced that the lower prices are there to stay, or because they want to avoid deflation losses at all cost. At the same time, however, production in many fields continues as before —partly because producers, too, consider the price fall as only temporary or because they cannot or do not want to close down and dismiss their workers. This circumstance creates an additional demand for credits to carry inventories over to the next recovery period; in the German literature these were called *Durchhaltekredite*. This demand for carry-over credits counteracts the contraction of the volume of money and of credit.

The result for the price level will be that prices at first hardly fall at all, in spite of the contraction of regular credits. The latter are to some extent replaced by carry-over credits— the difference being that now goods no longer pass into the hands of those who in the normal course of events would have bought them for further processing, or as distributors and consumers, but remain in the hands of entrepreneurs at earlier production and trading stages.

On the credit markets interest rates hardly recede in spite of a decrease in the demand for regular credits. If deflation is due to dearer credit supply, interest rates will even go up. Should the banks, in order to protect their own liquidity, be unable or unwilling to grant carry-over credits, i.e. to replace regular by carry-over credits, supply on the credit markets may become so scarce as to give rise to a real credit crisis.

As deflation proceeds, entrepreneurs lose hope for a return of the old boom prices. They no longer wait with selling, they even begin to hurry—especially if high interest rates deter from carrying swollen inventories indefinitely. The demand for carry-over credits dwindles, interest rates fall, and so do prices on the commodity markets.

The tightness of credit at the beginning of deflation, due to the sellers waiting, may be accentuated by some buyers hurrying with their purchases for fear of rising prices. In the later stages of deflation, the waiting of buyers expecting a price fall may accentuate the easing of the credit situation brought about by the liquidation of carry-over credits.

The whole deflationary process may even start with a buyers' strike. The ensuing demand for carry-over credits may be so strong that interest rates rise in spite of higher credit supply from quasi-saving.

Genuine Saving in Times of Inflation

Inflation causes not only quasi-saving through waiting, but also genuine saving.

To the extent to which inflation leads to higher employment and thereby higher aggregate income, savings obviously increase in absolute terms. From a higher national income more is saved, *ceteris paribus*.

But the savings rate, too, rises. It is true that in normal times an increase in total income does not increase society's average savings rate. However, in times of inflation this happens—not because of the Keynesian psychological law, according to which an increase in the living standard leads to an increase in the savings rate, but because inflation leads to a redistribution of income in favor of higher, and at the expense of lower income groups.

The lower incomes of workers and employees are reduced in real terms because they rise slower than prices. The higher incomes of entrepreneurs remain unchanged in real terms because they sell their products at inflated prices. Similarly the owners of bonds and savings accounts, pensioners and so on, on the average less wealthy, suffer losses through inflation —whereas entrepreneurs, on the average richer, make profits if they have contracted debts in good money. Thus the poor become poorer, the rich richer. Since the rich generally save more than the poor, the result of the redistribution of income must be an increase in the savings rate—at least as long as the public's inflation-consciousness does not destroy its propensity to save.

During deflation income is redistributed in favor of the lower, at the expense of the higher income groups. Falling prices mean that the real incomes of workers and employees— as long as they are still employed—grow; at the same time entrepreneurs generally suffer heavily. The savings rate falls.

But the spending habits of the population during inflation and deflation are probably much more affected by waiting and hurrying than by redistribution of income.

Multiplier Theory and Acceleration Principle

It has become customary to indulge in calculations of how much consumption expenditures will be induced by investment expenditures, and how much investment expenditures by consumption expenditures.

The effects of investment on consumption are dealt with by the multiplier theory, the effects of consumption on investments by the acceleration principle. In view of the great importance for theory and practice generally attributed to these concepts we shall examine them a little closer.

It is, of course, undeniable that investment and consumption are related. Every investment is so to speak eventually amortized into consumption, and every consumption is in the last instance the end product of investment. Nevertheless, the ratio of investment to consumption can vary, because it clearly depends on the length of the production detours. In an economy with longer average production detours a greater part of the product will, at any one moment, consist of capital goods than in an economy with shorter average production detours. Accordingly the amounts spent at the beginning of any production period on capital goods will be greater in the former than in the latter. This is illustrated by Figure 21.

The lengths of production detours are, however, not fixed once and for all. They are determined by the productivity of capital and the interest rate. These, therefore, determine in the last instance the ratio of investment expenditure to consumption expenditure.

If more is spent on consumption, entrepreneurs wishing to produce more consumer goods will, it is true, wish to acquire the capital goods necessary to produce the consumer goods in the same capitalistic way. Consumption induces investment, to use the customary expression. But the inducement can succeed only to the extent to which credit supply is elastic. If it is not elastic, entrepreneurs will have to produce the greater amount of consumer goods in a less capitalistic way. More consumption will not lead to more investment—contrary to the reasoning of the acceleration principle.

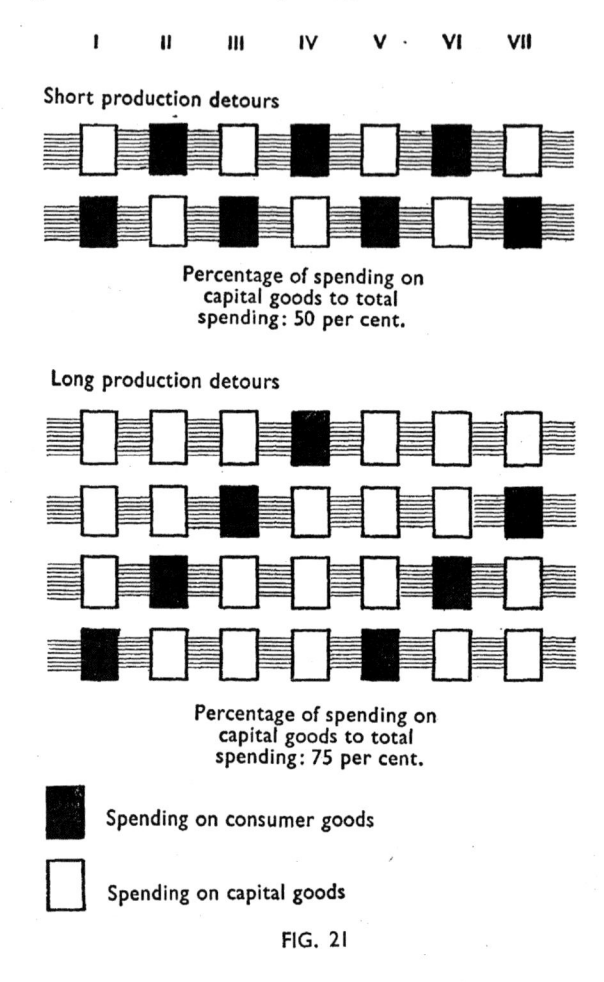

I　　II　　III　　IV　　V　　VI　　VII

Short production detours

Percentage of spending on
capital goods to total
spending: 50 per cent.

Long production detours

Percentage of spending on
capital goods to total
spending: 75 per cent.

■ Spending on consumer goods

□ Spending on capital goods

FIG. 21

If more is spent on investment, the incomes of those who have contributed to the production of the investment goods will rise. They will wish to spend more on consumption. But, again, they will be able to do so only if credit supply is elastic.

Otherwise interest rates will rise until more is saved or less invested. More investment, so far as it can take place at all, will not lead to more but to less simultaneous consumption—contrary to the reasoning of the multiplier theory.

Thus the multiplying and accelerating effects—the stimulating effect of investment on consumption and of consumption on investment—can at best take place only to the extent that Central Banks fail to defend the monetary system against inflation and deflation.

Multiplier and acceleration theories appear, therefore, to be valid only in an economy in which credit supply is highly elastic owing to easy money policy. For an economy which avoids inflation and deflation it remains true that more spending on investment leads not to more, but to less spending on consumption; and that more spending on consumption leads not to more, but to less spending on investment.

Even for an economy with elastic money supply the concepts of multiplier and accelerator are subject to considerable objections, theoretical as well as practical.

The very designations of both theories are misleading. The acceleration principle expresses nothing the old term induced investment did not express better. Furthermore, an increase in consumption would involve accelerated, i.e. over-proportional, increase in the aggregate expenditure of one period only if all the required intermediate products were produced in that same production period. Not only the production marked black in Figure 21, but all preceding intermediate productions too, marked white, must take place simultaneously. Such an assumption is technically and analytically inadmissible. For both technical and logical reasons we must assume that, when consumption increases, production of capital goods starts in the first production period, but reaches later stages of maturity only in later periods. Tools can be produced only after steel is produced. Investments are, therefore, not accelerated, i.e. do not increase over-proportionately but only proportionately. The accelerator is really an additioner. Correct and self-evident is that the expectation of higher demand or prices for consumer goods will spread to intermediate goods. The accelerator is thus at best a generalizator of improved price or demand expectations. But whether these improvements lead via higher credits to a concentrated higher effective demand for labor, raw materials and intermediate goods depends—quite apart from the technical consideration mentioned—as with every expansion of production, on price-cost relationships and thus especially on the elasticities of capital and labor supply. If price-cost relationships have become favorable, production expands, but this is not achieved through the working of an accelerator; it is in accordance with the general principle that production expands if expected prices go up more than costs.

The designation multiplier theory would be correct only if investment expenditures multiplied consumption expenditure in the same production period—as indeed circular flow analysis sometimes seems to suggest. But the idea of a timeless multiplier working instantaneously is nonsensical, as is increasingly acknowledged. The further effects of increased investment spending can at best be felt in subsequent periods. But the combined increase of incomes of later, future periods cannot be regarded as the multiplication result of the increased income of one period, just as the combined income of several periods together cannot be regarded as the multiplication result of the income of one period. A single dose of investment expenditure can, at best, add *once for all* a certain amount to the income of each period. It is not a multiplier but, again, an additioner—and an unreliable one at that. For practical purposes the designation multiplier has to be rejected because it leads to an enormous overrating of the beneficial effects of public investment. It may consciously or unconsciously have been chosen for this reason.

But there are more substantial objections. According to the older theories the amounts spent on investments and consumption in any future production period are dependent on all the data of the future, as well as on the psychological reactions of people to these data. Multiplier and acceleration types of analysis treat all these other data—under the heading propensity to consume or to invest—as given and constant or decreasing in the same proportion, and the amounts of original spending on investment and consumption as the variables of the system. This method concentrates attention quite unduly on these latter. In the dyanmic reality with which we are dealing when concerned with inflation and deflation problems, all propensities can have almost any strength or weakness. They change, furthermore, continually over time, in particular from one cyclical phase to another. And if, as a concession to reality, this is conceded then only the self-evident trivial statement remains that money received is sometimes spent and sometimes not.

Consumer and investment spending depend on many considerations other than whether entrepreneurs, through the additional spending of consumers, and consumers, through the additional spending of entrepreneurs, have received money. Life in an economy begins, so to speak, every day anew. If the price-cost relationships do not appear favorable, entrepreneurs will desist from buying services and capital goods regardless of whether consumers have previously spent money on consumer goods. And if consumers expect prices to fall, they will desist from buying consumer goods regardless of whether their incomes have risen or not. The correctness of this view was amply proved when in the first New Deal period the money spent by the government failed to create any additional demand, but simply disappeared in the banks.

It is the propensity to consume or to invest which in reality is the important variable of the system. The proper task for theory is to examine the changes and their reasons in this propensity rather than to treat it as given and constant, as the multiplier and acceleration theories do. Theory has to investigate whether and to what extent consumers spend in subsequent periods the purchasing power they have received through previous investment expenditure; and whether and to what extent entrepreneurs invest in subsequent periods what they have received through previous consumption spending.

Analytical work resting on multiplier and acceleration theories is guilty of a *petitio principii*. It presupposes precisely what really is in question: the spending in the future of money spent in the present. Such work is fundamentally no more than intellectual toying, neither necessary nor sufficient to solve the problems of a dynamic economy.

It is unnecessary to stress again that any accelerating or multiplying effects will be real only under the assumptions to be mentioned immediately. Under other conditions they will exhaust themselves in changes of the price level.

Compensating Reactions of Factors of Production

In everything said so far about the effects of inflation and deflation we have assumed that neither capitalists nor workers react by raising their demands correspondingly to the higher prices caused by inflation.

An analysis starting from this assumption is useful to clarify basic relationships. It also provides a correct description of what can happen during short transition periods. However, it is entirely misleading if used to describe the lasting effects of inflation and deflation. It is the chief mistake of the Keynesians to have taken the short-term transitory effects of inflation and deflation as basis for a general equilibrium theory.

The assumption that the demands of production factors remain stable in monetary terms even when the purchasing power of money alters, is unrealistic. It is hard to see why entrepreneurs, when engaging new workers, should take the changing price level into account, whereas on the other side the workers should not do likewise when offering their services. According to Keynes, it is just such a divergence that enables new workers to be employed. But labor leaders and their economic advisers are not as stupid as Keynes believes when he states that "the supply of labor is not a function of real wages." It is difficult to understand why this statement, instead of being greeted with deserved derision, was until recently accepted as gospel truth.

What happens when the factors of production, by compensating reactions, adjust their monetary demands to the real changes in the value of money?

THE ECONOMY IN INFLATION AND DEFLATION

Compensating Reactions of Creditors

Suppose prices have risen by 2 per cent during the last period. As soon as creditors no longer expect a reaction of prices but rather a continuation of their upward trend, they will raise their demands for interest on capital by 2 per cent, so as to be compensated for the loss of purchasing power expected during the lending period. The supply curve of credits will move upward.

If Central Banks, too, now raise the discount rates by 2 per cent, further inflation will be prevented. Although entrepreneurs may still expect higher prices and thus additional profits, credits will have become more expensive to the extent of these expectations. The demand curve for credits moves up, but so will the supply curve, and credits will not increase.

But if, as usual, the Central Banks do not raise their discount rate in spite of mounting demand for credits, the money-creating banks will expand their lending to meet the increased inflationary demand. At the same time those private creditors who are inflation-conscious will recall outstanding loans in order to invest their money themselves in goods expected to protect against inflation losses. The supply of non-inflationary credit is thus curtailed and demand has to be increasingly satisfied through inflationary credits. Thus the compensating reactions of private capitalists lend new impetus to the inflation. Such was the situation, for instance, during the last phase of the great German inflation from about 1922 onward. Private creditors either went on strike or demanded exorbitant interest rates, whereas the *Reichsbank,* failing to grasp what was happening, stuck to its low discount rates. The runaway inflation of that period was chiefly the result of these circumstances.

Compensating Reactions of Labor

By far the most important compensating reactions are those of labor. They are apt to happen very fast. The supply schedule of labor generally rises immediately after any increase in the cost of living.

As a rule, therefore, the margin between costs and prices

described above[3] will fail to materialize. There will be no inducement to employ more labor. Employment and production will not increase, and inflation will spend itself entirely on higher prices and not on higher employment and production. This agrees exactly with the opinion of classical economists. According to their so-called quantity theory of money, after a brief transition period during which supply prices are adjusted to the increased monetary demand, a greater volume of money simply raises prices correspondingly.

These facts were quite clearly illustrated during the last phases of the German inflation in 1922–23. Labor and management agreed on sliding wage scales. Wages were automatically adjusted to any increase in the prices of goods. As a result employment no longer increased, even though prices rose faster and faster. Employment even decreased when labor finally succeeded in raising real wages, which had lagged behind the depreciation of money during the whole inflation period.

The so-called escalator clauses, common in many labor contracts nowadays in the United States, practically rule out any employment-increasing effects of inflation. Thus the Keynesian employment theory is no longer valid even in transition periods.

When dealing in Part IV with the special case of inflation and deflation called the business cycle, we shall encounter exceptions from the rules just exposed. In the early stages of recovery, for instance, prices hardly move up, and even if they do, wages often lag behind rising prices. But there is nothing more unrealistic than the Keynesian statement that, as a general rule, "labor acquiesces in a diminishing real wage." Every union leader must consider such a statement as quite ridiculous.

Do Wage Increases Lead to Inflation?

It is often stated that higher wages enforced by trade unions lead to higher prices, and that this effect is cumulative when higher prices, in turn, lead to yet higher wages. If this were correct, union leaders rather than the Central Banks would

[3] See p. 117.

indeed be responsible for the value of the currency. It is, however, correct only in very special conditions.

In general, wage increases lower the marginal productivity and yield of capital. They have, therefore, a deflationary effect —unless we assume that cost increases cause price increases.

Cost increases, as such, do not raise the prices of the products, because the increasing costs can be shifted on to the consumers only if money inflation has meanwhile progressed further. If entrepreneurs—though perhaps mistakenly—expect the higher costs to be shiftable on to the consumers, they will indeed anticipate higher prices for the future. But then it is this belief, and not the wage increase as such, that prevents deflation or even leads to further inflation.

Wage Rigidities Downward

Whereas wages are generally immediately, or at least quickly, adjusted upward, they are these days indeed very rigid downward. In times of depressions, therefore, the Keynesian thesis according to which labor sticks to its money wages in spite of a changing price level does hold. Wage rigidities downward explain why unemployment increases in times of deflation and why it was so persistent during the Great Depression.

Wage Increases during Deflation Increase Unemployment. The Purchasing Power Theory

If wage rigidity downward during deflation creates unemployment, wage increases must do so even more. The contention of many labor leaders and their economic advisers that in depressions, when costs are in any case too high in terms of prices, wages should be raised in order to sustain demand is, therefore, nonsensical. It is nothing else but a replica of the often refuted purchasing power theory of which Professor Hansen, before he became a Hansenian, stated:

> It is, therefore, not surprising that the theory should become widespread that higher wages are the cure for the restricted market and declining price level of the last decade. This theory is accepted, one might almost say, by nearly every one in the

United States, not only by trade union leaders but also by leading business men, politicians, and journalistic economists. During the 1930 depression leaders of American public opinion in all walks of life were constantly urging that the surest basis for a revival of prosperity was a maintenance of wages or even an increase in wages. This state of affairs indicates a confusion of thought for which, it must be admitted, professional economists are in part to blame.[4]

You cannot raise the general level of prices by the simple process of raising wages. And it is an amazing fact that professional American economists have not come forward to point out the fallacy that lurks here.[5]

We shall not succeed in solving the depression through the soothing and agreeable device of inflation. We shall come out of it only through hard work, and readjustments that are painful. There is no other alternative.[6]

As the purchasing power theory has again come to be honored, although under another heading and in somewhat refined form, the following may be said.

It can be conceded that wage increases can, but do not necessarily, increase aggregate demand by shifting income from those of low propensity to consume (entrepreneurs, capitalists) to those of high propensity to consume. This is why the purchasing power theory—by which, incidentally, every wage increase could be rationalized—has always been popular with laymen, and not only with those of socialist leaning. The argument overlooks, however, the elementary fact—a typically circular analytical error—that income must be earned before it is either spent or saved. First comes the entrepreneur's decision to create income by engaging production factors, then comes the spending or saving. Now entrepreneurs as a rule expect the prevailing price level to stay. And under the prevailing price level wage increases must seem intolerable and lead to curtailing production. For the assumption of a perfectly or almost perfectly inelastic demand curve for labor is entirely unrealistic. Entrepreneurs will not pay *any* price for a given amount of work. Only for additional work are additional payments

[4] Alvin Harvey Hansen, *Economic Stabilization in an Unbalanced World*, New York, 1932, p. 279.
[5] *Ibid.*, p. 279.   [6] *Ibid.*, p. 378.

offered, even if only on a decreasing scale. This is, incidentally, why the recipe of the purchasing power theoreticians to raise wages during depressions—if not enforced by governments—is never carried out in practice. The individual entrepreneur does not feel able to grant higher wages and just does not do it.

But suppose, for argument's sake, the entrepreneurs were Keynesians and would anticipate that products of the past period—and also of the current period—would meet a demand or price increase resulting from the shift of income from the savers to the spenders. Even then they would curtail and not expand production. For the increase in demand or prices must always be smaller than the increase in costs. This follows from the simple fact that not all the additional costs become additional spent income. Even entrepreneurs and capitalists—whose income declines through the wage increases—had spent a part of what is now taken away from them.

Only if we assume that entrepreneurs pay higher wages immediately but curtail production only after some time could prices of or a demand for the products of the last period increase. But quite apart from the fact that it seems quite arbitrary to assume that entrepreneurs would react promptly to price increases but not to cost increases, entrepreneurs would shortly after realize that price increases are not sufficient to cover cost increases and would curtail production.

The same argumentation leads, incidentally, to the conclusion that even wage lowering in order to adjust costs to sunken prices would not be so self-defeating as Keynes expressly states and his followers repeat. With the prevailing price level in mind, entrepreneurs will expand production because of the cost saving through wage lowering. But let us again assume they were Keynesians and would expect the aggregate demand to sink under the impact of the shift of income from the spenders to the savers. Again they would have to realize, too, that aggregate demand would sink less than aggregate costs. For at least a part of the new income of the savers would surely be spent. Thus entrepreneurs would expand production.

Again, only if we assume, as is often done, that entrepreneurs would immediately lower wages but expand production only with substantial lags, could a deflationary effect on prices and demand for the products of the last period be expected. But again, quite apart from the arbitrariness of the assumption, entrepreneurs would react shortly after to the still-improved price-cost relation and expand production.

But this whole reasoning, assuming that entrepreneurs have either perfect foresight or react to price movements which are necessarily transitory, is of course entirely unrealistic. All depends on what the entrepreneurs expect the effect of wage lowering to be on the demand and price situation—which again depends on whether they believe that production in further production periods, which produces the income to buy the products of the current period, will increase sufficiently so that the addition to total income will at least compensate the demand deficit resulting from the income shifts from the spenders to the savers. Whether entrepreneurs on the average understand the economics involved or not, they will undoubtedly take an optimistic view so that even the transitory effects on entrepreneur psychology envisaged by Keynesians will not materialize. If tomorrow the rumor were spread at the United States stock and commodity markets that unions had agreed to a general lowering of wages by 10 or 20 per cent, a huge buying spree on all markets and a rush to invest would set in, in which everybody would participate except inveterate Keynesians. And buyers and investors, contrary to Keynes' contention, would not be disappointed. Nor would even the expectation of repeated wage lowering necessarily shake the optimism of entrepreneurs, contrary to a widely held belief. Wage decreases are by no means identical with price decreases. As a rule wage decreases are inflationary, not deflationary.

It is correct that, under certain conditions, the price level should be supported during depressions. But wage support is not only price support but also—and even more—cost support, and is therefore entirely contra-indicated as a means of price support.

The End of Inflation

Inflation stops when the Central Banks raise their discount rate to a level at which the inflation profits expected by entrepreneurs appear compensated by the higher cost of credit.

Inflation generally ends not with stabilization but with deflation of the monetary system. The so-called stabilization crises are really deflation crises. When prices no longer rise, hopes for higher prices, the characteristics of the later stages of inflation, dwindle and the demand for credit declines. If Central Banks were smart enough to lower their discount rates at once and to such an extent that the decrease in expected profits appeared to be immediately compensated, deflation would not be induced from the money side. The problem of swollen inventories would, however, still remain. As they can be liquidated only at lower prices a deflationary process must start. Therefore, monetary and credit policy does not, in practice, lead to stabilization of the economy. It can, at best, mitigate fluctuations.

Inflations can end for other reasons, too. The granting of inflationary credits to a government, for instance for war financing, will obviously stop when—but only when—the government succeeds in balancing the budget. If it does not succeed, this kind of inflation often ends with the public no longer accepting money as payment. Such repudiation of money leads to total destruction of the value of money.

A private inflation, i.e. an inflation to finance credits to private entrepreneurs, will one day stop even if the supply of credits is not curtailed or made more expensive by the banks. Demand for private credits is never unlimited. One day inflation loses its stimulating effects. Credit demand no longer expands, and the vicious circle of inflation is interrupted.

Every deflation, too, will end at some moment for similar reasons. We shall later deal in detail with the mechanism of the so-called upper and lower turning points of business cycles.

Who Gains and Who Loses by Inflation?

Inflation is in the last analysis a sort of tax—and the most unjust of all—on income and capital, levied on some members of the economy in order to shift purchasing power to others. In the case of inflation for governmental purposes purchasing power is shifted to the government, in the case of private inflation to some entrepreneurs.

These shifts in purchasing power succeed because, owing to the money illusion, some members of the community fail to recognize the change in the real value of money or cannot defend themselves against such a change. Therefore, inflation ends when the money illusion ceases to work. When all the creditors—including the Central Banks—raise their demands for interest, when all wage earners raise their demands for wages, and when all owners of real estate raise their demands for rent in accordance with the existing or expected inflation, then there is no further inducement for additional credit demand.

Whether an individual or a group profits or loses by inflation depends on the relative ability of individuals and groups to defend themselves against the inflation tax. This can never be determined in advance, nor once and for all. The following will, however, be the rule.

The Banks

At first sight, banks and Central Banks would appear as the inflation profiteers *par excellence*. They receive interest for loans granted to new debtors with bank money created by themselves and on which they pay no, or only very little, interest.

These profits are, however, nominal rather than real. They merely compensate for the money depreciation that is taking place. The assets of the banks grow roughly in proportion to the money and credit inflation, but so does the price level.

In real terms, banks not only fail to profit but even generally lose. Investment of the banks' own capital is generally not inflation-proof. It consists in the main of loans to clients, who pay interest and repay capital in depreciated money. In cases of governmental inflations the banks are, moreover, generally loaded with government bonds, so that they can lose also through bankruptcy of the government. The Hitler inflation, for instance, ended with the currency reform of 1948, which treated banks so badly that many of them suffered considerable capital losses.

Earners of Wages, Salaries and Fixed Incomes

All those receiving money incomes suffer from inflation. However, the losses of the various groups and individuals differ widely. Those able to make compensating reactions quickly will be hurt least, those able to react only with a substantial lag or not at all will be hurt most. At one end of the scale is organized labor; at the other end the rentiers, whose income derives from pensions, fixed interest securities, especially government bonds, savings accounts and insurances.

Let us suppose that these groups finally succeed in adjusting their incomes to the money depreciation. If, in this case, the banks continued to grant credits at the same low interest rates, inflation would proceed but employment would no longer increase. The inflation tax would still be levied, for prices continue to rise between the receipt and the spending of incomes.

During the last stages of the great German inflation (1922–23) entrepreneurs sometimes supplemented wages already paid with payments compensating the loss in purchasing power between receipt and spending of the wage. Such procedure, if carried through generally, must lead to complete disruption of the currency. If everybody insists on being compensated through new inflation for the effects of simultaneous inflation, then obviously a vicious circle is set in motion which soon raises prices infinitely high.

Entrepreneurs

Entrepreneurs having paid their production costs with uninflated money, but selling their products for inflated money, reap inflation profits. These are windfall profits (see p. 129 above) as the new prices were not, on the average, expected by entrepreneurs. Had the higher prices been generally expected, prices would have risen earlier, and not only following the money and credit expansion of the next period.

These windfall profits, however, are not necessarily profits in real terms. They may even represent real losses—namely if inflation makes further progress between receipt and re-spending of the money.

As long as labor does not achieve compensations for the fall of real wages, entrepreneurs profit from the increased margin between costs and present prices. Strictly speaking, these are not really profits; rather they represent additional earnings on capital due to the increased employment of "really" cheaper labor and the resulting higher marginal productivity of capital.

Monopolists will generally be able to adjust their monopoly rents sooner or later—mostly very soon—to the decreasing purchasing power of money. Enterprises of monopolistic or quasi-monopolistic character as a rule enjoy perfect protection from inflation losses, at least as long as price controls or other regulations do not establish ceiling prices for their products or services.

Debtors and Creditors

The situation becomes even more complicated by the fact that most entrepreneurs do not employ only their own capital, but also loan capital or credits. Unless the loan contracts provide for changes in the value of money during the lending period—and this is hardly ever the case—inflation creates real profits for the debtors and real losses for the creditors. If loans are repaid with depreciated money, less real purchasing power is returned to the creditor than he lent. The debtor, on the other hand, needs to sell less products in order to repay debts remaining nominally unchanged.

Such a redistribution of wealth through inflation can, of course, only happen to the extent that creditors are unable or unwilling to protect themselves. Inability to do so is mostly due to long-term contracts; unwillingness often to ignorance.

In the last phase of the great German inflation many creditors sought protection through so-called constant-value clauses (*Wertbeständigkeits-Klauseln*) in loan contracts. They stipulated that interest should be paid and capital repaid according to the diminished purchasing power of money as measured by some price index.

THE ECONOMY IN INFLATION AND DEFLATION 155

Deflation Profits and Losses

Deflation creates exactly opposite results. Stable money incomes grow in real terms. Debtors suffer losses while money creditors make profits at the expense of the former. The effects need not be described in detail. They follow from what has been said about inflation profits and losses.

Share Prices in Inflation

Share prices fluctuate around a level determined by dividends on the one hand, and by interest rates on the other. In the short run they are determined not so much by current as by expectations of future dividends. We shall return to this in Part V. Here we are concerned with the development of share prices in the long run.

Inflation must strongly influence share prices, since it influences both earnings and interest rates.

Profits due to Lagging Production Costs

We have just mentioned the profits of entrepreneurs through lagging production costs, particularly wages. Such profits are temporary by nature and can, therefore, influence share prices only temporarily.

Companies which are prevented by law or regulation from adjusting the prices of their products to monetary changes, can reap higher earnings only if and when the price ceilings are abolished. Therefore, the shares of public utilities with fixed tariffs do not rise during inflation except in special circumstances, and then often very late.

Windfall Profits and Share Prices

The windfall profits mentioned above are much more important for share price formation.

These windfall profits protect capital in times of inflation. They result in shares of many companies becoming perfect inflation hedges.

The rise in share prices due to windfall profits is not expected by the average investor, just as the windfall profits themselves are not expected. Otherwise share prices would be the same at the beginning and at the end of inflation.

Corporate earnings consist at least partly of monopoly rents, in general quickly adjustable to the declining purchasing power of money. This is another reason for stock market booms during inflation.

As a general rule, shares will protect the better against inflation the more the flexibility of prices of the products exceeds the flexibility of the compensation of the production factors.

The behavior of common shares depends, of course, also on whether and to what extent the individual companies are indebted to banks or have issued bonds or preferred shares. Since debtors benefit by inflation, bonds, bank credits, and preferred shares give so-called leverage to earnings and thus also to the price of the common shares.

Interest Rates and Share Prices

If the inflation is due to a fall in discount and interest rates, the rates at which dividends and the interests on long-term bonds are capitalized are altered. The prices of shares and bonds will move up accordingly.

However, even if inflation is due to increased credit demand, and interest rates therefore do not fall, inflation influences stock prices decisively for the following reason.

Part of the quasi-savings accumulating at the beginning of inflation are used to replace the inflationary credits granted by the banks. This not only dampens inflation, as described above, but creates also the phenomenon that at the beginning of inflationary war financing only a small part of government bonds remains in the hands of the banks while the greater part is taken up by the public.

However, only part of the quasi-savings are invested in government bonds. As the public is used to keeping a certain percentage of its funds liquid, interest rates on the free money markets begin to decline.

Soon the market for bonds becomes extremely firm. First-class corporate bonds, in less ample supply than governmental issues, sometimes rise above government bonds.

As the public usually wishes to invest part of its funds, increased through inflation, in shares, the demand for them increases. The interest rates at which dividends are capitalized decline. Share prices go up. Thus an extremely high demand for capital by the government is paradoxically accompanied by a stock market boom, and this even if earnings do not increase—for instance because of high war taxation.

Idle Money Boom

In times of inflation governments often resort to rationing of goods or to maximum prices. If this happens, the effects of voluntary waiting are reinforced by involuntary waiting. Rationing and price ceilings prevent part of the money in the hands of the public from reaching the markets. The funds so saved are spent by the public on the remaining free markets, mostly the security markets. A strong stock exchange boom, which can be called the idle money boom, develops.

When price ceilings and rationing are abolished, the public withdraws the funds invested on the stock markets. Although the pent-up demand for goods stimulates the economy, the stock exchange experiences what we could call an active money depression. The end of the war boom on the New York Stock Exchange in 1946 characteristically coincided with the end of rationing and price controls.

Hurrying and the Stock Market

But even when price ceilings and rationing are not first introduced and later abolished, stock markets are strongly influenced by the behavior of buyers. As soon as waiting turns into hurrying in the further course of inflation, the quasi-savings created through waiting are withdrawn from the capital markets in order to be spent on the commodity markets. Interest rates on the free market must, therefore, have a tendency to rise, bond and share prices to fall.

If now the Central Banks maintain their discount rate—as they regularly do if the government needs inflationary credits—treasury and commercial bills formerly bought by the banks and the public are offered to the Central Banks; as they have to buy them with newly created money, inflation is further stimulated. Money markets become easier again and stock prices rise sharply, unless capital flight is legal or possible. In this case, share prices lag behind prices of foreign currencies.

The third phase of the great German inflation—from about 1922 on—clearly showed the combined effect of buyers' hurrying and low discount rates maintained in flagrant misjudgment of the situation. The stock market soared in what was called at that time a catastrophe boom, and exchange rates reached astronomic heights.

Stock Prices in Deflation

Declining corporate earnings during deflation depress stock prices, just as their rising during inflation pushed them up.

But deflation influences stock markets also from the money side. If deflation is induced by higher discount rates, the capitalization factor for dividends and interests on bonds alters; bond and stock prices fall further. If deflation is induced by a diminishing credit demand, interest rates decline, thus supporting bond and share prices. Should a demand for carry-over credits develop, interest rates will rise more in the first case, and decline less in the second.

Money and capital markets can become so tight through entrepreneurs' demand for carry-over credits that a real stock exchange crash may ensue. Bonds and shares are dumped on the market to satisfy their urgent credit demand.

Later the demand for these credits dwindles because entrepreneurs begin to hurry with the liquidation of inventories. This, together with the quasi-savings of consumers, alleviates the situation on the credit markets. Money becomes easy. First-class bonds and sometimes also certain shares begin to move up under the impact of accumulating idle funds and low interest rates—much to the astonishment of the public expecting still lower prices because "business is still so bad."

Part IV

THE BUSINESS CYCLE

Business Cycles are Alternating Inflations and Deflations

Since the beginning of the nineteenth century the economies of industrial countries have experienced peculiar fluctuations at more or less regular intervals. Although showing many differences in detail, they had so many features in common that they are regarded as homogeneous phenomena. They are called business cycles.

Generally speaking, these common features are exactly those produced by money inflations and deflations. For this reason so-called monetary business cycle theories regard the business cycle as a monetary phenomenon, expressing the idea that the prosperity phase of the cycle is caused, or at least necessarily accompanied, by expansion, and the depression phase by contraction, of money circulation.

Inflation and deflation result from changes in credit demand and supply, as described above in detail. The inflationary prosperity phase and the deflationary depression phase of the cycle result from the same changes.

However, cyclical inflations and deflations have some peculiar features. In the first place, cyclical deflation brings the economy back to, or very near to, where it was before inflation started. The movement closes like a circle. Second, the individual cycles exhibit if not the same then at least similar wavelengths; this fact is generally referred to as periodicity. Third, as soon as one cycle is completed, a new one begins. The individual cycles follow each other in certain rhythms like measures in a musical score; cycles are, therefore, also called rhythmical phenomena.

Changes in the economy generally lead after a certain time —just as in nature—to adjustments and thus to new equilibria. Contrarily the changes creating business cycle fluctuations do not lead to new equilibria. For endogenous reasons prosperity creates depression, and depression creates prosperity in eternal sequence. The pendulum of economic activity does not come to rest but continues to swing, like a *perpetuum mobile*—or at least it has done so until now.

Why is the business cycle self-perpetuating? Many economists have tried to solve this so-called riddle of the cycle, but no one answer has so far found general acceptance.

Maldistribution of Monetary Demand over Time

During the prosperity phase demand for goods and services is far above and during the depression phase far below the intracyclical average level. But over the whole of the cycle monetary demand does not dwindle and money does not disappear into death traps. For the business cycle as a whole, therefore, Say's law remains valid. The income of all factors of production is always sufficient—and is used—to buy all goods produced. The cycle is characterized by a maldistribution of demand over the various phases of a cycle rather than deficiency of demand during the whole cycle.

What are the reasons for this maldistribution of monetary demand over time?

Under-consumption Theories

The most popular answer to the question of why demand suddenly falls off at the end of a prosperity phase and remains low during depressions, is provided by the so-called under-consumption theories. They are as old as the business cycles themselves. They were considered as definitely refuted until Keynes' unemployment theory—which is at least partly an under-consumption theory—made them fashionable again.

Under-consumption theories have been presented in the most various forms. Their basic idea, however, is always the same. People in upper income brackets have a higher propensity to save and a lower propensity to consume than people in low income brackets. Therefore, the increase in incomes during the boom prevents investment from keeping up with growing saving; "over-saving" develops and deflation ensues. Under-consumption theoreticians consequently see the most important remedy against depressions in a redistribution of income in favor of lower brackets. One economist, the "free money" man Silvio Gesell, even went so far as to propose the creation of a money with melting value, so as to discourage saving and thereby prevent an interruption of the money flow.

It may be conceded that under-consumption might in certain conditions create deflation. But under-consumption, or over-saving, can never lead to those phenomena which have been characteristic of business cycles in the past. Nor can they above all explain cyclicity.

If increased savings were responsible for the end of a boom, obviously interest rates would be low at that juncture. In reality the upper turning point is marked by high and even rising interest rates. Furthermore, changes in saving are usually slow processes, whereas at the onset of a typical depression demand falls off abruptly and, so to speak, out of a clear sky.

Over-investment Theories

The so-called over-investment theories try to explain depressions as a lack of new investment opportunities. Their argument runs as follows. During the prosperity phase entrepreneurs expand their plants because they expect higher demand for their products. But once the plants are constructed, the additional demand for goods and services created by their construction disappears. Deflation must ensue. Spiethoff explained the end of a boom in this manner long before the Keynesians developed their types of over-investment and stagnation theories. He gave, incidentally, an additional reason for the break. Once the new capital goods—especially new industrial plants and equipment, and all installations for a long-term use, such as railways and electricity and water works—are operating, the production of consumer goods increases suddenly and excessively; demand can no longer absorb the supply of goods at prevailing prices. The ensuing price fall forces entrepreneurs to restrictions.

Many objections can be raised against this line of reasoning. It is, for instance, as we shall see later, by no means self-evident that the production of capital goods should expand by jerks rather than be spread evenly over time. But more important: if additional capital is applied in an economy, the structure of the economy changes once and for all. It becomes more capitalistic. A new equilibrium with longer roundabout ways of production is established, provided no credit contraction is enforced by new developments. At the beginning of every new production period entrepreneurs spend the same, now increased, amount of money on capital goods. Therefore the demand for capital goods cannot suddenly fall off. The funds required by entrepreneurs to maintain such demand are provided by the proceeds of the consumption goods sold, into which the capital goods of earlier period are, so to speak, amortized. There is no reason why amortization and new production of capital goods should not balance.

The Theory of Unnatural Interest Rates

The over-investment theories being entirely unsatisfactory, the Swedish economist, K. Wicksell, developed a theory according to which cyclical inflations and deflations are due to, or at least made possible by, fluctuations in credit supply. For Wicksell and his followers the credit policy of the banks and Central Banks is primarily responsible for the business cycle. Their theory runs roughly as follows. If demand for credits picks up for one reason or another, the interest rates on the free markets—which appear as the natural rates to Wicksell—have a tendency to move up. If the Central Banks, and with their support also the commercial banks, fail to adjust their interest rates and keep them unnaturally low, the increased demand for credit will partly be satisfied by the banks' inflationary credit expansion. Later on, but too late, the Central Banks and consequently also the commercial banks raise their interest rates—either because they are losing gold or foreign exchange, or for other reasons. Now demand for new credits is discouraged, and at the same time the credits granted earlier appear less profitable and are repaid. Deflation ensues. In other words: delay in adjustment of the bank rate to the increased credit demand opens the death trap for money with the result that the volume of money grows; the subsequent belated adjustment forces the money back into the death trap so that the volume of money shrinks.

The Wicksellian argument is basically correct. His theory should be regarded as the most decisive progress in the field of economics. Much of what has been taught later appears retrogressive in comparison.

Wicksell's reasoning might be contested for not stressing enough the importance of changes in credit demand. In times of permanent cheap money policy, interest rates obviously cannot rise at the end of a boom, and therefore cannot be responsible for the turning of the tide. The short but steep American depression of 1937 happened with interest rates moving hardly at all. It was an "easy money depression." But Wicksellian reasoning remains valid in so far as even the strongest demand for credits cannot lead to inflation if it is checked in time by a restrictive interest and credit policy, i.e. by raising discount rates so high as to counteract even the most optimistic profit expectations of entrepreneurs.

Psychological Business Cycle Theories

Every business cycle consists of two distinct parts—an upswing and a downswing. Each of these parts, in turn, is divided in two sections: during the latter section of the upswing and the first section of the downswing production exceeds, and during the latter section of the downswing and the first section of the upswing, production falls short of the intracyclical average. Thus there must be forces at work which prevent an equilibrium at the average level. If this were not so, any increase in credit demand or supply, for instance, would lead to a single and lasting credit and monetary expansion, but not first to inflation and then, as a reaction, to deflation. Such forces, first strengthening the effects of certain changes only to damp them after a certain time, exist in economic and social life. They are of a psychological nature. When prices rise, people expect further rises. They go on paying and demanding higher prices, until one day the exaggerated price expectations break down. Over-speculation must then be liquidated. The price level falls.

Psychological business cycle theories, for which the cycle is essentially the result of uncertainty, error and psychological epidemics, are not new. Almost all contemporary descriptions of the cycles in the nineteenth century treat crises as the results of over-speculation of producers and consumers. Mass optimism is regarded as responsible for the boom, mass pessimism for the depression.

After a lifetime of practical experience I am inclined to consider the psychological business cycle theories in combination with Wicksell's credit supply theory necessary as well as sufficient to solve the riddle of the cycle. I am strengthened in my opinion by the observation of the so-called secondary stock exchange movements, where prices fluctuate in waves around a trend line without any change in objective data. I do not, of course, deny that changes in objective data may start a cyclical movement. But why is this movement first exaggerated, only to be reversed later? Why does it lead to maldistribution over time rather than to a single and lasting change in the volume of consumption and production? These facts can be explained naturally only by a psychological theory. A brilliant exposition of such a psychological business cycle theory can be found in Professor A. C. Pigou's famous book, *Industrial Fluctuations*.[1]

Psychological Cycle Theories are Realistic

If business cycles are the result of a maldistribution of monetary demand over time—and there can be no doubt that they are—then they are in the last analysis nothing else than the expression of hurrying and waiting on a gigantic scale, embracing the whole economy. Whatever may induce the upward movement, producers and consumers hurry to buy goods and services. And whatever may induce the downward movement, producers and consumers wait with buying.

Later, when dealing with stock market phenomena, we shall

[1] 1st edition, 1927; 2nd edition, 1929.

examine in detail the mass psychological reasons for such hurrying and waiting. Here it suffices to point out that the psychological theories are identical with the explanation of the cycle given by business men. They know from practical experience how decisively their own, their fellow entrepreneurs', and their clients' decisions are determined by moods, i.e. by optimism or pessimism; they also know how strongly their own decisions are influenced by the decisions of others.

As far as I can see, only psychological theories can explain the suddenness and abruptness with which the boom ends in most cases. Only they offer an explanation for what is really the riddle of the cycle: why the movements do not peter out but continue like a *perpetuum mobile.*

Error about the Reversibility of Price Movements a Necessary Condition for the Cycle

Even those who do not consider the fluctuations of the cycle as caused mass psychologically must admit that a certain mental attitude of the people, and especially of entrepreneurs, is a necessary condition for their happening. Aberrations could not develop if people regarded the occurring changes in prices and demand as only temporary. Nobody will invest, or even consume, beyond his most urgent needs at rising prices if he expects prices to collapse during the period for which he is planning. Nor will anybody sell at falling prices, except under compulsion, if he expects prices to recover later. One of the main shortcomings of all non-psychological explanations of the cycle is not taking into account that maldistribution of demand over time cannot develop unless people are unaware of it. A mass error concerning the character of the market movements has to prevail. Otherwise single erratic changes could develop, but never those periodical reversible and cyclical phenomena which have characterized the economies of industrial countries, at least until now. These presuppose error.

Economists who believe they can forecast and calculate in advance the end of investment demand, and thus of the boom, must turn out to be false prophets, and most of them have indeed done so. If economists can recognize the temporary character of high demand, business men can, too. For the world does not consist of economists who know and business men who err. It is rather the other way round. But when business men cease erring, they alter their plans. They postpone certain investments and the calculated depression does not happen.

Some people, of course, speculate on the short run. They buy at rising and sell at falling prices, although they realize the price movements to be short-term. They hope to be able to unload on to others before the prices break, or to re-purchase from others before they recover. But then they err in believing that the others will err in believing that the price movement will continue rather than be reversed. Their belief in the errors of others is a necessary condition for their short-term speculation.

Liquidity Preference not a Helpful Concept

Since the appearance of Keynes' *General Theory* some economists have tried to explain the cycle through so-called liquidity preference. However, this concept confuses rather than explains the issue.[2]

It is true that business men at times refrain from spending and keep their money at home or in banks. They also prefer short-term to long-term money claims. According to the liquidity preference theory this is due to the business men's wish for protection against the uncertainty of the future. It could be added that for this reason they also prefer to repay debts.

However, business men in particular and the public in general preferring at times to be liquid, i.e. to own money and short-term claims rather than capital or consumer goods or long-term claims, are not seeking special protection against the uncertainty of the future. The future is always uncertain and not only at times. Their behavior is simply the result of their being bearish at that particular moment, i.e. expecting prices —possibly also of bonds—to decline, and their liquidity preference will be the greater, the greater they judge the probability and extent of the price fall.

[2] For more details see my *Economics of Illusion,* Chapter 13, "Anachronism of the liquidity preference concept."

If this is so, then it is unnecessary, misleading and alien to the whole system of our economic thinking to introduce the preference for liquidity, i.e. for cash and short-term money claims, as a new and special reason why producers and consumers abstain at times from purchase. Those who consider a preference for cash the reason for depressions are, therefore, guilty of a sort of double accounting. The disinclination to own goods and the preference to own cash are taken as two separate phenomena, whereas they are really two sides of the same phenomenon: people prefer not to own goods because they fear the exchange rate of goods and money will move to the advantage of the latter.

Multiplier Theory, Acceleration Principle and Business Cycles

Some economists believe that the riddle of the business cycle can be solved in terms of the acceleration principle and/or the multiplier theory. We have already dealt with the objections to these concepts. Here we wish to add a few words on the weaknesses of the so-called oscillation models.

The explanation of the business cycle in terms of the acceleration principle runs somewhat as follows. If consumption increases by an amount x, a multiple of x of capital goods must be produced, because production detours are, on the average, very long in a highly capitalistic economy. The consumption induces investment. In order to carry out these investments credits must be sought. A credit inflation will ensue. But once the new capital goods are produced, the additional credit demand falls off. There will be credit deflation.

As mentioned above, these arguments have to be refuted because they presuppose a highly elastic credit supply and a world in which the interest rate has lost its function to control the distribution of capital over time. And, furthermore, because they presuppose as certain an inducement which really has first to be explained and proved. As an independent explanation for reversibility they are without value. An acceleration boom could come about only if entrepreneurs failed to realize that they were faced with just such a boom, i.e. a reversible phenomenon. In other words, entrepreneurs must not be acquainted with the acceleration principle. If the entrepreneurs recognize the working of the accelerating mechanism, they will not trust the boom and will abstain from investing at rising prices. If they know that an increase in the annual production of automobiles requires only a single increase in automobile factories, they will certainly not construct steel mills with a capacity for an annually recurring increase in automobile factories. Capacities are never calculated on the basis of a single non-recurring use. Only in so far as entrepreneurs believe the rise in prices and demand of steel to be lasting will they act as assumed by the acceleration principle. The investment boom which later collapses is thus not caused by the increase in consumption, which, as such, never leads to a reversible phenomenon. It is rather caused by entrepreneurs' faulty judgments about the duration of the price and the demand increases for capital goods. Many cycles of individual goods, such as the pig cycle, the construction cycle, and others, are caused simply by errors.

As regards the multiplier theory, a credit expansion for investment purposes results indeed in higher incomes of those contributing to the production of capital goods. But it does not follow that these incomes are really spent. The problem of the cycle is just why at times these incomes are spent and why at other times they are withheld from the markets. Allusion to the power of additional investment to create additional consumer income only re-formulates, but does not solve, this problem. But let us not go further into the dreamland of the acceleration and multiplier theoreticians and their abstruse models. Their unrealistic speculations of how a boom must— or should—collapse for purely mechanical reasons are too far away from our way of thinking.

Responsibility of Money-Issuing Institutions

Unnaturally low or high interest rates may often not be sufficient causes for inflation and deflation, but they are certainly always necessary conditions. Unless the money-creating institutions supply money at inflationary low interest rates no credit demand, however strong, could lead to inflationary booms. Similarly, unless these institutions enforce repayment of credits by deflationary high interest rates, deflationary depressions could not normally develop.

Central Banks are responsible for every inflation, but not for every deflation. If the demand for credits weakens to such an extent that interest rates on the free market sink to near zero without the credit supply being absorbed by demand, then deflation develops, even if Central Banks and banks pursue an extremely easy money policy. They cannot lower their rates below zero.

We have already treated this case of death traps opening in detail (pp. 111-112). We recall that outside of typically cyclical movements it can happen only under very exceptional conditions, such as prohibitive taxation of production. A structural decline in the propensity to consume due to changing saving habits will, as a rule, lead only to an insignificant, gradual decline in interest rates, as will a structural decline in the propensity to invest due to changing productivity of capital. Only the combination of a simultaneous decline in the propensity to consume and to invest, such as occurs in cyclical depressions as a result of general pessimism on prices and demand, can lead to such abundance of credit supply and such scarcity of credit demand that deflation ensues.

Keynesians are apt to lump together genuine saving and waiting due to pessimism on demand; they speak of both as a declining propensity to consume. This can lead only to general confusion, since it obscures the necessary distinction between structural and cyclical phenomena.

The Start of an Upswing

A cyclical upward movement can start theoretically and, as historical observation has shown, also practically in totally different ways.

Recovery can start from an easing of the money situation. When the investment excesses of the previous boom have been liquidated and the interest rates have fallen, certain projects, unprofitable so far, can be carried out. The volume of credit and money begins to rise.

Recovery may also start from changed conditions on the side of demand for credits. A new invention enhancing the productivity of capital will increase the demand for credits and hence the volume of credit and money. This happened, for instance, when the railroads and later the automobile were invented and taken into use. War booms, too, are started by high credit demand—for destructive rather than for productive purposes.

Recovery can, of course, also start from a combination of changes on the supply and the demand side for credits.

By far the most important cause of recovery, which has at least reinforced all upswings of the past, is of a psychological nature. After depressions have run their course for a certain time, pessimism some day reaches proportions which cannot be surpassed. Deflation ceases to be cumulative. Prices no longer fall. Certain entrepreneurs, therefore, now hope to produce again at a profit, or at least without loss. They may wish, furthermore, to replenish their excessively run-down inventories. Consumers, in turn, no longer hope to buy cheaper later on. Their waiting ends also because their stock of non-durable consumer goods dwindles and their durables are worn out.

The result will be inflation—or, as it is sometimes called in this case, reflation.

According to Keynes depression comes to an end when an under-employment equilibrium is reached, i.e. when a fall in employment reduces incomes and thereby savings to the point where they can be absorbed by investment demand. An upswing is not necessarily supposed to follow. This whole idea is unrealistic. Depressions are neither reinforced by over-saving nor halted by under-saving. Depressions end when, for the above-mentioned reasons, people no longer wait with spending. And every depression has so far been followed by an upswing.

From Recovery to Boom

What forces lead an economy from recovery to boom, and finally to that state of hypertension which ends in crises or depression?

The answer is given by what we have said above in connection with psychological business cycle theories. It can be summed up in the French saying: *"la hausse amène la hausse"* (the boom creates the boom). For reasons of mass psychology an inflation once begun does not—except in very special circumstances—lead to a new equilibrium but to ever stronger inflation and finally to deflation.

We have already spoken of this self-intensifying mechanism of inflation. Here we just want to recapitulate. When the prices for finished products increase under the impact of inflation—while production costs, especially wages, lag behind—entrepreneurs will strive to expand production because such expansion will now appear profitable. Credit demand rises. This demand will be satisfied by the banks granting inflationary credits. The new money reaches the markets directly or via wage earners. The price level will be lifted anew, with the result that in the next production period expansion is further stimulated—provided that at least some of the costs remain stable.

As long as costs rise proportionately, the price rise as such will not lead to increased credit demand. A new equilibrium is established. But when prices have risen for some time more and more people will expect the upward movement to continue. These people, too, now wish to buy—not for immediate consumption or use but for re-sale at a later time. Additional credit demand now emanates from these speculators. If not deterred by higher interest, the speculators will now, too, enter the markets as buyers and join in bidding up prices, thus further reinforcing the stimulus to yet greater credit and production expansion in the next period. The process continues as long as the boom can intoxicate ever new parts of the population.

The End of the Boom

Recovery, as we have seen, can start from changes in demand for credits as well as in the supply of credits. So can prosperity end.

The supply of credits is curtailed when Central Banks raise

their discount rates. They may do so because they lose gold or foreign exchange to other countries, or just because they finally recognize the inflationary consequences of unnaturally low interest rates. Discount rates are hardly ever sufficiently raised to check a credit demand fanned by optimistic price and profit expectations of entrepreneurs and speculators. Therefore the effects of tighter money are generally not felt until somewhat later, when the demand for credit, in its turn, collapses.

The demand for credits breaks down when the optimism of entrepreneurs and speculators has become so universal that the fever cannot spread to new layers of the population. From this moment on credit no longer expands. Prices no longer rise. As the calculations of many speculators and entrepreneurs were consciously or unconsciously based on the expectation of ever increasing prices, the former credit expansion will now turn out to be unprofitable—especially if the costs of credit, the interest rates, increase. Total demand for productive and speculative credits will contract. All production—and also all inventory accumulation—profitable only in inflationary condition—buyers' resistance, or buyers' strike. Prices appear sud-

Some depressions clearly begin with a collapse of consumption—buyers' resistance, or buyers' strike. Prices appear suddenly to have risen too high. Or stocks of goods in the hands of consumers begin to be excessive. Money which would normally have been spent flows back to the banks. Unless the banks are able and willing to expand immediately their credits according to this increased credit supply, deflation must ensue.

Such changes on the demand and supply side of credit are able to break the boom quite independently of any tightening of credit supply by Central Banks. In times of permanent easy money the interest policy of the banks does not change anyway. None the less, even then the boom must collapse sooner or later—contrary to the expectations of certain easy money enthusiasts.

It has become fashionable nowadays to predict the end of booms on the basis of so-called objective data. An attempt is made to determine, for instance, when a new plant to meet a certain demand will be completed, or when government rearmament expenditure will terminate. As already explained changes in demand calculable or calculated in advance cannot cause cyclical fluctuations, since adjustments will be made in the meantime. The erroneous belief that the boom is there to stay, coupled with a lax credit supply policy, causes the economic activity to expand above average during prosperity. The end of the boom will, therefore, generally coincide not with changes in objective data but with the collapse of the inflation mentality or with changes in credit policy. But the end of an optimistic mass psychology or of a lax monetary policy can never be calculated in advance.

A war boom is only partly a cyclical, i.e. reversible, phenomenon. When the government stops spending for war purposes, not a deflation but a post-war boom generally follows. Pre-war prices seldom return. War booms are erratic, inflationary phenomena caused in the last instance by lax taxation policy.

Delayed Deflation

In most of the historically known depressions starting with a buyers' strike, deflation did not set in immediately. Just as inflation does not "catch on" fully as long as many still do not believe in the upturn, so does deflation not fully operate as long as many entrepreneurs and speculators do not believe in the recession.

Additional credits are needed to carry inventories growing through unsold production. Later, when the hope of price recovery and of avoiding inventory losses vanishes, these additional credits are liquidated. The credit volume contracts, deflation sets in with full force. Prices fall.

Interest Rates during the Cycle

Generally speaking interest rates tend to rise during the upswing and to fall during the downswing. However, cyclical interest movements have some peculiarities which we have to mention repeating partly what we have said in Part III.

At the beginning of recovery interest rates rise less than would correspond to the increased demand for credits. During the depression part of the money no longer needed disappeared into private hoards, the small death traps. This money is now dishoarded and returns to circulation. Thus a part of the new credits is financed by the money coming out of the death traps.

Free money market rates are, during the recovery phase, generally lower than the discount rates of Central Banks. Later, interest rates stiffen. For those debtors having direct or indirect access to the Central Banks interest rates never rise much above discount rates. Other debtors may have to pay higher rates.

When Central Banks eventually raise discount rates to the level of the natural rate, the whole interest structure stiffens, sometimes very substantially.

Toward the end of the boom interest rates are very high unless Central Banks have maintained their unnaturally low rates. The beginning of the depression is usually accompanied by a further rise in interest rates. In spite of the declining credit demand, money stringency can reach the proportions of a real money crisis. Lack of confidence in the banking system can induce people to withdraw banknotes from the banks. Lack of confidence in the currency can induce people to convert, in turn, banknotes into foreign exchange or gold. Money crises from such causes will hardly be tolerated in the future. As soon as lack of confidence involves many or all the banks of the country the government is likely to step in and provide the banks with all the banknotes needed. The conversion of banknotes into foreign exchange or gold will be forbidden, if it is not already forbidden as it is nowadays in most countries.

When the money crisis subsides and carry-over credits are liquidated, interest rates decline. But again they decline less than would correspond to the decreased credit demand. Part of the money disappears in the small death traps, so that the credit supply decreases.

Thus, due to the small death traps, the volume of credit fluctuates during the cycle more than the interest rates.

Not all interest rates fluctuate to the same extent and simultaneously. As a rule, long-term rates (capital market rates) fluctuate less than short-term rates (money market rates), because people generally do not expect extreme tightness or extreme easiness to last. During prosperity capital market rates go up later than do money market rates. During depression they fall later. The reason is, again, that the tightness and easiness of money are at first regarded as only temporary.

Rates for loans to debtors of lower quality are always higher than for those to debtors of higher quality, because the former include risk premiums. They do not decline as quickly during depression as do the rates for first-class risks. The memory of losses suffered during the depression leaves risk premiums very —sometimes even prohibitively—high. At the end of a depression the money market is characterized by extreme easiness, while many debtors still have to pay high rates for their credits.

Money Circulation during the Cycle

Another phenomenon which we have already discussed in general terms in Part III, when describing inflation and deflation, can be observed very clearly during the cycle. Prices and production fluctuate more than the quantity of money, or conversely the quantity of money is more stable than prices and production.

This phenomenon, too, is due to the decrease in private hoarding during recovery, and to its increase in depression. Because of this so-called change in the velocity of circulation, prices and production may increase in the first case and decrease in the second even when the amount of money issued by the money-creating institutions—the official inflation, as we have called it—does not increase or decrease correspondingly.

Toward the end of the last war increase in the amount of banknotes issued by the Federal Reserve system was far in excess of increase in production and prices. This phenomenon was, however, only partly due to an increase in private hoarding owing to waiting. It was essentially the result of a change in paying habits. Black market operators and tax evaders, for obvious reasons, preferred cash to checking accounts.

Cyclical Phenomena are Results of Maladjustments

Prosperity differs in nearly every respect from depression. The most important and most conspicuous differences concern the general price level, employment and the capital structure of the economy.

All these differences are the results of changes in credit supply and demand. They develop only under one further condition, namely, if at least part of the population fails to react—or to react at once—to these changes in credit supply and demand. If, for instance, labor immediately adjusted its wage demands to higher prices, employment could not fluctuate.

Business cycles with all their sweeping changes can thus also be defined as changes in credit demand or supply, to which at least a part of the population does not adjust—or does so only belatedly. They are maladjustment phenomena.

Changes in the Capital Structure

During the upswing the capital structure of the economy deepens, the roundabout ways of production lengthen. The contrary happens during depression. For during upswings the use of capital is—or appears—more profitable. A new invention may have raised the productivity of capital. Or the expectation of higher prices creates hopes for inventory profits. Unless the cost of capital is adjusted to the higher profit expectations, increased amounts of capital will be used per unit of finished goods, or increased inventories will be carried.

During the downswing the use of capital is—or appears—less profitable. Unless interest rates are adjusted to the lower profit expectations, the capital structure flattens.

In the special case of a war boom the capital structure does not deepen as a rule. The proceeds of genuine saving, as well as of inflationary credit expansion, are made available to the government against war bonds. The government uses the amounts received mostly for war purposes, i.e. unproductively. As a further peculiarity of war booms commodity prices—and thus rents on land—rise much higher than prices in general, whereas during every post-war period raw commodity prices fall much lower than those of industrial products. The reason for this phenomenon is that, on the one hand, a great waste of agricultural products takes place during wars, and, on the other hand, production of raw materials is much less elastic than industrial production, so that the prices of the former are much more sensitive to changes in the demand.

Changes in Employment

The most characteristic phenomenon of the cycle is the fluctuation in employment. It is, as explained above, due to margins between costs—especially of labor—and prices. When, during the upswing, money wages lag behind rising prices, thus lowering real wages, entrepreneurs are able to employ workers so far unemployable because insufficiently productive. When, during depression, wages decrease more slowly than prices, entrepreneurs must dismiss workers. The tendency of real wages to decrease during upswings has been weakened during the last twenty years through union action. The fact that the United States, at the peak of the boom in 1936, still had several million unemployed can be explained only by excessive real wages. The tendency of real wages to rise during depression, on the other hand, has been reinforced by union resistance against any lowering of money wages. The result must be an increase in cyclical unemployment during depression.

Significance of the Elasticity of Labor Supply

As already mentioned, any increase in employment through inflation largely depends upon the elasticity of labor supply. The less elastic the labor supply, the less inflation increases employment—even though wage demands may lag behind price rises.

During recovery, labor supply is apt to be very elastic. Additional labor is available at the same wage rates. The supply curve of labor runs horizontally, because unions strive to maintain a uniform wage level during depression. While under such conditions employment is strongly curtailed during depression, it increases significantly during recovery, even if the demand for labor grows only slightly. Through the increase in employment, and hence in output, during the early stages of the upswing, the price-raising effects of increased demand are at least partly compensated by an increased supply of goods. This, and not the alleged Keynesian real wage unconsciousness of labor, is the reason for what is called in German *Mengenkonjunktur* (volume prosperity). It is a purely cyclical phenomenon and cannot be made the basis of a general theory —not even of a general inflation theory, as already explained in p. 94.

Unliquidated Inventories and Idle Fixed Capital

In the early stages of recovery, prices generally increase rather slowly for a further reason. The increased monetary demand meets the products not only of the immediately preceding production period, but also of earlier periods. There are always some inventories of finished or semi-finished goods which have not been "liquidated at any price" but held in the expectation of better times. Similarly, some capital goods —fixed capital—have not as yet been amortized into consumer goods. Thus, products of earlier periods are in supply during the first stages of recovery. The new workers' additional demand for consumption goods, and the new entrepreneurs' additional demand for capital goods, are at least partly satisfied by this supply.

Decreasing Unit Costs

The relative price stability during recovery is often attributed to the simultaneous decrease in unit costs, which results from fixed costs being spread over a larger output. Unit costs, it is true, decrease in many enterprises during recovery, until the best combination of fixed and variable costs—the combination for which the plant had been planned—is re-established. But in the short run (and the cycle is a short-run phenomenon) unit costs are no more decisive for pricing than are total costs—the variable costs plus fixed costs. Even if fixed costs are not covered by revenue, entrepreneurs continue to produce as long as variable costs are covered, for they have to pay the fixed charges in any case. Therefore the *increasing marginal* variable costs, and not the decreasing unit costs, determine the supply price of goods. The decrease of unit costs during recovery only diminishes the losses of the enterprise but does not lower the supply price of goods.

Profits and Losses during the Cycle

Since cycles are essentially alternating inflations and deflations, entrepreneurs reap inflation profits during prosperity and suffer deflation losses during depression. As we have seen such profits and losses are due to three reasons: the increase (or decrease) of prices; the lag of production costs such as wages, interest rates and rents behind rising (or falling) prices; and the increase (or decrease) of real debts through inflation or deflation.

The lag of production costs behind rising or falling prices is greatest at the beginning and smallest at the end of boom and depression. The psychological and institutional obstacles to adjustment weaken in the course of the movements. Therefore inflation profits and deflation losses are larger at the beginning than later on. Inflation and deflation, nonetheless, continue because subjective factors now gain strength. The hope of ever higher prices and the fear of ever lower prices lead to cumulative increases or decreases in credit demand, as long as credit supply is not tightened or eased correspondingly.

As recovery proceeds, unutilized or under-utilized equipment is put into use. As soon as industrial plants produce the output for which they were originally built variable and fixed capital are again employed in optimum combination. Marginal enterprises now produce without loss. Intra-marginal enterprises make profits or higher profits. The extraordinarily strong fluctuations of profits during the cycle are in all probability caused chiefly by fluctuations in the utilization of fixed capital.

Most entrepreneurs complain, except at the height of the boom, that their equipment is not fully utilized. The question of why industrial equipment is, on the average, seldom used to capacity has been discussed quite often lately. The only satisfactory answer seems to be that entrepreneurs tend to plan for maximum rather than for average output.

Is There Still a Cycle?

Many economists believe that the traditional cycle is a thing of the past. They maintain that the fluctuations of economic activity have, during the last two decades or so, been erratic rather than periodic and rhythmic. They contend that the forces causing periodicity and rhythm are no longer working. It is correct that in this age of armament races and other government interventions, fluctuations in demand emanating from the private sector of the economy can no longer affect the overall situation as they used to. Nevertheless, some features of the cycle are still likely in the future. The maldistribution of demand over time, even when emanating from exogenous, erratic factors, will still be exaggerated by mass psychological reactions of the people, both upward and downward. Human beings are still human beings. Otherwise, for instance, the post-war boom in the United States would not have been interrupted by the recession of 1949. The demand pent up during the war would have been spread much more evenly over the entire period from 1945 to 1953.

The study of the nineteenth- and twentieth-century cycles therefore remains of more than merely historical interest: the good old business cycle is still with us.

Stabilizing the Business Cycle

As a means for the stabilization of the business cycle, American literature stresses the importance of what is called functional finance. Functional finance is nothing else than a new version of the old prescription that governments should increase their expenditures during depressions and diminish them during booms. I have elsewhere dealt extensively with the problem of business cycle stabilization by deficit spending.[3] Here I would only like to repeat that, in my opinion, most advocates of functional finance are guilty of gross oversimplification of the business cycle problems. Every boom witnesses cost-price relationships appearing normal and bearable only during general optimism. This condemns every boom to death sooner or later. It is, therefore, naïve to suppose

[3] See *Economics of Illusion*, Chapters 6 and 14.

that the boom can be kept alive indefinitely by compensatory government spending, unless this is done on a scale that would transform the free into an entirely socialized economy.

Effective counter-cyclical interventions must set in before extreme situations have developed. They, therefore, presuppose early prediction of future developments. The exaggerations of an inflationary boom, for instance, can only be prevented if its coming is recognized well in advance. Otherwise the counter-inflationary measures will work only *post festum*. The early recognition of a boom presupposes all those qualities which are required for correct business or stock market forecasting. In particular, it presupposes independence from mass opinion which, at this juncture, does not yet expect extreme developments. Are the economic advisers of governments on the average particularly well qualified in this respect? It is not very probable. People with the rare gift of being able to recognize coming economic developments at an early stage will hardly enter government service. Nor does there seem to be any reason why government advisors should be less susceptible to mass opinion than private business men and investors.

Governmental economic forecasts are, on the average, just as mistaken as those of the business world. During the war government experts in the United States predicted post-war deflation—incidentally with complete disregard of historical precedent. Instead, a strong post-war inflation developed. In the spring of 1949 the government warned against impending runaway inflation, at the very moment when the commodity markets broke. The inflation predicted for 1951 failed to materialize. Raw material prices fell continuously from the spring of 1951 to the end of 1952. On the other hand, the end of the so-called second post-war boom which began in 1949 had been forecast ever since 1951 but did not actually occur until mid-1953 and then for other reasons than had been anticipated. Nor has the reaction been as strong as predicted.

In matters of business cycle stabilization, the spirit may be willing but the flesh tends to be weak. Strong political resistance regularly develops against any anti-inflationary fiscal policy. As to an anti-inflationary credit policy, the political resistances seem to be insurmountable.

Breaking a boom is always unpopular. Politicians will not seek to end a situation which can develop precisely because the business world regards it as normal and harmless. The year-long fight of conservative economists against the permanent easy money policy was, therefore, bound to be unsuccessful. The strong post-war inflation of 1945–51 could easily have been prevented by a restrictive credit policy.[4]

Attempts to shorten a deflationary depression are, of course, always popular. Deficit spending by governments, after the misinvestments of the preceding boom have been largely liquidated, may have very beneficial effects. It may change the psychological attitude of the people and thus prevent a secondary deflation. But the effects of such government spending begun too soon will be practically nil. The additional money immediately flows back into the banks. In any case, no deficit spending can have a lasting success as long as costs have not been adjusted to lowered prices. To combat wage rigidity, however, is the most unpopular of all measures.

Business Cycle Consciousness as a Stabilizing Factor

Certain stabilizing forces in the private sector of the economy may prove more important than governmental efforts.

It is a well-known fact that in economic and social life a phenomenon caused or reinforced by mass error has a tendency to disappear, or at least to weaken, once it has been observed for some time and begins to be understood. It would seem as if something of this kind has happened in the field of business and stock market cycles. Consumers and entrepreneurs have become business cycle conscious. They expect a depression long before it is actually due. Stock market speculators have learnt that no bull market and no bear market lasts forever and that both are reversible. People look, so to speak, through the mountain of the bull market into the next bear market

---

[4] For a detailed study of the post-war monetary policy in the United States until the end of 1952, see Appendix I, pp. 217ff.

valley; exaggerated movements in both directions are thereby avoided.

Much of what happened during the past few years is easily explicable by the public's greater business cycle consciousness. On the New York Stock Exchange prices fell from 1946 to 1949, although the first post-war prosperity phase continued until 1949. It was, no doubt, greater business cycle consciousness which prompted the stock market to discount the 1949 recession two-and-a-half years in advance. The bull market which started in mid-1949 and lasted to the end of 1952 never gave rise to prices out of proportion with yield in spite of a lax credit and monetary policy, the reason being that many stock exchange operators had been expecting a new depression ever since the beginning of 1951. Whether in the easy money boom that has been going on since September 1953 the lessons of the past will be heeded or forgotten remains to be seen.

Does Economic Growth Guarantee Lasting Prosperity?

It is often maintained that the growth of an economy, i.e. in the first instance the population growth, protects against depression.

During the war most American experts predicted a post-war depression. Then the growing population argument was used to support pessimistic forecasts. It would be impossible after the war to integrate fully into the productive process the discharged soldiers as well as a growing population. After ten years of almost uninterrupted prosperity the same argument is now, paradoxically, used to support optimistic forecasts. Growth of population is supposed to lead to increased demand and thus to guarantee a market for expanded production.

Population growth, as such, leads neither to excessive labor supply nor to a particularly strong demand for goods. If the latter were the case, the under-developed countries with their large birth rate would be the soundest economically because least subject to crises.

Population growth, as such, is neutral for an economy. Every producer is a consumer and every consumer a producer. Population growth appears important only under certain assumptions concerning the simultaneous growth of capital. In countries with slow capital formation, population growth lowers the standard of living, or, if wages are rigid, causes unemployment. In countries with strong capital formation, population growth increases the demand for capital. The expected decrease in population growth was, in fact, one of the main arguments of the stagnation theory. However, it seems very doubtful whether such structural support of the demand for capital could compensate for a cyclical deficiency of demand at the onset of the depression. That population growth guarantees prosperity is probably no more than one of those pseudo-arguments regularly appearing after a few years of good business in order to rationalize the prevailing confidence in the future.

In the same way it appears doubtful that a necessarily slowly proceeding development such as an increase in population can play a decisive role at the beginning of an upswing.

The contrary statement that a stationary population leads necessarily to a cyclical depression seems equally of doubtful value. A slow lowering of the demand for capital will lower the interest rates but will never lead to the sudden deflations which are characteristic of the upper turning points.

It follows, from what we have said above (p. 112) about secular deflations (stagnations) in general, that a stationary population can never lead to long-term deflations.

Easy Money Policy and the Cycle

It may be appropriate to add a few remarks about the influence of easy money policy on the course of the business cycle.

Before deliberate adoption of easy money policy, discount rates failed to be adjusted to free market rates because of institutional rigidities and misjudgments. The theoretical aim of discount policy remained the stabilization of the internal and/or external value of the currency through anti-inflationary or anti-deflationary measures. Since 1932, however, and even more since the appearance of Keynes' *General Theory* in 1936, discount policy—at least in Great Britain and the United States—has been influenced by a belief in the beneficial effects of easy money on employment and public finance. This belief was strongest in the United States when Secretary of the Treasury Morgenthau directed war financing, and in Great Britain under the Labor Government after the war. Lately the enthusiasm for easy money policy seems to have waned somewhat. A return to common sense in theory and practice has taken place. I doubt whether the return has been decisive enough.[5]

Easy money policy is a combination of two different policies: a policy of stabilizing interest rates, and a policy of stabilizing them at very low levels. There are various reasons for the popularity of the latter policy—among them the naïve belief that easy money guarantees full employment, the equally naïve belief that the burden of the public debt could with impunity be alleviated by artificially low interest rates, and last but not least resentment against unearned income in general.

Stabilizing Interest Rates

Stability of interest rates always means instability of the economy. Stability of interest rates causes the death traps for money to remain open much too long. Fluctuations in the demand for credit are no longer checked by compensating movements of interest rates, so that money can freely flow into and out of banks and Central Banks. Thus, the introduction of stable interest rates has led to the paradoxical result that a generation speaking and writing continuously about stabilizing the economy has destroyed, or at least weakened, the most important weapon in the fight against inflation and deflation—namely, interest rate policy.

Stabilizing Low Interest Rates

Interest rates could be stabilized at a level where credit demand and supply would balance at least over the average of

[5] My opinion on the monetary policy from 1953 on will be gathered from the article in Appendix II (pp. 229ff.).

a cycle. Such stabilization would be neutral in the long run. But if stabilization is achieved at a much lower level, the result will obviously be a long-term trend towards inflation.

The post-war inflation in the United States and in Great Britain was chiefly the result of a totally unjustified maintenance of low interest rates.

It is not astonishing that permanent easy money policy should have created inflation. Once easy money is considered legitimate and eternal, it is inflationary not only because it lowers the cost of credits, but also because confidence in permanently cheap money leads to belief in permanently rising prices.

In these circumstances it is, on the contrary, astonishing that price increases during the period of extreme easy money were not even greater and sharper. The reason may have been that people in their historical subconsciousness still reckoned with the possibility of reversals. This historical subconsciousness would eventually be destroyed if—as is often recommended—even "light" inflation became the object of deliberate government policy.

Securities during the Cycle

Quite generally speaking, common share prices depend on the one hand upon the dividends paid or expected, and on the other upon the prevailing yield of long-term bonds, i.e. the interest rates of the capital market. The prices and yields of long-term bonds depend in the last instance upon interest rates for short-term credits, i.e. money market rates, and—indirectly —upon discount rates.

Money Market Rates during the Cycle

Short-term interest rates as a rule rise with the upswing and fall with the downswing. But they do not rise and fall immediately after the turning point. We have already mentioned the reasons for this lag: the relative stickiness of the discount rates of Central Banks and the existence of private hoards, out of which and into which money flows at first.

Bond Prices and Capital Market Rates

During depression long-term interest rates decline and bond prices rise, but not immediately after the easing of money markets. The lag has psychological reasons. Investors having witnessed declining bond prices for a protracted period of time, remain at first bearish on bonds, i.e. bullish on long-term interest rates. They do not yet believe that the easier money is there to stay. A considerable margin between long-term and short-term interest rates therefore persists until investors gain confidence in the easing of the money markets and begin to switch from short-term to long-term investments.

In the later stages of prosperity money market rates rise considerably. Again bond prices do not decline until some time later. Investors who have seen rising, or at least stable, bond prices for a long time do not believe that tight money is there to stay. Later they begin to realize that the easy money period is over. Only then bond prices decline.

Common Share Prices

We shall discuss the laws governing share prices in detail in Part V. Here we may anticipate that share prices, quite generally speaking, equal dividends capitalized at the prevailing long-term interest rate. Share prices are pushed up by rising dividends or declining interest rates. They are depressed by declining dividends or rising interest rates. The forces pushing share prices upward and downward sometimes work in the same direction, thus strengthening each other; and sometimes in opposite directions thus weakening each other. They sometimes do not work immediately but with a psychological lag. The picture of stock price movements during the cycle is therefore a complex one.

Although individual cycles differ from each other in share price movements more than in any other respect, we may perhaps venture to formulate the following general rule.

Toward the end of depression long-term interest rates decline, i.e. bond prices rise. Share prices are not as yet affected. As long as business stagnates and profit expectations are bad, people have no confidence in the maintenance of dividends at even a low level.

Once business recovers, share prices move up vigorously under the double impact of higher profit expectations and lower and sometimes still declining interest rates. In the course of prosperity long-term interest rates tighten, bond prices begin to decline. But share prices still remain high because higher dividends, and expectations of still higher dividends, compensate the higher rate at which they are capitalized. Finally dividends decline, and now share prices, too, decline under the double impact of lower dividends and higher capital market rates.

Sequence of Interest Rate, Bond and Share Price Movements

The sequence of the changes in short-term interest rates, bond and share prices, and in economic activity may be illustrated by Figure 22. The curves roughly correspond to the old so-called Harvard business barometer. They do not, of course, give a picture of what really happened during the historically known cycles, nor even of what happened "averagely" or generally. They do show, however, what would happen if the forces responsible for cyclical movements were allowed to work unhampered. Nor is the graph purely speculative, for every cycle observed during history showed at least some of the sequences represented. But whatever the theoretical objections to the graph, it has often proved useful for practical investment decisions. Although one can never rely on events following each other as shown, the graph helps to bring home the forces at work, and the delays with which they may become operative.

The curves of business activity and of share prices coincide in our graph. Contrary to a widely held opinion, it was not typical of most past business cycles for share price movements to precede business activity movements.

In our graph money market rates begin to fall about the middle of the depression, and the inverse curve of interest rises. When money market rates have fallen to a certain extent, bond prices begin to move up. Economic activity and share prices

THE BUSINESS CYCLE

begin to pick up when the inverse curve of money market rates has reached its peak, i.e. when interest rates are at their lowest.

When business is at its peak, short-term interest rates harden. The inverse curve of interest rates goes down. Later, long-term

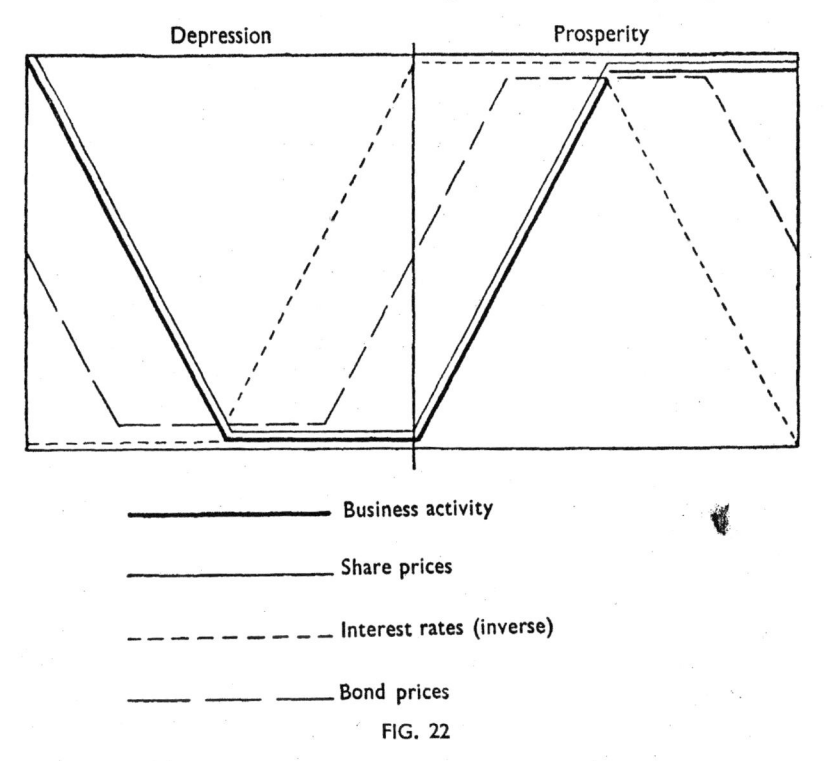

FIG. 22

interest rates join the movement and bond prices begin to decline. Business activity and share prices remain high in spite of hardening short-term and long-term interest rates. This is due to the fact that profits are still increasing and compensate for the higher rates of capitalization. Later, when depression sets in, business and share prices fall and bonds decline even further. Business activity and share prices remain low during the further course of depression, although interest rates soon decline and bond prices later begin to rise. This is because still declining earnings counteract the lower rates of capitalization.

Fluctuation in the Yield of Common Shares

Theoretically and *a priori* prices of common stock should always stabilize at a level where their yield exactly equals the yield of long-term bonds. This, however, is not what happens in reality. Share prices are generally lower. Their yields are normally higher than the yields on long-term bonds. In recent decades, yield differentials have been substantial in the United States, for a variety of reasons such as high income taxes, fear of labor unrest and other troubles.

Share yields fluctuate over the course of the cycle. At the depth of depressions they are usually high, and share prices therefore relatively low, because investors fear dividends will fall further. At the height of the boom yields are usually low and prices relatively high because investors hope that dividends will increase further. At such moments it may happen that share yields drop below the yields of long-term bonds.

Share prices do, in fact, fluctuate over a much wider range than indicated by our curve—and over a much wider range than interest rates. This is by no means self-evident. Theoretically, earnings on invested capital cannot exceed the interest rate at which new credits are demanded. However, for the above-mentioned psychological reasons, the supply price of equity capital may differ from that of loans. At the height of a boom, funds for bonds may be provided at 5 per cent, whereas shares may be bought on a 4 per cent yield basis. In a depression, funds for bonds may be provided say at 3 per cent, whereas shares are bought only on a higher than 7 per cent yield basis.

Earnings, Dividends and Share Prices

Companies generally pay out only part of their earnings as dividends. They use the rest to create or increase reserve funds, or they plough it back into the business in order to increase their fixed and variable capital. In recent years, and especially under the impact of high personal income taxes, the percentage of earnings distributed to shareholders in the United States has diminished so that undistributed earnings are now often greater than dividends.

Generally speaking, earnings fluctuate much more than dividends because the managements of companies with cyclically fluctuating earnings wish to stabilize their dividend payments in the interest of their stockholders. On the other hand, share prices fluctuate less than earnings though more than dividends. The least volatile of the three are the dividends, the most volatile are the earnings, whereas share prices move somewhere in between.

Independent Share Price Cycles

The correlation of stock market movements and changes in business activity has become less close in the past two decades than it used to be. According to some writers such a correlation no longer exists at all. This would not be astonishing. Net earnings are nowadays affected by corporation taxes and other burdens imposed on business much more than by purely economic changes in gross earnings. The New York bear market of 1939–42, for instance, was created through fear of impending war taxation rather than fear of bad business. The bear market of 1946–49 preceded the 1949 recession by more than two years; the bull market since September 1953 began a full year in advance of recovery. Only the future will tell whether and to what extent stock exchange bull and bear markets will continue to occur independently of business cycles.

Part V[1]

PRICE FORMATION ON STOCK MARKETS

Significance of the Problem

The study of price formation on security markets, and particularly common stock markets, is as interesting and important for the economist as for bankers or investors. The study of the stock market more than that of any other market can help the theoretician to understand the interrelation between the world of facts and the world of expectations—so much discussed just now. The business man, on the other hand, may learn through such study some useful rules which, otherwise, he might have to acquire by lengthy and possibly costly experience.

Much of what I have to say here is concerned with the laws of mass psychology influencing the formation of stock market prices. Although my exposition may help the business man to a clearer understanding of what, in the past, he may have realized instinctively and indeed used profitably in business nothing I say is really new. It would, therefore, perhaps hardly be worthwhile to return to these problems were it not for the fact that most people are impressed by studies in the field of mass psychology only in an abstract and, so to speak, theoretical way. Everyone knows that mass errors exist, yet there are few who seem able to apply this knowledge to practical situations. This is so not by accident, but as it were by definition. The majority of people are identical with the erring mass and, therefore, not able to recognize their own errors. This is why each generation seems to repeat at least some of the errors of its predecessor.

Shares as a Source of Long-Term Income

Most of those contemplating the purchase of common shares look to the regular and permanent income from dividend

[1] Part V is a translation of a lecture delivered at the Schweizerisches Institut für Auslandsforschung in Zürich and published in *Schweizerische Zeitschrift für Volkswirtschaft und Statistik*, vol. 88, No. 2, 1952.

payments. Consequently, it has been concluded that share prices must, in principle, be such that dividends guarantee a yield, i.e. a ratio between income and price, which equals the yield on long-term bonds. This also means, roughly, that the yield on shares must equal the long-term interest rate on loans. Given full confidence in the maintenance of the dividends, there would at this price, be no reason for switching from stock to loans or bonds, or vice versa, and thus for stock market transactions which would lower or raise prices. Share prices would, therefore, be bound to fluctuate with dividends, provided no changes in the long-term interest rate influenced share prices from the money side.

How far is this conclusion confirmed by actual price movements on stock markets? A glance at two charts from Moody's Investment Service representing developments on the New York Stock Exchange from 1929 to the spring of 1956[2] shows that the thesis of a close correlation between share prices and dividends is valid only with severe restrictions.

Let us compare—in Figure 23a—the development of dividends and share prices. We immediately see that the broad upward and downward movements on the stock market, the so-called bull markets and bear markets, do indeed correspond with the upward and downward movements of dividends in many, though not in all, cases. The great bear market of 1929–32 was accompanied by a strong fall in dividends, the bull market of 1932–37 by a substantial recovery of dividends. The subsequent pre-war bear market of 1937–42 coincided, paradoxically, almost all the time with rising dividends. Again, paradoxically, the strong war bull market from 1942 to 1946 coincided with relatively stable dividends. Still paradoxically, the post-war bear market of 1946–49 experienced a significant rise of dividends. The post-war bull market from 1949 to the end of 1952, on the other hand, returned to the normal pattern of simultaneously rising share prices and dividends. The short bear market which lasted from the beginning of 1953 to

[2] The lecture was given in the spring of 1952. The original charts showed developments up to the end of 1951. The first has been replaced by one published on April 2, 1956, and the second continued on the basis of other Moody publications. The text has been brought up to date correspondingly.

FIG. 23a

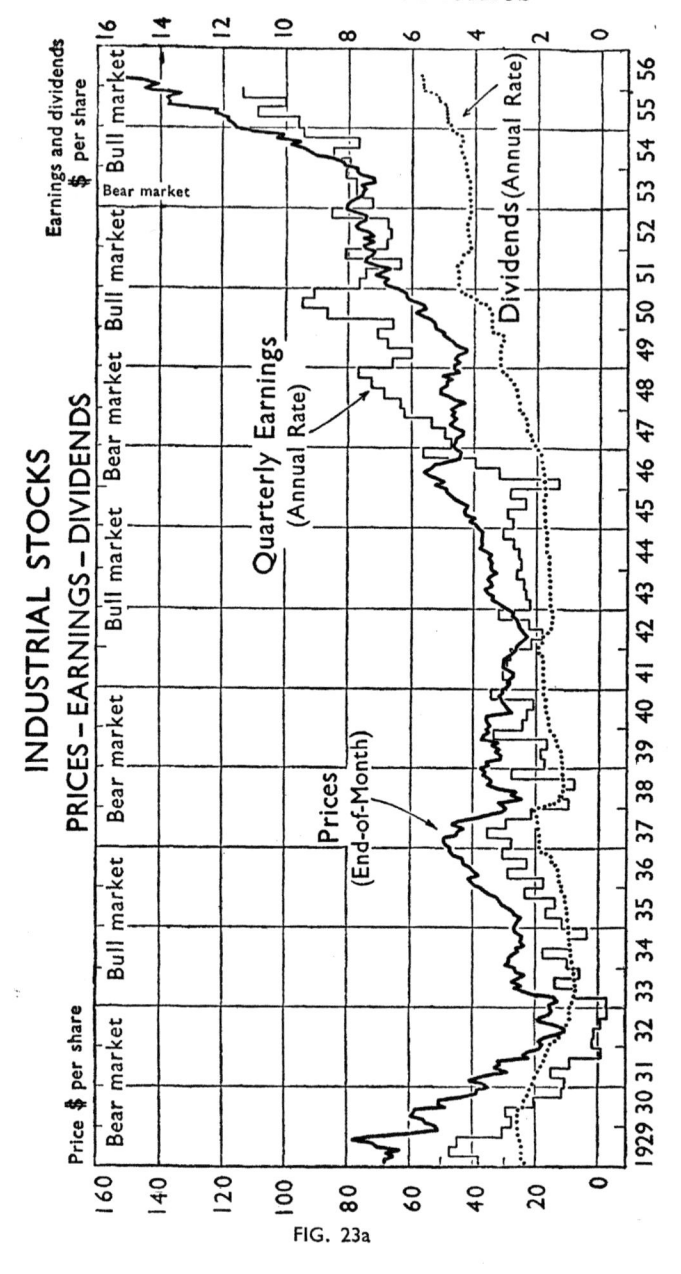

September 1953 saw falling share prices with more or less stable dividends. During the subsequent bull market, since September 1953, both share prices and dividends have been rising.

Something else can be seen from the chart. Though dividends and prices often moved in the same direction, the movement was by no means parallel. The curve of share prices regularly rises and falls much more than the curve of dividends. The yields, i.e. the dividends expressed as a percentage of price, rise in a bear market because share prices fall more than dividends, so that the latter represent a higher percentage of prices. In a bull market the yields decline because share prices rise more than dividends, so that the latter represent a smaller percentage of prices.

Figure 23b provides an even better illustration of the development of the yields. The dotted line represents the development of yields from 1929 to spring 1956.[3] Note that the curve is inverted, so that high yields are represented by a lower point on the curve than low yields. We see that by and large the lowest yields (about 3 per cent) coincide with the highest share prices in 1929, 1937 and 1946, whereas the highest yields (mostly 7–8 per cent) coincide with the lowest prices in 1932, 1942 and 1949.

Incidentally, Figure 23b shows also that changes in yields were hardly ever influenced from the money side. Only the rise in yields in the bear market of 1929–32 and the fall in yields in the bull market of 1932–37 correspond to similar developments of bond yields, and may therefore have been influenced—at least partly—by the latter. Since 1937 the yield on bonds did not change significantly, thanks to a deliberate easy money policy. The strong ups and downs of share yields can, therefore, not have originated from the money side. The 1953 bear market and the subsequent recovery are, however, again clearly connected with the yields on bonds, which first rose and later declined. Since 1955 bond yields have increased whereas stock yields continued their downward movement as the bull market proceeded.

[3] See footnote on p. 193.

FIG. 23b

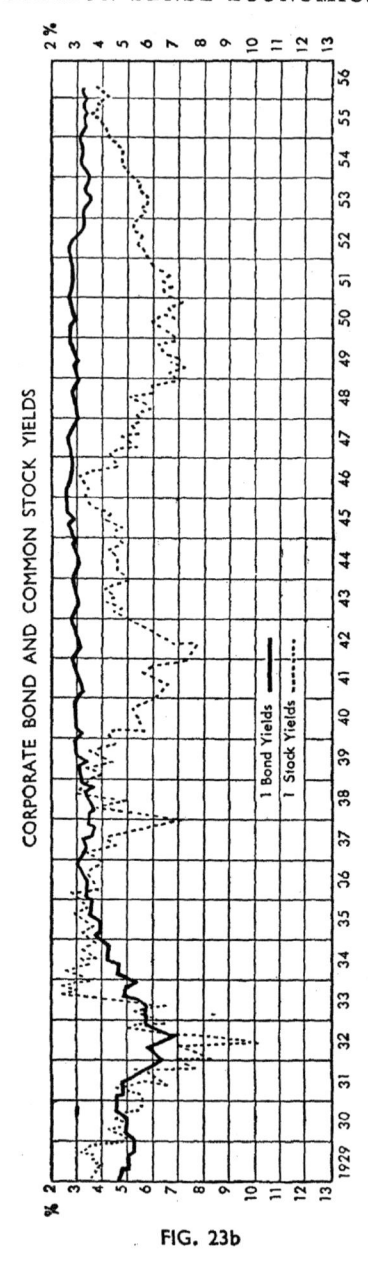

Corrected Price Curves

Thus the correlation between actual price movements and dividends is in reality only very loose. We gain an entirely different picture, however, if we compare dividend curves with price curves from which the exaggerations of boom and depression have been eliminated by some statistical methods—in other words with curves of intertemporal price averages. Such corrected curves run almost completely parallel with the dividend curves.

Thus results so far may perhaps be formulated as follows. Share prices are not just dividends capitalized at current interest rates, but they do fluctuate around a level determined by capitalization of current dividends at the current interest rate. Share prices may at any particular moment be higher or lower. But share prices coincide with dividends capitalized at the prevailing interest rates every time the market capitalizes dividends at an *average* yield rate.

Dividends, Net Earnings and Share Prices

A third curve in Figure 23a represents net earnings of corporations. We immediately see that net earnings and dividends move generally in the same direction, but that the former fluctuate over a much wider range. This is simply an expression of the fact that managements, aware of the temporary character of exceptionally high or low net earnings, pursue a policy of more or less stable dividends and distribute during prosperity a smaller—during depression a higher—percentage of earnings as dividends. As share prices, too, generally fluctuate more than dividends, they must move more with net earnings than with dividends. This is so although only dividends create income for the shareholder, and the undistributed part of earnings is important to him only in so far at it improves the quality of the dividends and the ability to produce future dividends.

Figure 23a shows that until about 1938 share prices and net earnings did, indeed, move in a fairly parallel way. However, between 1939 and 1942 the development of prices corresponded as little to net earnings as it did to dividends. From 1942 to

1944 prices and net earnings corresponded somewhat. From 1946 to the end of 1950 earnings rose much more than prices; instead of running below the price curve as usual, the earnings curve ran considerably above the price curve. A very much smaller part of total earnings was then abnormally high. In the general sentiment that earnings were abnormally high. In 1951 no parallelism between net earnings and share prices is observable. Since then, earnings and prices have risen, but the latter much more steeply than the former.

The generally greater stability of the price-earning ratio as against the price-dividend ratio explains a peculiarity of stock market literature. If future prices are to be forecast on the estimate of future earnings, the previous price-earning ratio, i.e. the relation of share prices to earnings, is taken into consideration. If, for instance, net earnings of a share are expected to be $10.00, and if the average price-earning ratio of the share has so far been 12 : 1, then the future average price of the share is believed to be $120.

The Significance of the Past for the Future

If share prices at a given time are identical with dividends capitalized at a certain yield rate, then stock market forecasts must obviously include prediction of future dividends as well as of future yield rates. Can such forecasts be made on the basis of past dividends and past yield rates?

Any forecast of the future must always start from a study of past developments of the market as a whole as well as of individual corporations. However, the experienced investor will always keep in mind that analogy conclusions from the past are permissible only within narrow limits. Dividends fluctuate not only within each business cycle, but also from one cycle to another. As regards yields, the year 1952 afforded a splendid example of how one can be mistaken. According to all precedent, average yields after three years of bull market should not have been higher than 4 per cent. Instead they were almost 6 per cent. The Dow Jones Index should have stood at about 375, rather than at about 275 as it actually did—a difference by no means unimportant for investment and speculation.

Yields were exceptionally high, nearly 8 per cent, at the beginning of the bull market in 1942, and exceptionally low, around 3 per cent, at its end in 1946. In such cases some reversal of price trends is indeed very probable—toward a bull market in the first case, toward a bear market in the second. However, such extreme cases do not often occur. And then there is always the possibility that high yields may be corrected by lower dividends rather than by higher prices, just as low yields may be corrected by higher dividends rather than by lower prices. Unfortunately, neither future fluctuations of the economy nor the extent to which the stock markets will over- or under-discount these fluctuations can be scientifically or objectively determined in advance.

If this is true of the stock market as a whole, the subject of so-called market analysis, it is even more true of prices of individual shares, the subject of so-called securities analysis. The dividends of individual corporations fluctuate quite differently in each business cycle. Whole industries, moreover, may profit or lose from one cycle to another. Different industries may also show quite different secular developments. Some become important and prosperous, others wither away as time goes on. To anybody who has doubts in this respect, perusal of the well-known work by Mead and Grodzinsky, *The Ebb and Flow of Investment*, is strongly recommended.

Expectations as the Cause of Market Distortions

The fluctuations of share prices are essentially due to two causes: the fluctuations in dividends and net earnings, and the fluctuations in the rate of interest at which the fluctuating dividends are capitalized. We have, in earlier sections, discussed the reasons for fluctuations in earnings and resulting dividends within a cycle and in the long run. Here we shall deal with the distortion of share prices by fluctuations in yield. Every investor and speculator knows that a correct forecast of the rate at which dividends will be capitalized is decisive for the success or failure of almost any transaction. It is extraordinarily difficult to act against the general market tendency resulting from changes in yield.

Why does the stock market capitalize dividends sometimes at an excessively high, sometimes at an excessively low rate? It is because the stock market always discounts the future dividends and never the present.

It is not easy to answer the question of how long in advance the stock market discounts future developments and changes. It has been maintained that the usual advance is about twelve months. This is a fairly reasonable assumption. It must be borne in mind, however, that if any future change is to lead to changes in the valuation of a share—or of all shares—it must be expected to be permanent. Increases or reductions in the dividends of highly cyclical shares which are expected to be only temporary, do not influence the price level. The prices of such shares generally fluctuate less than their dividends. Any actual rise or fall in the prices of such shares is due to an expectation of a long-term rise or fall of their average dividends.

Model of a Typical Stock Market Movement

All stock market movements known from historical observation differ, particularly with respect to the margin between current and expected dividends. Some correlations do, none the less, return with such regularity that we may speak of typical stock market movements.

Such a typical movement may concern one particular share, and may perhaps be due to the expectation of a new invention. Or it may concern the market in general, in which case the movement is usually called a bull or a bear market.

Any typical bull market starts with dividends being low and yields high. Yields are high because even lower dividends are expected in the future.

The reasons for such pessimism have often been discussed. We wish here to point to only two facts. First, in mass psychology, a sort of law of inertia seems to prevail; if the economic situation has deteriorated and dividends have fallen for a long time, then people expect this downward movement to continue until they are proved wrong by very drastic contrary experiences. Second, the very fact that share prices fail to move upward in spite of high yields seems in itself to create a mass suggestion that prevents objective judgment and reinforces the prevailing pessimism. Each individual investor is led to conclude that if share prices are low, they are so because there are good reasons why they should be.

The bull market starts with a phase which we may call the adjustment phase. Dividends rise; in addition, future expectations improve as a result of the rising dividends. General pessimism vanishes as the public begins to react to the slowly improving situation. As share prices rise more than dividends, yields fall. Share prices become adjusted to dividends.

The next phase may be called the normal phase. The future is expected to be neither better nor worse than the present. It is generally believed that current dividends will by and large neither rise nor fall. Share prices move up with dividends. Yields remain stable at levels neither excessively high nor excessively low.

The exaggeration phase follows. The rise in dividends and prices for a protracted period leads to general optimism regarding future dividends. The market discounts not only the current high level of dividends, but a still higher level in the future. Once more the law of inertia in mass psychology is at work. Rising dividends create expectation of further rising dividends. The fact that prices continue to rise in spite of continuously falling yields reinforces this expectation. More and more people begin to buy just because others buy—although some of them may do so against their own better judgment. All this ends in the well-known vicious circle of rising prices and further willingness to buy. We again recall the French saying: *La hausse amène la hausse.*

Eventually share prices reach a level entirely out of line with the dividends, which may already have started to fall. The situation begins to look unsound—first to a few, eventually to more and more people. No new buyers turn up, and some of the former buyers become sellers. Quotations weaken. The infection of mass optimism no longer spreads. Expectations which but yesterday appeared irrefutably correct, now seem fantastic. The reaction phase follows the former upward movement. This phase is, at the same time, the adjustment phase of the beginning bear market. Share prices, too high compared to dividends, now adjust to the latter.

The adjustment phase is followed by its normal phase and finally by its bearish exaggeration phase. Later, the adjustment phase of a new bull market starts.

Figure 24 schematically illustrates what we have said.

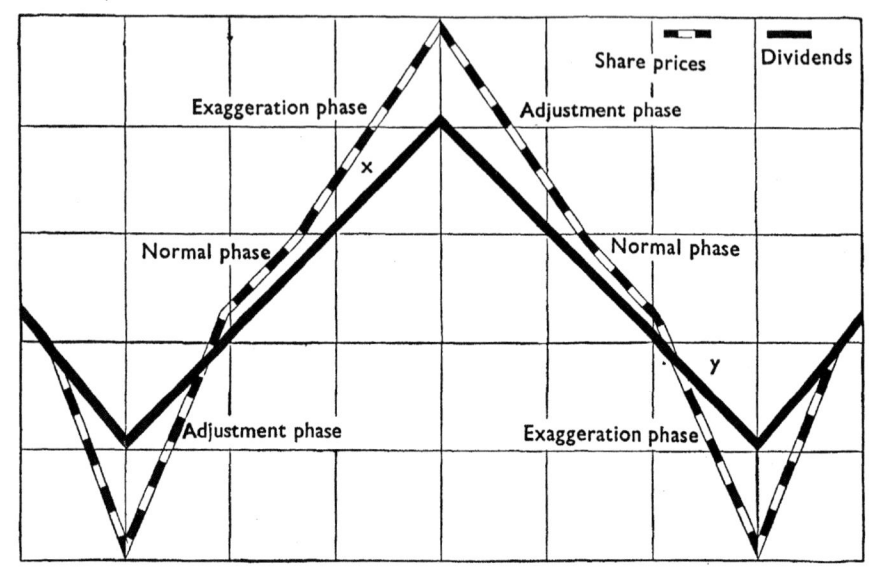

FIG. 24

Our description of a typical stock market cycle, incidentally, agrees with the widespread opinion that any upward or downward movement on the stock market is divided into three distinct parts: one in which shares are under-valued, one in which they are correctly valued, and one in which they are over-valued.

Are the Market Expectations Correct or Wrong?

Our graph shows that expectations coincide with the current situation only during the relatively short normal phase. At the same time it provides an approximate answer to the question whether and when current prices correctly discount the future, and when and to what extent the stock market makes mistakes. Let us assume that investors and speculators really discount the future about twelve months in advance. Let us assume further that each of the phases we have described lasts one year. Paradoxically, share prices anticipate correctly the factual situation a year later only at points X and Y. At all other times the market is mistaken. Up to point X the bull market takes too unfavorable a view of the future, beyond point X too favorable a view. Up to point Y the bear market takes too favorable a view of the future, beyond point Y too unfavorable a view. There is nothing to the alleged prophetic gifts of the stock market. The stock market does, indeed, try to guess the future, but it usually fails.

Uncertainty and Error as Price-Forming Factors

In the last analysis the stock markets err simply because the future differs from the present—a stationary state exists only in theory—and because human beings have no knowledge of the future in this or any other field. Future developments may be expected as more or less probable; they can never be recognized as certain. If it were possible to foresee the future correctly, say one year in advance, then the movements in share prices would simply precede the actual changes by one year. And if we had the perfect foresight of which theoreticians speak, that is to say, if we could correctly foresee an indefinite future, then all future changes would be discounted by present prices. Prices would never change again. This is, however, clearly an unrealistic assumption. The distant future cannot even be assessed by probability judgments; it lies, shrouded in mist, beyond the horizon of time. The nearer future may, however, be gauged by probability judgments. As time goes on, the near future becomes the present and can be recognized as certain. At the same time, however, a new segment of the future rises above the horizon of time. Men wishing to make decisions involving the future, must again try to guess its probable course. There is no point in deferring economic decisions "until the future is clear". The future is never clear.

Single features of the future may be visible with certainty

in the present. But only isolated events are thus visible, and never the whole complex future upon which earnings of any security depend. In these cases the margin between probability judgments and actual knowledge becomes small, and share prices reflect the objective situation more correctly. No event, however, is ever fully discounted as long as it is not recognizable with absolute certainty.

Purchases of Stocks are Purchases of Chances

All this leads to a conclusion which may seem awkward but is nevertheless indisputable. Purchases on the stock markets, as indeed on any other markets dealing with commodities of uncertain future value, are purchases of chances. In buying the share, the buyer really buys the chance of rising coupled with the risk of declining prices. All stock market transactions are thus based on probability judgments.

About the nature and the subject of such probability judgments much has been thought and written during the past few years. Much ingenuity, indeed perhaps too much ingenuity and certainly too much mathematics, has been deployed to reach, in the end, results by and large long known to any business man endowed with a reasonable measure of common sense.

Mathematical Probabilities?

The following paradox is responsible for the extraordinary difficulty in forming an opinion on the nature of probability judgments in business. On the one hand, the law of large numbers undoubtedly does not apply to forecasts of individual market situations. The probabilities entering, for instance, into judgments about the future course of an individual business cycle are not, strictly speaking, probabilities in the mathematical sense. Cycles are never completely uniform phenomena, and only few of them happen during a man's lifetime. One can never reckon with a mathematical probability of 1:1 that the market will go up rather than down. The case is comparable not to that of the bank in Monte Carlo, which can and does rely on red and black turning up equally often in the long run, but rather to that of the individual player, who cannot know whether the ball will stop on red or on black. He has to take his chance. He may be playing red ten times in succession, although black may win ten times.

On the other hand, each player, and each stock exchange "player" as well, behaves *as if* he were faced with mathematical chances. He may speak of a 10:1 chance that General Motors will double its dividend, although he knows perfectly well that he is faced with an individual situation and not with a large number of interchangeable cases.

David Hume has already discussed this paradox. He held that such judgments were not really probability judgments proper, but a kind of feeling representing a purely subjective assessment of the chances of success, based, it is true, on experience in numerous similar cases. A roulette player considers quite subjectively the chances for red to win as being very good—1:1; and the chances of a particular number to win as being very poor—1:32. As a result he will be content with a much smaller gain when playing a color—yet the very next turn of the wheel may throw up the individual number he had in mind.

It seems to me that since Hume nothing much has been said or written which transcends his explanation of the paradox. I am afraid we shall have to accept it, although it is admittedly not quite satisfactory. We would add only that a player, as well as a stock market speculator, will often play the chance of doubling his stake not only when he considers the odds as 1:1 but also when he considers them to be poorer. This is due to the gambling spirit of man. Without it, there could be no games of chance or lotteries whose total prizes are smaller than corresponds to mathematical probability.

Weighing the Chances

Offer and demand prices on stock markets may perhaps be explained fairly realistically by the following example. Suppose someone believes the chance that the shares of General Motors may rise to $70 is 1:4, and the risk of their falling to $30 is 3:4. Now, according to a widely held view, the value of a chance is equal to the expected profit multiplied by its probability. Provided our buyer's judgment is distorted neither by a passion for gambling nor by unusual anxiety, his purchase limit will not exceed $40, because at this price the chance of profit and the risk of loss will appear equivalent. A 1:4 chance of gaining $30 is worth 7:5 as is the 3:4 risk of losing $10.

We must, of course, always keep in mind that the underlying probability judgments are highly subjective. An optimistic buyer will over-estimate the chances of gain and under-estimate the risks of loss. A pessimistic buyer will do the contrary.

Finally, in the real world, people normally do not envisage only two probabilities. Expectations of the future are usually concerned with several favorable or unfavorable possibilities. The question, of how these different chances are weighed against each other and what the economic consequences will be, is highly controversial. In our example the buyer may believe that, besides the probabilities mentioned, there is a further 1:8 chance that the shares of General Motors will move up to $80, and a 3:8 risk that they will drop to $20. What, then, will be the upper limit for his buying order? It would seem realistic to assume that he will value the share at a price at which all the chances toward the up side together, and all the risks toward the down side together, appear to him equivalent.

Facts or Expectations as the Basis of Stock Price Formation

We can now give a more detailed reply to another question. Are stock prices—and indeed all prices depending upon expectations—ultimately determined by objective facts or merely by subjective opinions, however fantastic?

Many theoreticians have justly pointed out that if prices were dependent only on subjective considerations and no longer on objective facts, equal for all men, total anarchy of the markets and chaos in the economy must ensue. The very existence of the economy would be endangered, and with it economics as a science.

On the other hand, Keynes has clearly stated in his *General*

Theory that stock market prices are essentially the result of purely subjective anticipations. Indeed he went so far as to assert that these anticipations are not concerned with the objective facts themselves, but with the anticipation of the facts. This would be subjectivity squared. Stock price formation would appear to be the result of the general opinion on what the general opinion is going to be.

It is interesting to note that in practice business men, too, partly adopt the one and partly the other view. We find stock market forecasts based entirely on the prediction of facts. We find others exclusively concerned with whether and how the public will react to coming events. This latter attitude explains the behavior of many speculators who carefully watch how the market reacts to any given event and then quickly jump on the band wagon—a dangerous procedure—since the band wagon often stops or even reverses soon after. Market opinion is not reliable.

Figure 24 shows that neither of the two extreme views, but a compromise between the two, is correct. The objective situation is as important for price formation on the stock market as is the running hare for the hunter. At the same time, subjective distortions cannot be denied any more than the fact that marksmen often miss their targets. The hare exercises a sort of attractive power on the marksman; it does not prevent a lot of shots from going astray but it focuses the hunter's eye. In the same manner prices are shown in our chart to differ frequently and widely from the situation determined by objective facts. The latter, however, always pull prices back from their extremes. The normal phases, it is true, tend to be short because new events rising above the horizon of time always create new errors. But the duration of the phases of error, too, is limited.

Is the Economy a By-product of a Gambling Casino?

In a widely known passage of his *General Theory*, Keynes has drawn from the undoubted dependence of stock market prices upon subjective factors, moods and errors the conclusion that the flow of savings into investments is no longer dictated by long-run expectations of yield, but rather by short-run expectations of stock market gains, particularly in the United States. Thus, he thinks, investment has become the by-product of a gambling casino! Foolish investments were made or reasonable ones omitted depending on whether speculators were pushing up or depressing prices. Keynes recommends as a remedy that the bonds between investor and investment be made as indissoluble as those of marriage, which can be separated only by death or for very important reasons. In other words, Keynes opposes negotiability of investments in securities so as to prevent short-term speculation.

Once again Keynes, the brilliant generalizer of half-truths, has succumbed to the temptation of expressing a paradox at the cost of stating untrue facts and of giving dangerous advice.

Keynes' reasoning confuses two different things: short-term investment or speculation in investments planned for the long run, and short-term investment or speculation in investments planned for the short run. It is simply not true that an investor, or even a speculator, is not interested in the long-term prospects of, say, a new plant to be installed. On the contrary, any calculation of earnings submitted to investors is based on very long-term estimates indeed. The fact that the more distant future cannot be assessed so clearly never leads to its being neglected. It only results in the attempt to reduce risks by providing for rapid amortization. However much anyone may invest for capital appreciation, he still invests with a view to the long-term earnings. Capital appreciation can ultimately be realized only by sale to an investor who, in his turn, buys the security for the sake of its long-term return.

It is true that during a bull market long-term prospects are, for a more or less limited period, considered more favorable than during a bear market. Some of the investments made during a bull market, therefore, turn out to be faulty investments in the long run. During a bear market, on the other hand, some investments fail to be made which would have been profitable in the long run. But none of this is due specifically to the fact that securities represent liquid assets. It is the expression and the result of the cyclical fluctuations in a free economy. In the last analysis the stock market is neither the heating nor the refrigerating installation of the economy but its thermometer.

It is also true that there are always some people whose decisions are not based on present or future yields, but simply on the hope that prices will rise during the boom. These so-called camp followers hope to unload the "black Peter" onto another buyer before the prices break. Now it is by no means certain whether speculation by camp followers always reinforces the prevailing tendency, i.e. that it raises prices in a bull market and depresses prices in a bear market. Those who buy at low and sell at high prices mitigate rather than reinforce the price fluctuations. This is precisely what so-called professional speculators do. They buy when the public dumps its shares on the markets in a state of exaggerated pessimism, and they sell when the public, in equally exaggerated optimism, scrambles to buy.

Were the link between investor and investment to be made as indissoluble as marriage, fluctuations of prices would indeed be reduced. But the cost of such reduction would be a contraction of investment to the small volume of early capitalism and an obstruction of economic progress, which is decisively dependent upon the free flow of venture capital from the saver to the entrepreneur. Stricter divorce laws, too, would not only protect some existing marriages from dissolution, but also deter people from new marriages.

It should, however, hardly be necessary to dwell on anti-stock-exchange arguments, often disproved, just because an influential author has revived them in an admittedly entertaining manner.

Interpersonal Differences of Expectations

Booms are due to a raising of the prices at which stocks are demanded and offered by individual buyers and sellers, depressions to a reduction of these prices. These changes in price limits are the result of changes in expectations.

If the expectations of all parties to the markets changed simultaneously and to the same extent, prices would rise in the boom and decline in the depression without any turnover. Any buyer's higher or lower limit would be matched by a seller's higher or lower limit. The quotations would change; but no transactions would take place.

As is well known, neither booms nor depressions proceed without large, though fluctuating, turnover. It follows that the upward or downward adjustment of limits by buyers and sellers must vary from one person to another.

This is indeed what happens, and it is easy to explain. Both the subjective and the objective conditions for rising or decreasing prices are continuously assessed differently by the different groups of investors and speculators.

The result is, in any case, that during every boom and depression the distribution of securities between individuals, and groups of individuals, changes continuously.

Shifts in the Distribution of Securities

Shifts in the distribution of securities are hard to trace. We can, however, gain a general if simplified idea of what is happening if we consider that in every bull or bear market there must obviously be two groups of investors and speculators: the successful and the unsuccessful. The successful will buy near the trough of the price curve and sell near its peak; during most of the bull market they will hold shares, and during most of the bear market they will hold cash. They will make considerable profits. The unsuccessful, on the other hand, will sell somewhere near the lowest price and buy somewhere near the highest; they will hold cash during most of the bull market, and shares during most of the bear market. They will suffer considerable losses. In between there must be, and indeed are, innumerable mixed groups—for instance the half successful who hold shares during only half the bull market and cash during the other half, because they either bought too late or sold too early or both; and their counterpart, the half unsuccessful, who hold shares during half the bear market and cash during the other half, because they either sold their shares too late or re-purchased them too early or both. Most of the in-and-out traders who buy and sell continuously during any stock exchange movement belong to these groups. We shall ignore these groups, since they are not homogeneous in respect to the special qualities leading to success or failure.

The successful groups are distinguished first by being better informed, second by having the ability to resist the forces of mass opinion so that they manage to buy when the majority is deeply pessimistic and to sell when the majority indulges in exuberant optimism. At the same time, they do not underrate the power of mass opinion, so that they neither sell too early, i.e. long before mass optimism ends, nor buy too early, i.e. long before mass pessimism has run its course.

The unsuccessful do just the opposite. They succumb to mass pessimism when prices are lowest and sell; they succumb to mass optimism and buy when prices are at their peak. At the same time, they underrate the force of mass error. If, exceptionally, they have bought in good time during the bull market they get out too early; if, exceptionally, they have sold in good time during the bear market they get in again too early.

The qualities leading to success are rare. The majority simply cannot place itself outside the forces of mass psychology which condition its behavior. It cannot observe and judge them coolly from without. Neither the strength nor the weakness of mass opinion will be recognized in time by the majority. Regularly the majority fails to buy, or even goes on selling, at low prices because prices are expected to fall still further. Similarly the majority will not sell, or will even go on buying, at high prices because prices are expected to rise yet further. Therefore, when prices are low, stocks and shares must move out of the hands of the many into the hands of the few, and when prices are high, they must move out of the hands of the few into the hands of the many. This is indeed what happens in reality. At the end of a bear market and the beginning of a bull market the number of share owners is usually small and the average holdings of each owner large. This situation persists throughout the bull market when shifts occur mostly within the various groups of half successful and half unsuccessful. Toward the end of the bull market the number of share owners grows and the average holdings decline. Cash, on the other hand, is held during the bull market by the many who have sold out at low prices, and during the bear market by the few who have sold out at high prices. One speaks of accumulation in the case of the shares being bought by few, and of distribution in the case of the shares being bought by many. The smaller speculators are in the habit of closely watching whether shares are accumulated or distributed on the market. Correctly so, because there is a strong presumption that the mass is wrong and that the few are right. Moreover, a bear market rarely comes to an end as long as the securities are in so-called weak hands, that is to say in the hands of people financially and temperamentally ill-equipped to sustain further price declines.

Emancipation from Mass Opinion

As every experienced market operator knows, success on the stock market depends decisively on the ability to go against the prevailing tendency, i.e. against mass opinion, at the very moment when its correctness is least in doubt. The ability to go against the prevailing tendency, however, presupposes in the first instance that the individual remains conscious of the persuasive influence of mass opinion on his own opinion. This, in turn, presupposes a correct assessment of its force.

Everyday observation shows the strength of mass opinion to be very great indeed. It engulfs not only those who easily succumb to foreign influences but even those with normally detached views and sober judgment. An almost superhuman effort is needed to evade the influence of mass opinion—particularly in the United States, where price movements and thus the opinions of others are continuously reported to the farthest corners of the country by the ticker. The ticker assembles, as it were, all the buyers and sellers in one room. The ticker influences speculation as the flag influences troops. As long as the flag is carried forward, every single man knows that the others still have the courage and strength to go on, and this knowledge sustains his own courage and strength. Once the flag retreats, every man concludes that the others' courage and strength is waning. As he knows that he cannot advance alone he, too, retreats, even though he would not himself be forced to.

There is, of course, no general rule on how to counteract the influence of foreign opinion on one's own opinion. One of the most important aids for emancipation from mass opinion and its influence is to bear in mind that all prices are almost always necessarily wrong. It is further important to remember that mass suggestion wields its strongest influence when only *one* opinion is stated and discussion is prohibited. An experienced stock market operator will always listen with special attention to any arguments in opposition to the prevailing opinion.

Mass Opinion as an Objective Datum

It would be wrong to reach the conclusion that one should always follow one's own judgment against mass opinion. We have seen that mass opinion does sometimes, and for certain periods, constitute a force operating either with or against objective data and whose great strength must be taken into account. Faith displaces not only mountains but also price levels. It does so at times—although usually not for long—contrary to the objective situation. Woe to those who always mean to be right in opposition to mass opinion! They may be right in the long run, but may lose their money and their nerves in the meantime.

From the point of view of each individual mass opinion is indeed a datum until it collapses or reverses itself. He has to make guesses and forecasts about it just as if it were an objective datum.

This, incidentally, is the reason why some economists have recently compared economic decisions to gambling decisions, where much depends on the unforeseen action of others and on sheer chance. I believe that this approach constitutes an altogether unjustified exaggeration of a correct idea. I doubt whether it will prove to mean a real progress in economics. The actions of economic subjects are hardly ever accidental and arbitrary. They are fashioned by definite psychological laws even in the short run. This is especially true of economic subjects on the average.

The Basic Principle of Successful Investment

With the help of our model it should, in theory, be quite easy for investors or speculators to time their purchases and sales correctly. They have to go against mass opinion and buy toward the end of the exaggeration phase of the bear market and at the beginning of the adaptation phase of the bull market. They should then follow mass opinion and hold their securities through most of the bull market. Toward the end of its exaggeration phase they should again go against mass opinion and sell. Thus it is as wrong always to oppose the prevailing tendency as it is always to follow it. In a nutshell, the right rule is: first against the tendency, then with it, and finally against it.

The difficulty in practice is, of course, to feel exactly when the forces of mass opinion run out at the end of every exaggeration phase. Is there any way of determining this moment objectively?

The truth is that there is no scientific way of predicting how far psychological waves will carry. Stock market forecasts will therefore always be an art, never a science. And those who pretend to be able to calculate in advance, in a scientific and objective way, the length of a bull or bear movement are guilty, consciously or unconsciously, of charlatanry.

Only Minority Forecasts are Useful

It is too often and too easily overlooked that stock market forecasts can lead to gains only when they are minority forecasts.

As soon as any opinion about future developments and their effect on the behavior of investors and speculators becomes general, both factors are discounted in the price. The margin between present and future prices, the basis of any stock market gain, vanishes.

There is another interesting phenomenon. A forecast may become wrong by being generally accepted as being right. Suppose, for instance, that economists calculate that capital investment will be higher next year than this year and that the general price level will therefore rise. This may lead entrepreneurs to invest more this year than next, in an attempt to benefit by the prevailing lower price level. As a result, this year's price level will turn out to have been higher than next year's. The world simply does not consist of knowing economists and ignorant business men.

The beginning of the Korean war in 1950 provided a good example of the way the general expectation of certain events can alter the course of events. At that time everybody expected prices to rise and bought in advance. As a result, inventories were too large in 1951 and prices tended to fall. Any information which becomes accessible to everybody kills itself, so to speak. Since most information nowadays is accessible to the public, it fails to be useful to any individual. Only really secret and personal information is of value. However, nine-tenths of all strictly confidential information is, in fact, accessible to all and sundry.

Forecasts are Always Highly Subjective

Many mistakes are made by overrating the importance of historical analogies. Just because event A led in the past to effect B, A will by no means need to have the same effect today. Conclusions by analogy may at best indicate probabilities; they can never guarantee certainty. The future always remains uncertain, because we are unable to survey *all* the links which connect the past with the future. Things always turn out just a little different—the more so when, exceptionally, all the causal relations have for once been recognized. For it is just then that people take counteraction to protect themselves against repetition.

Some people think they can enhance the objectivity of their conceptions by consulting a great number of experts and then taking an average of all they have heard. One investment service in the United States, in fact, systematically collects the views of all the other investment services and combines them in a united opinion. To consult many is no worse and no better than to consult none. Those who consult many merely ascertain the average opinion, as it is reflected in prevailing prices. To ascertain a united opinion is useful only for the purpose of acting against rather than in agreement with it.

Investors often consult their broker. He, too, is no more than one unit of the mass. Moreover, brokers and bankers always tend to be unilaterally bullish—if for no other reason than because they regard pessimistic utterances as unpatriotic.

Others consult the so-called business leaders among their acquaintances. They forget that business leaders, with few exceptions, are always surprised by any reversal of tendency. And this not accidentally but inevitably. If business leaders in general were able to recognize coming cyclical changes, the business cycle could not develop. Nobody would buy at high prices and sell at low prices. Uncertainty regarding strength and duration of cyclical movements is their necessary precondition.

Some investors follow certain systems, for instance the so-called Daw theory. This theory has many adherents and as a result it often proves right, if only for a short time. If many believe in a rising market their purchases will bring it about. Many thorough investigations have shown the practical value of this theory to be very limited. The same is true, in my opinion, of the innumerable other systems. The Daw theory, in particular, does no more than register the existence of a bull or bear market—it does not predict them.

Every investor or speculator believes, as the result of his experiences, in certain rules. If he succumbs to the temptation of publicizing them in writing or speech, they will lose the little value they might possess.

The following articles are reproduced here as Appendices I and II because they give a picture of the events in the field of monetary and credit policy in the United States from 1949 to the middle of 1954, and of the comments they called for.

Appendix I

PROSPERITY BY INFLATION[1]

The United States is again flooded with forecasts on the economic future. The consensus, at least until recently, seems to run as follows. The year 1953 will be one of continued high level economic activity; a depression of moderate extent and duration is bound to set in during 1954 at the latest. The boom will end mainly for three reasons: armament spending will decline, industrial investment for enlarged and improved production will have reached its peak, housing construction will be lower.[2] A protracted depression, however, is not to be feared if for no other reason than the fact that the government will be able and willing to replace dwindling demand by deficit spending and other devices.

To a younger generation of economists brought up to think along the lines of the Keynesian employment theory, such a forecast and argumentation seem entirely normal and in order. For they consider employment as depending on demand, and demand in turn as depending on propensities to consume and invest which appear predestined or at least calculable in advance. And they believe in the ability of the government to prolong a boom indefinitely by deficit spending.

To the older generation of economists, who have not forgotten their neo-classical education and have managed to keep their heads clear of the Keynesian neo-mercantilism, this whole approach seems highly perverse. They are shocked in the first place by the distinctness of the forecasts and by their presentation as scientific and objective, whereas they are, at best, only rationalizations of subjective feelings. I have dealt with this illusion lately in an article "Predicting the Unpredictable."[3] Here it suffices to recall that in an economy still free in essential parts, the maldistribution of demand over time

[1] Appeared first in *The Commercial and Financial Chronicle*, New York, February 19, 1953.
[2] Contrary to predictions, the recession took place in 1953, not for the reasons expected but because the Republican administration resorted, if only temporarily, to a policy of credit restriction.
[3] *The Freeman*, October 6, 1952.

—called the business cycle—is dependent on the behavior of innumerable individual consumers and producers. But who believes seriously in the possibility of forecasting, for instance, future consumer spending which directly and indirectly influences aggregate demand more than anything else? Especially after the unexpected saving spree of the past two years, it should be clear to everyone that the consumer's waiting or hurrying with spending can be less accurately forecast than the weather six or twelve months hence. And as to investment-spending no prediction is possible without definite knowledge of the future in general, and future wage and monetary policies in particular. For they determine the all-important cost calculations—and therefore the profit expectations—of the entrepreneurs, as also does, incidentally, the so-called political climate which can change overnight.

Errors in judging the future made by the majority of the people are a necessary concomitant of and one of the chief reasons for cyclical movements. Therefore forecasting future markets can always only be a highly subjective art, never an objective science. It is not pure chance that all forecasts by the overwhelming majority of economists, analysts and statisticians since the war have turned out to be wrong. A sort of law of necessity of forecasting errors seems to be at work. It is highly probable that the present studies of "Markets after the Defense Expenditures" will prove, for all practical purposes, as valueless as the wartime studies of "Markets after the War" on which so much money and work were spent.

The prevailing approach shocks old-fashioned economists furthermore by the fatalism with which the let-down of the economy after the exhaustion of the momentary stimuli is considered as unavoidable. There is, at least in theory, nothing unavoidable in a slump. For an economy is not a sort of lame horse that slows down from a maximum speed if not continually whipped. It is rather a horse that a reckless driver allows to run quicker at times than its forces allow, with the result that a speed below average is occasionally needed in order to recover the force spent during the above average speed. If the present boom leads a year hence to a depression, this would only prove that consumers' and producers' demands had been allowed to grow too strong in the present, that the horse had not been reined in in time. In other words, the banks, with the assistance of the Federal Reserve System, have through the granting of inflationary credits created in the present an excess of effective demand which will be lacking at a later date. If this is correct, then the logical attitude toward a future depression is not to forecast and await it fatalistically, but rather to prevent it by putting brakes on the boom before it enters its excessive phase.

If neo-classical economists do not share the fatalism concerning the inevitability of the slump, they share still less the optimism of the Keynesian planners concerning the ability of governments to prolong a boom indefinitely by artificial devices such as deficit spending. They rather believe that such spending, if begun before the maladjustments of the preceding boom have been liquidated, can only lead to needless exhaustion of valuable ammunition to be used against the so-called secondary deflation, and ultimately to the ruin of the credit of the State.

A Crucial Moment in the Current Prosperity Phase

But is not all this only of theoretical interest? Has the current prosperity phase really reached or even already over-reached the point where restrictive measures have to be applied?

I personally think that it is indeed high time to take steps toward a restrictive monetary policy which would transfer part of the present effective demand to the future. I believe that if we let the boom run, we are just repeating the mistakes of the war (which cost the dollar 50 per cent of its purchasing power), and of the period following the outbreak of the Korean war. The recent increase in the re-discount rate undoubtedly is a step in the right direction. But if the demand for credits should not subside, much more drastic steps would have to be taken. Still no interests are paid on demand deposits and only very low ones on time deposits—and a change is not even considered. This proves how far off we still are from what in the pre-easy-money days would have appeared a necessary condition of any fight against inflation.

In order to support our view, we shall first examine the features and the strength of the present inflation as it has developed since the autumn of 1949, the period usually referred to as the second post-war boom—the first post-war boom extending from the beginning of 1946 until the end of 1948. We shall also confront the present second post-war boom with the second post-war boom from 1921 to 1929 after the first war. Comparisons between the two second post-war periods are indeed illuminating. In spite of all differences in detail, history seems to repeat itself in a somewhat frightening way.

Industrial Production Since 1949

As is well known, industrial production as measured by the Federal Reserve Index has risen from about 175 to about 234. Whatever the shortcomings of an index based upon the so-called physical volume may be, one cannot fail to be very impressed by this increase of almost 33 per cent, especially if one considers that the new top surpasses the top of the first post-war boom at the end of 1948 by roughly 40 points.

This tremendous increase has been achieved with an increase of non-agricultural employment from roughly 50 to only 55 million persons, or only roughly 10 per cent; and with hardly any increase in the average weekly work-hours. It must therefore to a large extent be the result of higher productivity through rationalization of the productive process, higher capital investment, and maximal and optimal utilization of all resources through their full employment.

An achievement of this sort is as such, of course, highly commendable. There remains, however, the question whether and to what extent this achievement is due to the special conditions of inflation, and also whether the same high production could not have been obtained without it. In other words, whether we never "had it so good" only because of an unnecessary inflation.

Loan Inflation

How strongly has inflation progressed since 1949? When we examine developments in the field of money and credit, our attention is immediately drawn to the appalling increase in loans of commercial banks during the last three and a half years. These loans have increased from roughly $40 billion to well over $60 billion, i.e. by more than 50 per cent. This compares with an increase from roughly $25 to $35 billion during the eight years of the 1921–29 boom.

Not all the additional loans granted during boom periods are inflationary, i.e. granted through new demand deposits, new bank money. Some parts of bank loans are granted out of genuine savings and are therefore not at all inflationary, as for instance loans granted by savings banks against mortgages.

It is, theoretically and practically, extremely difficult to decide which part of an increase in loans of commercial banks is inflationary and which not. Obviously loans are not inflationary which only replace other assets in the balance sheets of the banks, as happened from 1946 to 1949. At that time the increase in loans was accompanied by a decrease in the holdings of government securities, with the result that the total of loans and investments remained pretty stable. Since 1949 the holding of government securities no longer decreased, so that the net effect of the loan increase of $20 billion, plus the increase of some other assets, is an increase in total loans and investments of commercial banks from roughly $114 to roughly $145 billion, an increase of $31 billion. This corresponds to an increase from about $38 to $50 billion, i.e. $12 billion, during the whole eight-year period from 1921 to 1929.

But how much of this increase of $31 billion in total assets and of $20 billion in loans has been financed by inflation? Some—but unfortunately not quite sufficient—light can be shed on this question by the debit side of the balance sheets of the commercial banks.

Total deposits with commercial banks increased since 1949 from roughly $145 to about $176 billion, demand deposits increasing from $96 to about $112 billion, and time deposits from roughly $35 to $43 billion. As people hardly ever save genuinely in demand deposits from which they receive no interest, the increase in demand deposits may roughly correspond to the increase in circulating bank money. We can, therefore, conclude that of the $31 billion increase in the total assets of commercial banks, $16 billion, or 50 per cent, have been financed through inflation.

Bank Money Inflation

Looking at the situation from the money side, we find that since 1949 demand deposits of *all* banks have increased from about $96 billion to about $112 billion, or almost by 20 per cent. This compares with an increase from $18 to $21 billion, or only 15 per per cent, during the eight-year period from 1921 to 1929.

But in order to judge the extent of inflation, not only the quantity but also the velocity of turnover of bank money has to be taken into account. The annual rate of turnover of demand deposits at member banks in New York increased since 1949 from about 28 per cent to about 36 per cent, and in other leading cities from about 18 per cent to about 22 per cent—on average, therefore, somewhere between 20 per cent and 30 per cent. We may, therefore, conclude that effective demand emanating from bank money during a unit of time has increased from $96 billion to say 125 per cent of $112 billion, or $140 billion, i.e. roughly 50 per cent.

Currency Inflation

People pay, of course, not only with bank money but also with cash. Currency in circulation increased during our period from about $27 billion to about $30 billion, or roughly 10 per cent. Thus currency has increased much less than bank money.

It is interesting to compare what happened during the period from 1921 to 1929. Although bank money increased from $18 to $21 billion, or 15 per cent, currency in circulation did not increase at all; it even declined slightly. The obvious explanation is that some of the money hoarded during the war was still coming back into circulation, as, incidentally, it also did during the first post-war boom from 1945 to 1949, when demand deposits increased whereas currency in circulation dropped. The return of hoarded currency may explain why circulating bank money now again has increased much faster than circulating currency.

Our contention that the quantity of bank money has increased almost 25 per cent is, incidentally, confirmed by the movements of the counterpart of demand deposits, the reserve balances of member banks with the Federal Reserve Banks. These have increased from roughly $16 to roughly $20 billion, or 25 per cent.

Price Inflation

What have been the effects on the price level of such a credit and money inflation?

Consumers' prices have risen from about 170 per cent to about 190 per cent of the 1935-39 averages—or about 12 per cent. Wholesale prices rose at first—until spring 1951—from about 99 per cent to 115 per cent of the 1947-49 averages. They have since declined to 110 per cent, with the net result that wholesale prices, too, have over the whole period increased roughly by 12 per cent. Thus price inflation has been much weaker than money and credit inflation.

This development has again an interesting parallel in the second post-war boom period of 1921-29. In spite of the strong credit inflation consumers' prices remained practically unchanged during the whole period, whereas wholesale prices, after some increase in 1925 and a persistent fall from then on, returned to where they started. This inflation without inflation was at that time widely discussed and various explanations advanced—the best being that productivity per man-hour had increased simultaneously. Whatever the explanation, the development during the twenties shows that price stability is quite commensurable with strong inflation. Price stability alone can therefore never prove the absence of money inflation.

Money Inflation With and Without Price Inflation

Money inflation since 1949 which—taking into account the increase in the velocity of turnover—was in the magnitude of roughly 50 per cent, has undoubtedly been partly a money inflation with price inflation, the price level having risen by roughly 12 per cent. But it has obviously been, too—repeating the phenomenon of the twenties—partly a money inflation without price inflation. As far as this is the case, the higher monetary demand must have spent itself not on higher prices but on the larger product which indeed came to the markets as a result of the tremendous increase in productivity mentioned above.

This leads to the very important question: is a money inflation going along with price stability an inflation at all? Does it create all the dangers of a money inflation *with* price inflation, especially that of a later deflationary slump? In other words is inflated money neutral money as long as it has no effect on the price level? This is maintained nowadays by even conservative economists. I think the experiences of the twenties have given a clear answer. In spite of an almost total price stability over the whole period the credit inflation of the twenties ended with probably the biggest deflationary crash of all time.

Thus neutrality of money cannot be judged without taking into consideration whether or not cost-lowering factors working simultaneously have counteracted the effects of money inflation on the price level. If they have, money is not neutral and the boom is inflationary in spite of price stability. It is an important criterion of an inflationary boom that entrepreneurs expand production under the impact of profit-margins increased by inflation. It is irrelevant whether the increase has come about by higher prices with costs remaining stable or lower costs with prices remaining stable. The latter is just what happens in the case of inflation without inflation. Costs decline through increased productivity of production factors—at least as long as these have not adjusted their demands fully to the change. And prices remain stable because demand expanded by inflation prevents them from declining in accordance with sinking costs.

Inflation with price inflation must at some time come to an end in one way or another. Inflation without price inflation can no more go on forever than inflation with price inflation. A credit system cannot expand indefinitely, if for no other reason than the fact that every stimulus must exhaust itself. When inflation no longer progresses, goods produced under the assumption of ever-rising demand become unsalable. Depression sets in.

Greater Production and Higher Employment During Inflation

If this is correct—and the experiences of the twenties seem to prove the accuracy of the statement—then also the popular argument, that a higher bank money and currency circulation is justified and made innoxious by higher production, must be considered an error. It is due to thinking along the lines of a very crude quantity theory of money. If production increases with employment unchanged, it is because the employed have become more productive and unit costs have thus declined. Declining costs lead in a noninflationary environment to lower prices. If, in spite of lower costs, prices remain stable, it can only be due to a simultaneous inflation without inflation not less dangerous than any other.

Nor does an increased labor force justify a higher quantity of money and/or a higher velocity of its turnover. In order to employ, say, 10 per cent more labor at the same wages entrepreneurs need 10 per cent more funds—not taking into consideration the capital needed to buy the material and the equipment to work on and with. If such funds are provided by newly created money, this means inflation, even if through a rising productivity prices remain stable on the markets where the new money is spent. The inflation profits mentioned above and all their consequences will thus appear in spite of an increased labor force. Although this fact will hardly be grasped by our inflation-minded generation, the labor force can be increased without recourse to inflation only if either genuine saving furnishes the funds necessary to pay and equip the workers, or if wages are reduced as the number of employed increases.

Every Cycle is Inflationary

There is nothing astonishing in the serious credit and money inflation experienced since 1949. Credit and money inflations are —this is the essence of all so-called monetary business cycle theories—if not the sufficient reason then the necessary condition for every cyclical upswing. But this does not solve the question of whether the present inflationary prosperity is not, or has not already

PROSPERITY BY INFLATION

been, moving for some time above what could be called the trendline of long-term economic growth.

The decision on whether this is the case or not depends on the judgment of where and when the boom would collapse anyway. The middle of a way can obviously be determined only after the length of the whole way is estimated. Such an estimate is, however, as mentioned, wholly subjective and dependent on the business cycle feeling, the *Konjunkturgefühl* of the individual observer.

I can, therefore, in the following give only the reasons why, in my own opinion, any further increase of bank credits should be prevented by all means, and why even some reduction in the present level of inflation should be aimed at.

As already mentioned, entrepreneurs decide during the upswing to expand their production mainly under the impact of extra profits resulting from inflated demand. If production is to be expanded, new loans have to be asked for and granted. This brings new money into circulation, with the result that demand for the products coming to the markets is again higher than expected. A new impulse to expansion is given—*la hausse amène la hausse*.

This situation can still be regarded as sound as long as expectations of future prices are based on what has happened in the past on the markets. But after a certain time entrepreneurs, having experienced over and over again—maybe for years—that demand turns out to be stronger than expected, begin to reckon with a permanent repetition of such favorable developments. They plan and carry out investments meant to meet an ever-increasing demand. The result is a still stronger inflation. The boom is now carried forward by a sort of mass psychological infection to the optimistic side.

This is just what is happening nowadays. The thirteen pre-war, war and post-war years, with their almost uninterruptedly increasing demand, seem to have rendered entrepreneurs unable to believe that this increase can one day stop or be reversed.

In such a psychological situation enterprises are founded or expanded although the new plants can only show profits within an inflationary environment. Again this is just what, to my mind, has happened during the past years. This cannot, of course, be proved objectively as long as the boom lasts. It is only after the collapse that it becomes clear which of the new investments have been mistakes. But we should consider that abnormally high break-even points were allowed to develop even in the best situated enterprises

—which, incidentally, will have to be corrected through a painful cost-price adjusting process. This strongly suggests that many marginal ventures have been undertaken which will have to be liquidated.

To summarize my diagnosis: there is no doubt in my mind that since about a year or so we have entered what may turn out to have been the later and critical phase of the upswing. Comparing the present post-war boom with the post-war boom of 1921–29 I believe the year 1952 can be considered as roughly corresponding to the years 1926 or 1927.

Business Cycle Consciousness

To such a pessimistic prognosis it is often objected that entrepreneurs are, in fact, on the average not over-optimistic nowadays; that they do not expect demand to stay high indefinitely. Now, there is indeed a profound difference between the situation of today and that of the twenties. Whereas at that time the new era idea of eternal prosperity prevailed, our generation of entrepreneurs has learned the hard way that there is nothing like an eternal prosperity. It has grown business-cycle conscious. And this cycle consciousness has indeed prevented until now the boom from becoming excessive.

However, if we analyze closely what can be called the present general opinion, we see that, in fact, people anticipate the coming of a depression, but that they are also convinced that it will be only a very short and mild one. In other words, it is expected that demand will be lacking only in the short and not in the longer run. Consequently entrepreneurs seem in fact in the aggregate not to be over-optimistic in their decisions for the nearer future. They watch very carefully, for instance, whether inventories are not excessive. But for the more remote future their decisions are by no means based on pessimism. They are committing themselves to long-run investments that seem warranted only under the assumption of a permanently expanding demand. In short, entrepreneurs are adjusting to a short and mild but not to a long drawn out and severe depression.

But in the past few weeks even a short and mild depression seems no more to be envisaged. The fact that the depression expected by many for 1951, and then for 1952, has not materialized until now has not only induced the forecasters to postpone the day of reckoning further into the future, but after the future has approached it has also induced some of the official and semi-official forecasters to postpone the moment of the depression to *Calendas Graecas*. Already a fresh "new era" slogan allegedly justifying permanent optimism is beginning to appear. We hear of the "inherent strength of American economy," of "increasing needs of a growing population," of "consumer needs being really unlimited if only newer and better products are offered." In short, people are slowly forgetting the lessons of 1929. Expectations turn again toward an eternal prosperity.

Objections to a Restrictive Money and Credit Policy

A really restrictive money and credit policy will, of course, be met by many with strong resistance.

They are first those eternal skeptics who, as they did during the strongly inflationary first post-war boom, doubt that a higher interest rate would have the desired counter-inflationary effect. They can pride themselves on having prevented until lately even the weakest attempt to curb inflation indirectly rather than artificially through price ceilings, rationing and so on. Interest rates have become somewhat flexible during 1952, although only on a homeopathic scale. The effect of even this slight departure from permanent easy money may have, or should have, convinced the easy-money economists of the effectiveness of higher interest rates as an anti-inflation weapon.

Nor can it be argued that while higher interest rates may have been effective during the first post-war boom, when investments in the private sector increased rapidly, they cannot be successful in times when government and industry spend huge amounts directly or indirectly for armament. It is correct that such spending is insensitive to changes in the interest rates. But during the past years a tremendous amount of long-term investments have been made in the private sector quite independently of rearmament. Such long-term investments—most sensitive to change in interest rates—could and would have been deferred into the future under the impact of high interest rates. But the will to really curtail credits was lacking, as clearly shown by the fact that restrictions on consumer credits were loosened and the construction boom kindled rather than dampened.

Another objection to an anti-inflationary money and credit policy—paradoxically often advanced by the same economists—contends that such a policy would, on the contrary, be too effective, that once deflation started "no one knows how far it will go." To this we shall only reply that it is still much easier to stop a so-called secondary deflation, if the boom is curtailed voluntarily before it has become too excessive than when it has been allowed to run unhampered to the inevitable collapse.

Many other objections, mostly concerning the debt management, are heard. The allegedly strongest argument against a deflationary or even anti-inflationary policy is, of course, that such a policy would be incompatible with the full employment policy to which the government is committed. Conservative economists agree, of course, on the paramount importance of avoiding unemployment. But they do not agree with the Keynesian way of achieving full employment. There are obviously two ways. Keynesians analyze the economy in terms of effective demand only. They naturally conclude that only by preventing monetary demand from declining from high levels can full employment be maintained. Full employment on a lower level of monetary demand is (as they consider wages as fixed) unthinkable, and a restrictive money policy therefore taboo to them. Conservative economists analyze an economy in terms of demand *and* supply. They believe that at every level of monetary demand full employment can be maintained if only the supply prices of the factors of production are adjusted to the price level. To them the propensity to work and not the propensity to spend is the foundation of full employment for any length of time.

In an economy that has been doped by the poison of inflation for twenty years a sort of stabilization crisis with some unemployment could, of course, develop. But it should prove, as all stabilization crises do, of very short duration. To endure it means to pay the price for the avoidance of further inflation and the crash that looms at its end.

The most serious hindrance to a sound money policy that would brake a boom voluntarily in time is, of course, that such a policy is extremely unpopular. Great courage and fortitude are required by those who wish to adopt it. It is much easier to let things run, and to represent the inevitable deep depression following an exaggerated boom as an unavoidable fate under the unholy capitalistic system, and then to cry for government intervention.

Appendix II

THE ECONOMIC SITUATION IN THE UNITED STATES[1]

Since about the middle of 1953 production in the United States has been receding; unemployment has been rising and has reached quite substantial proportions in some places and in some industries. In some circles of entrepreneurs, but above all in circles of trade unions, the future is regarded with apprehension. A number of theoreticians of standing, including the Australian economist Colin Clark, forecast a further very severe deterioration of the situation. On the other hand, the government and the majority of economists assert that the situation will very soon improve, that it is in fact improving already. In their opinion, what is happening is just an adjustment, especially an adjustment of excess inventories.

There is no doubt that it is, for the economic and political fate not only of the United States but also of Europe, of the highest importance who will prove to be right in this controversy.

I have described developments of the monetary sphere until the end of 1952 in my article "Prosperity by Inflation."[2] What developments have taken place in the meantime?

The Reactions of Economists and Politicians

It will be remembered that long before 1953 the question was strongly discussed in the United States as to whether the credit expansion which was then obtaining should be curtailed, or whether its further advance should be tolerated. Two diametrically opposite opinions were put forward. The one demanding curtailment can be described as the Conservative Neo-classic. The other, which considered a further expansion as permissible or unobjectionable, can be described as the Keynesian New Dealistic. For both opinions are in fact nothing else but the expression of those opposing conceptions of economic life which, during the past two decades, have

[1] Translation of an address delivered at the University of Francfort in June 1954, and reprinted in Issue No. 15 of the *Zeitschrift für das gesamte Kreditwesen* (1954).
[2] See Appendix I.

put a stamp on all economic and political discussions in almost every sphere.

Conservative neo-classical economists diagnosed the situation as a clear case of highly inflationary prosperity. They compared the situation with that of 1927, when by an energetic credit restriction the development of the super-boom of 1927–29, and thus the great crisis, should have been prevented. Therefore they now demanded, too, the braking of the boom through higher interest rates and other means of credit restrictions.

This demand of the conservative economists was the logical consequence of their ideas about the business cycle and the methods for its stabilization. For neo-classical economists the business cycle is basically nothing else but an intertemporal maldistribution of aggregate demand. In contrast to the so-called stagnation theoreticians, who believe that the demand for credit can in the long run vanish through lack of investment opportunities, these economists are of the opinion that short-term phenomena are at stake. What is too little invested during the depression is too much invested during the boom. They contend that by preventing an excess investment during the preceding boom the investment deficit of the following depression can be avoided. By making the supply of credit more expensive, the exaggeration of the prosperity phase of the cycle, and thus the following depression, could and should be prevented. This is the method of fighting the depression by fighting the preceding boom. One can describe it also as a method of stabilizing the cycle at the average level. In principle it works, in the case of recession, with the means of cancellation of the preceding increase of interest rates. It considers this—provided that the preceding boom has been braked by raising the interest rate—as necessary and sufficient to increase, by stimulating the use of credit, the aggregate demand of the economy and restore full employment. Governmental deficit spending is rejected as unnecessary and damaging in principle.

Keynesian New Dealistic economists, in spite of many reservations, do not recognize the necessity of braking the boom before it begins to collapse by itself. They speak of stabilizing the cycle at the level of highest employment. They know, it is true, that one day the demand must dwindle and the reaction set in. But many rely for fighting it on planned governmental interventions, especially deficit spending, or, as it is sometimes called, the policy of functional finance. This is indeed the position which before

1953 was taken by New Dealistic economists like Hansen, Harris, and, above all, by the leaders of trade unions who denounced every possible increase in the cost of credit as a wicked interference in the full employment policy and an unwarranted gift of advantages to the capitalist class.

One can describe the method of business cycle stabilization demanded by the Keynesians also as the method of stabilizing the cycle at its highest possible level.

The Dream of all Laymen

To stabilize the boom at its highest level, or to prolong it in all eternity, is the dream of all laymen. My friends and I have in the period prior to 1953 pointed out that this dream is utopian and have fought the easy money policy which would lead to the exaggeration of the boom. Our reasons were the following. During prosperity a development sets in which the French characterize by the slogan *la hausse amène la hausse*. The entrepreneurs try to expand their production because their profits rise under the influence of the inflationary demand. They use additional credits or loans which the banks again grant "inflationary." The new money increases the demand, prices and profits rise further. A vicious circle upward is released. But the moment comes when the expectation of the continuation of the boom no longer gives a new stimulus to expand production. Now there are no new layers of entrepreneurs or speculators who, by use of additional credits, could carry the boom further. Now all enterprises have to be liquidated and all speculative positions have to be dissolved which were profitable only under inflation, i.e. with rising demand or prices. The boom is followed by depression and this depression cannot be fought with the classical method of lowering the interest rate. For, contrary to the case in which the cycle was braked at an average level, in the case of the stabilization of the cycle at the highest level there is no more potential credit demand which has been left unsatisfied, because the interest rate was too high, and which can be satisfied after it has been lowered. In any case, lowering of the interest rate cannot be applied for the simple reason that these rates have already reached their lows.

Functional Finance

All this does not disturb those who believe in the possibility of missing an eternal boom. According to them, the government which can disregard profitability of its investments, has the right and the obligation to replace the failing demand of the private economy as soon as the boom recedes. As long as effective demand can be held at its previous level by governmental deficit spending, full employment is considered as guaranteed.

This application of governmental finance policy is called functional finance and praised as a new invention. One can say that in so far as it is correct it is not new, and in so far as it is new it is not correct. The idea of concentrating governmental expenditures in times of depression in order to mitigate the fluctuations of the cycle is an old one. The idea that such concentration guarantees full employment is, however, incorrect. It is based on an over-simplification of the problem. If the State compensates the failing demand of the private sector of the economy, immediately, and not only after liquidation of the boom, it not only has to spend extraordinarily high amounts but the spending has also to be repeated permanently. For a part of the amounts spent by the government trickles away by the building up of savings and has to be replaced by new governmental expenditures. Permanent deficit of the State, however, means permanently increasing governmental debts. What permanently increasing government debts mean for the financial situation of the State and the currency need not be further explained, especially after the results of the Nazi experiment have been recognized. A permanently increasing intervention of the State must, incidentally, also lead to a displacement of the private sector of the economy by the governmental sector, and by doing so to total socialization.

In all this we have not considered that under the prevailing political conditions there exists the further danger that wages are pushed upward during the depression in order to strengthen the purchasing power of the masses. To compensate for the cost increase which follows, it is not sufficient to re-establish the old price level—the inflation has to be pushed so far that the price level even goes up. A race between prices and wages develops which, in the long run, must be even more catastrophic for governmental finances and currency.

Republican Credit Policy I

One of the chief objections of the Republicans to the Democratic economic policy was concerned with the permanent easy money policy of the New Dealers, which, it was argued, robbed the dollar of 50 per cent of its purchasing power since 1939. The leading Republicans, so far as they are concerned with economic policy, adhered unconditionally to the neo-classical conservative view described above, according to which the inflation should be curtailed immediately by an energetic increase in the cost of the credit supply.

In accordance with this opinion the Republican administration, when it came to power in January 1953, allowed the interest rate to rise in such a way that the yield of the so-called A.A.A. bonds went up by the middle of the year from 3 to $3\frac{1}{2}$ per cent—a very substantial increase in view of the former stability and low level of the yields.

As far as the braking of the inflation is concerned, the measure was a full success. Contrary to the opinion of most of the New Dealistic economists, according to whom raising of the interest rate has no effect in preventing inflation—an argument by which they had resisted every raising of the interest rate—the effect was strong and spontaneous. The money circulation which had increased markedly for years, increased only negligibly. The same applied to demand deposits. Total investments and loans, it is true, still increased during the year 1953 by about $6 billion, but this increase was evidently no longer financed by inflation. The general price level remained for the first time entirely stable.

Depression of Production without Deflation

Not so satisfactory, and for many quite unexpected, was the effect on production and employment. When in the middle of 1953 the anti-inflationary effect of the interest rate policy materialized, production began to decline. The index of production fell from about 138 to about 122 by March 1954. Unemployment, which until then had been negligible, increased by about 3 million. Only this March (1954) has the movement seemed to have reached its low point and perhaps even to have turned upward.

These developments are almost uniformly described as cyclical in character and called, according to the mood of the observer, adjustment, recession, or depression; and diagnosed as a consequence of the deflation induced by the Republicans' monetary policy. The Democrats try to profit by what has happened. New Dealistic Keynesian economists, especially Professor Harris, demand the return of a policy of extreme cheap money which allegedly has brought so many years of magnificent prosperity.

This diagnosis seems to misjudge the situation entirely. The figures of the developments in the monetary sphere that have just been mentioned clearly show that inflation was indeed curtailed—although perhaps not completely—but that there is no question of deflation. This easily recognizable fact seems to have entirely escaped all observers, with only one exception as far as I know—all others speaking always only of deflation. However, what has been deflated are production and employment; prices have remained entirely constant and money circulation pretty much so, and total loans and investments by banks have even gone up substantially. What had set in was an employment depression without a money deflation or, better, no depression at all—at least not a cyclical one.

There is in my opinion only one explanation for these phenomena, i.e. that the prevailing unemployment is of a stabilized or structural character such as develops when wages increase too quickly compared with prices. Unemployment was the result of the monetary situation only in so far as the progress of inflation was prevented for the first time for many years. A similar unemployment had been observed in Germany in the years 1926 to 1929. At that time unemployment increased substantially, whereas the inflationary boom progressed until 1929. Then, just as today, the reason can only have been that wages increased correspondingly more than prices and productivity. Then, just as today, labor which had become too expensive was replaced by relatively cheap capital investments.

If this diagnosis is correct, then the prevailing unemployment only confirms the year-long fears and warnings of conservative economists who regarded the permanent raising of the wage level with concern. They contended that the high wages were made only partly tolerable by higher productivity, but for the greater part only by inflation. The moment inflation would end unemployment would appear, if wages were not reduced in time, or at least prevented from rising further. However, wages have in fact steadily continued their steep rise which began in 1949, as becomes clearly evident by a look at the curve of hourly wages which in 1953 showed the same upward angle as in previous years.

The Dilemma of the Republicans

What was to be done in view of this development in the realm of production and unemployment?

Again minds were divided. Conservative economists, wishing

to prevent the resumption of inflation by all means, believed the only possible way of reducing unemployment was through an adjustment of costs to the price and demand level which now showed no signs of further inflation. They demanded—in an utopian fashion perhaps—the reduction of wages to the level prevailing at the beginning of 1953, or at least their stabilization at the level of the moment, so that an increase of productivity would be able to absorb the wage rises which had taken place until then.

Keynesian New Dealistic economists demanded, as already mentioned, the immediate return to a policy of permanent easy money, and thus, consciously or unconsciously, to further inflation. They demanded, therefore, the adjustment of the price and money level to the cost level, instead of conversely the adjustment of the latter to the former. This demand was only the consequent expression of the Keynesian employment theory, or, as I would say, mythology. For Keynesians do not consider employment, as neo-classical economists do, essentially a function of the propensity of the people to work but of the so-called effective monetary demand for products. In order to increase or maintain employment, an increase of the monetary demand is considered necessary and sufficient. In reality, an increase of the demand is by no means necessary. Full employment can also be attained by adequate regulation of the labor supply. Nor is the increase of the demand sufficient: even a strong inflation does not produce an increase of employment if wages go up with prices.

Republican Credit Policy II

The decision of the Republicans in this dilemma is known. From the middle of the year 1953 the administration again followed a conscious easy-money policy which has lowered the yields of A.A.A. bonds below the level prevailing at the beginning of 1953, with the characteristic result—very much reminiscent of the year 1927—of an extraordinarily strong upward movement of the stock market. The decision was rationalized with the argument that the lowering of the interest rate is meant to prevent a real deflation which could perhaps develop. So far as this is the aim, the new credit policy can be approved. But I am afraid that, within these limits, it will prove to be insufficient to absorb the prevailing unemployment. The new policy, if it wants to succeed, must not exhaust itself in preventing deflation, but must have inflationary effects. In so far as the Republicans allow the development of a further inflation, or even consciously create it, they act contrary to their own pre-election program. But it is perhaps too much to demand that they remain faithful to it. The population is through the Keynesian economists educated in the belief that unemployment is always the result of a failing demand for labor and never the result of a too expensive supply, so that not the wages but the monetary policy must be responsible. In democracies, however, the opinions of the masses are decisive. Consequently, the Republicans could obviously banish the evil spirit of inflation which the Democrats called in only at the price of their own election defeat.

Will the Inflation Catch?

Quite another, by no means self-evident, question is, of course, whether by lowering the interest rate one will succeed in revitalizing an inflationary boom which has been interrupted by a raising of the interest rate. The question is identical with the question of the future course of the business cycle in the United States. To answer it means forecasting the future course of the cycle.

Unfortunately I have now to disappoint severely all those who hope to receive from me an objectively founded, and not only a purely subjective, reply. For the question can never be objectively answered. We have to face the regrettable fact that we are in general, and particularly at this moment, not able to make scientific forecasts about further developments. Even now (spring 1954), when the recession is one year old, the uncertainty is not less than it was. The slight improvement of the last weeks could just as well be the beginning of a new upswing as a secondary upward reaction in a primarily still downward movement.

Reasons Suggesting a New Upswing

I can, therefore, only express the opinion to which my own business cycle feeling leans. I think that the government will succeed in starting the inflationary credit expansion anew, and that under its influence unemployment will decrease substantially.[3] But my opinion is, as I want to stress again, purely subjective and possibly quite erroneous. Nevertheless I may, perhaps, mention the reasons with which I rationalize my feeling.

(1) The end of the inflationary boom in the middle of 1953 did not coincide by chance with the height of the interest rate but was

[3] My forecast regarding the attempt to rekindle the inflationary boom has, in the meantime, proved to be correct.

caused by the high interest rate. Although, in my opinion, all sins were committed which can be committed in matters of business cycle stabilization, it still was a stabilization somewhat at the average level of the cycle, as described above, and not at its highest level. Historically viewed we were still in the year 1927, not in the year 1929.

(2) Never until now have deep depressions set in at the moment when they were expected. Depressions come, so to speak, out of the clear skies. Now the average of the entrepreneurs in the United States have expected the coming of a depression for many years, and particularly since 1951. Therefore, the so-called business-cycle consciousness has, by its dampening effect on the credit demand, compensated—at least partly—for the mistakes of the governmental credit supply policy; with the result that heavy exaggeration of the boom, and, thus, the danger of a deep depression no longer correctible through interest rate lowering, have been avoided.

(3) All the characteristic features of a genuine cyclical turn were absent. The usual credit demand of a crisis, with its strongly rising interest rate, was not observed. Employment did not fall off suddenly and commodity prices did not recede at all. The slow decline of employment and production which could be observed was in contrast to the sudden interruption of production and dismissal of workers regularly observable at the beginning of a typical depression resulting from financial difficulties.

No Boom Will Last Eternally

This optimism concerning the course of the cycle is, to put it quite clearly, no optimism for a very long period. Nor would I like it to be thought that I approve of absorbing unemployment by methods coming very near to the New Dealist Keynesians. In this realm the principle of "Time is won, all is won" is not a good one, and the Keynesian sentence "In the long run, we are all dead" is valid only for individuals and not for economies and nations.

The path which is now followed will not be eternally successful. Once all the reserves of the boom—of an objective and psychological nature—are exhausted, a depression will set in which it will be possible to mitigate only by the strongest governmental intervention. How much time will pass until then I do not wish to forecast even approximately. Only those who believe they can predict the unpredictable will think they are able to do so.

INDEX

Acceleration principle, 139–144; and business cycles, 167–168
Agriculture, 42, 177
Analysis, 25–26, 115–116, 142
Anticipatory buying, 131

Balance sheets, 25
Bank deposits, interest on, 219; and money turnover, 134–135
Bank rate, 108–110, 162–163
Banknotes, 114–115, 118, 132; during business cycle, 174–175
Banks, 28, 38; and business cycles, 168–169; cash holdings in, 107; cash withdrawals from, 134; during deflation, 137; growth financed by, 123; and inflationary credits, 132, 151–152, 162; lending restricted by, 136; loss of confidence in, 135–136; and price level, 130; private, 114–115; savings by, 118–119
Bear markets, 182–183, 191, 193, 199–200, 202, 208–209, 212
Black markets, 107
Bonds, 62; government, 108, 110, 156–157; liquidity factor in, 63; prices of, 100–101, 186, 187–190, 195; yields on, 104, 186, 196
Brokers, 216
Budget deficits, 110
Budget surpluses, 110–111
Bull markets, 182–183, 191, 195, 198–201, 208–212
Business cycles, x, 94, 108, 112, 130, 159–191, 318; consciousness of, 226–227; definitions of, 159, 176; and inflation, 224–226; interest rates and, 168–169, 172–175; savings and, 86; share prices during, 187–191; stabilization of, 180–183, 228, 231; theories of, ix–x, 66, 109, 160–168
Business management, x–xi
Buyers, effect of inflation on, 134
Buyers' strikes, 138, 173

Capital, accumulation of, and production, 27–34; during business cycles, 176–177; fixed, 40, 48–52, 123, 178; frozen, 101; growth theories and, 123–127; idle, 178; and labor, 38–39, 124–125; labor-saving effect of, 88–89; need for, 126; productivity of, 41–55, 78, 80–82, 169; substituting for labor, 81–82; use of, income distribution and changes in, 91–92; variable, 40, 48–52, 123; venture, taxes and, 91
Capital demand, 87–89, 91, 100–102, 160, 169
Capital goods, 26, 31, 99; land as, 43; over-investment in, 161–162; and production detours, 139; spending on, 140
Capital structure, 116, 119, 174–176
Capital supply, changes in, 83–84; and demand for labor, 89, 124; fixed, 125; by inflationary credit expansion, 123; and interest rate, 85; and security prices, 100–103
Capitalists, 26–27, 41; and corporation taxes, 103; and entrepreneurs, 27, 31; and income taxes, 90–91, 104; and interest rates, 78; and production, 55
Cash, 107, 113–115, 175
Cash reserves, 106
Central Banks, 109–111, 118–119; and business cycles, 168–169, 171–172, 174, 186; during inflation, 141, 145, 151–152; power of, 109, 114; reserves of, 106–108, 115
Cheap money policy, 110
Checking accounts, 113–115, 118, 132, 134–135
Child labor, elimination of, 72–74
Circular flow analysis, 26, 115–116, 142
Clark, Colin, 229
Coal fields, 42, 45
Commercial bills, discount rate for, 108
Community, the, capital of, 26, 37; income of, 25, 85–86; payment habits of, 107; and savings, 112; standard of living of, 86
Competition, 21–22, 81

238

INDEX

Consumer goods, 1, 6, 26, 31, 35, 99; change of taste and, 66, 98; and credit supply, 139–140; demand for, 119; spending on, 140
Consumption, and business cycles, 172; changes in, 66, 92–93, 96–97; forced restriction of, 119; future, 84–85; investment and, 93–94, 139–144; lack of, 111–112; production and, 5–16, 28, 34–36, 56; savings and, 84; total, 67; under-, 160–161
Consumption exchange, 34–35, 54–55
Corporate earnings, 90–91, 102, 156; in deflation, 158; and interest rates, 102; net, after taxes, 103; share prices and, 190–191, 197–198
Corporation taxes, 90–91, 102–103
Cost of living, rise in, 145
Costs, fixed, 51–54, 60; marginal, 52–53; and revenue, equality of, 56–57; unit, 51–54, 178–179; variable, 51
Credit, bank, 114–115; carry-over, 137–138, 172–173; during depression, 109; inflationary, 114–115, 132–133, 156; new, ix; non-inflationary, 132–133; from savings, 78; short-term, 62; in stationary economy, 62; during upswing, 108, 131, 169–171; use of, 33, 38–39
Credit contraction, ix–x, 117
Credit demand, 109, 111, 121–122, 131, 158, 163, 169–172, 176; deficient, 113; during deflation, 136–138, 162; weak, death traps and, 111
Credit expansion, ix–x, 117; inflationary, 123–128, 145, 162, 236; purchasing power and, 119
Credit market, and budget surpluses, 110; during depression, 111, 136–138; interest rates on, 108–109; supply and demand on, 136
Credit restrictions, 108–109, 227–228
Credit supply, 109, 111, 121–122, 126, 132–134, 139–141, 169–170, 172, 176; theory, 162–164
Creditors, 145, 154
Crises, over-saving and, 111
Currency inflation, 222
Cyclical deflation, 111–112

Daw theory of investment, 216
Death traps, 93, 96, 163, 169; large, 107–108, 111, 135; small, 106–107, 174; (*see also* Hoarding)
Debts, 27, 31
Debtors, 154–156, 175
Deficit spending, 111, 180, 182, 219
Deficits, 93, 110
Deflation, x, 64–65, 93, 96–97; and business cycle, 159–160, 170–173; causes of, 136; Central Banks and, 109–110, 114; credit demand in, 136–138, 162; cyclical, 111–112; delayed, 173; economy in, 105–158; effect of, analysis of, 115–117; employment and, 94–95, 117; end of, 151; hoarding and, 136; money, 108, 136; preconditions of, 105; of price level, 105, 119–120, 130; production in, 130; profits and losses in, 155; and recovery, 170; savings during, 138; secular (stagnation), 112–113, 184; short-term, 64; under-consumption and, 161; wages and, 147–150
Deflationary gaps, 109
Demand, during business cycle, 160; consumption and investment changes, effect on, 92–93; "effective," ix; income and, 54–55; misjudgment of, 59–60; supply and, 3–4, 8–13, 98, 119; wealth of nations and, 65
Demand curves, 8–10, 15; for credits, 39–40, 113; for goods, 119; for labor, 75–77, 79–80, 117
Demand theory of employment and production, 67
Democratic party, 232, 236
Depression, vii, xi, 175; and deflation, 111–112; end of, 170; hoarding during, 107; interest rate during, 108–109, 187; inventories accumulated during, 120; of production, without deflation, 233–234; prosperity and, 65, 134, 160, 176, 182–183, 218–219, 226–227; share prices during, 187–191; of the '30s, 113, 147–148; (*see also* Deflation)
Diminishing marginal returns, law of, 40, 44, 48, 75, 82
Diminishing marginal utility, law of, 2, 7
Discount rate, business cycles and, 172, 186; for commercial bills, 108; during inflation, 145, 151,

Discount rate—*contd.*
157; and interest rate, 133, 174; and market rate, 133, 174; raising of, 110, 121, 128, 133, 151, 163
Dividends, 62–63, 188, 193–195, 197–201
Dow Jones Index, 198

Easy money policy, 163, 184–185, 187, 232–233
Ebb and Flow of Investment, The, 199
Economic advisers, 181
Economic data, variability of, xi
Economic laws, of diminishing marginal returns, 40, 44, 48, 75, 82; of diminishing marginal utility, 2, 7; Keynesian psychological, 139; Say's, 6, 64–66, 109, 160
Economic Stabilization in an Unbalanced World, 148n.
Economic Theory of Bank Credit, viii, xii
Economics, fundamental problems in, 35; knowledge of, importance of, x; of nature, 1–13, 18–20; theories of, viii–ix, xi–xii
Economics of Illusion, The, viii, 67n., 107n., 166n., 180n.
Economists, classical, 48, 146; and the future, 97–98; Keynesian, vi, 93, 97, 111, 113, 144, 149–150, 169, 219, 228, 230, 235–237; neoclassical, 117, 217–219, 235; New Deal, 97, 143, 229–231, 235, 237
Economy, the, barter, 20, 24, 37; capitalist, xii, 29–33, 35; changing, 5, 64–104; in equilibrium, costs and revenue in, 56–57; forces affecting, ii, xii; gambling as factor in, 207–209; in inflation and deflation, 105–158; money, 22–26, 37; Robinson Crusoe, x, 6, 10, 18, 34; stationary, ix, 1–63; time element in, 25–28; with two workers, 10–18, 34
Efficiency of workers, 20–21
Employment, basic law of, 68–72; and business cycles, 177; consumption and investment changes and, 96–97; decrease in, capital and, 50; demand theory of, 117, 217; effects of inflation and deflation on, 117; full, vii, 67, 122, 228; increase in, capital and, 27–28, 94–95; during inflation, 224; Keynes' theory of, 160, 217, 235; labor supply and, 70–71, 73–74; production and, 67, 76, 121–122; productivity of labor and, 79–80, 82–83; wages and, 67–68
Entrepreneurs, anticipation of future by, 98–99; and capitalists, 27, 31; competition among, 81; definition of, 18; during deflation, 148–150; functions of, 18–22; income tax and, 90; during inflation, 151, 153–154; investment by, 92; land and, 42–46; money and, 23–25, 28, 31, 38–39; productivity and, 20–22; profit and, 21–22, 24, 57–60, 77–78, 129–130
Equilibrium theory, 144
Escalator clauses, 146
Europe, 97, 113, 131
Exchange of goods, 13–18, 23–25

Farmers, 43
Feather bedding, 80
Firm, the, optimum size of, 50–51
Forecasts, economic, 217–218, 226, 229, 237; stock market, 198–199, 214–216
Foreign exchange, 172, 174
Foreign trade, 105
Free markets, 80
Functional finance, 180, 231–232
Future, the, anticipation of, 97–99; changes in, 97–99; economic, 217–219; profits in, 100; spending in, 142–144; and stock market, 198–199, 203–204, 214–216

General Motors, 205–206
General Theory of Employment, Interest and Money, viii, 26, 65, 87, 94, 97, 115, 166, 185, 206–207
Germany, 97, 145–146, 152–154, 158, 234
Gesell, Silvio, 161
Goods, exchange of, 13–17, 26; intermediate, purchase of, 55–56
Government bonds, 108, 110
Government debts, 110, 232
Great Britain, 110, 185, 186
Gross national product, 67
Ground rent, 46–47
Growth theories, 123–127

Hansen, Alvin Harvey, 147–148, 231
Harris, Professor, 231, 233

INDEX

Health, labor laws and, 74
Hoarding, 106–107, 135–136, 174–175, 186
Hume, David, 205
Hurrying, 131–134; business cycles and, 164–165; and credit demand in inflation, 136–138; inventories during, 136; spending and, 139; and stock market, 157–158; and velocity of money turnover, 135

Immigration, labor market and, 69
Income, community, 85–86; distribution of, 6, 54, 55, 66, 82–83, 91–92, 138–139; fixed, 153; high, 138; individual, 25–26, 35–36, 85; long-term, from shares, 192–195; low, 138; national, 25, 138; real, 25, 138; saving and, 85, 138
Income statements, 25
Income taxes, 90–91, 103–104, 113
Indifference curves, 8
Industrial Fluctuations, 164
Inflation, vii, 64–65, 93–94, 96; and apparent profits, 129–130; and business cycles, 159–160, 170–173, 224–226; Central Banks and, 109–110, 114, 145, 151; cheap money policy and, 110; credit supply in, 132–134; creditors' reactions to, 145; economy in, 105–158; effects of, 115–117, 123, 224; employment during, 224; end of, 151, 161, 171–173; forced saving and, 118–119; and general price level, 119–121; growth financed by, 123–124; hoarding and, 106–107; investment and, 104; loan, 220–221; money (*see* Money inflation); money turnover during, 134–136; neutral, 105; official and unofficial, 135; original, 122, 129; preconditions of, 105–106; price, 94, 222–223; private, 151; production during, 115, 224; prosperity in, 217–228; results of, 152–154; runaway, 131, 145; savings and, 133, 138–139; second, 129; share prices in, 155; short-term, 64; slow, 85; wages and, 146–147, 149–150; war and, 130–131, 151, 219, 222, 226
Interest, 33, 43, 45, 48, 55, 60, 107, 152
Interest rate, and bank rate, 108, 133; and bond and share prices, 188–190; and business cycles, 168–169, 172–175, 236; capital supply and, 38–40, 83, 85; consumption and, 84–85; demand for capital and, 87–88, 91; during crises, 111; during depression, 108–109, 137, 187; dividends and, 62–63; fixed capital and, 49; hoarding and, 107; labor supply and, 78; for land, 45–46, 48; low, 110, 134, 185–186; productivity of capital and, 80–81; rents and, 61; rise of, vi, 121, 126, 134, 141, 227; savings and, 84–85, 101–102, 161; and share prices, 156–157; unnatural, theory of, 162–163
Inventions, new, capital and, 121
Inventories, accumulated during depression, 120; carry-over credits for, 137, 173; at end of boom, 172; swollen, 151; unliquidated, 178; during waiting and hurrying, 136
Investable funds, 38
Investment gap, cause of, 112
Investment management, x–xi
Investment services, 215
Investments, and business cycles, 165–166; for capital appreciation, 208; changes in, 92–93, 96–97; consumption and, 93–94, 139–144; during depression, 111; interest rate and, 100–102; liquidity factor in, 63; long-term, 62–63, 227; over-, 161–162; risk in, 204–206; savings and, 117–118; short-term, 63, 208; successful, 214–216

Keynes, Lord, viii–ix, xii, 26, 65–66, 85, 87, 91, 94, 106, 109, 112, 115, 144, 149, 170, 185, 206–208
Keynesian psychological law, 138
Keynesian theory of economics, viii–ix, xii, 65–66, 110, 146–147, 160, 178, 217, 235

Labor, agricultural, 44, 47–48; compensating reactions of, 145–146; demand for, 67, 68, 76, 78, 83, 89; demand curve for, 75–77, 79–80; division of, 13–16, 22–23; goods and, 1; machine, 29–31, 33; production and, 5–13, 36–39, 41, 55, 67; productivity of, 5, 41, 76–82, 84, 89; supply curve of, 2–4, 37, 69–71, 73–74, 94; and taxation, 91

INDEX

Labor contracts, escalator clauses in, 146
Labor market, 69, 72–73
Labor supply, 68–69, 89, 121–122; changes in, 69–72, 75–77, 88; elasticity of, 67, 177–178; production and, 125; restriction of, 96–97; scarcer and costlier, reasons for, 72–73
Labor unions, 68, 73–74, 81, 97, 146
Land, 41–50, 61
Leisure, 2, 7, 72
Liquidity as factor in investment, 63, 167
Liquidity preference theory, 106, 166–167
Loan inflation, 220–221
Loans, 26–28, 38; contracts for, 154; on land, 45–46, 55; rates for, fluctuations in, 173
Losses, anticipation of future and, 99; during business cycles, 179; deflation, 155; demand and, 58; national, 59–60; output and, 53, 60

Machines, 29–31, 33, 42–43, 45, 61
Mass opinion, investment and, 212–213
Mead and Grodzinsky, 199
Minimum wage laws, 73–75
Minors, employment of, 73–74
Monetary policy, anti-inflationary, 181–182, 219; and business cycles, 184–185, 187; Republican, 232–236; restrictive, 109, 227–228
Monetary system, ix, 108
Money, xii, 22–25; bank, 114–115, 134; cheap, 110; circulation of, 23, 93, 94, 105, 119, 175; and consumption exchange, 54–55; easy, 163, 184–185; elasticity of, 65, 94, 141; entrepreneurs and, 23–25, 28, 31, 38–39; and exchange, 22–23; flow of, illustrated, 32; "free", 161; functions of, 22, 24; hoarding of, 106–107, 135–136, 174–175, 186; idle, 157; as indicator of profits, 24–25; during inflation, 131–132, 134–136, 145–146, 152–153, 163; lack of confidence in, 174; lending of (see Loans); need for, 124–126; paper, 114–115; and prices, 37; purchasing power of, stability of, 131; quantity theory of, 54, 146; scarcity of, 28; and utility, 34, 36; value of, changes in, 105
Money inflation, 94, 105, 108, 130, 147, 159, 223–224
Money markets, 173, 174, 186–189
Money substitutes, 106, 113–115
Monopolies, 154
Monopoly profits, 102
Moody's Investment Service, 193
Morgenthau, Henry, 185
Multiplier theory, 139–144, 167–168

Nature, economics of, 1–13, 18–20
New Deal, 97, 143, 229–231
New York Stock Exchange, x, 157, 183, 191, 193

Oil fields, 42
Optimism, business cycles and, 163–165, 173, 227, 237
Output, changes in, and unit cost, 52–53; illustration of, 20–21; increased, 16–17, 80; input and, 56–57; losses and, 53, 60; productivity of labor and, 80, 82
Over-investment, 161–162
Over-investment theories, 161–162
Over-speculation, 164
Overtime pay, 71
Ownership, 26

Pessimism, 163–165, 169–170, 200, 211, 226
Pigou, A. C., 164
Plant, 40, 43, 102, 161
Political unrest, capital demand and, 89
Population growth, economic effects of, 123–125, 183–184
Price ceilings, 157
Price-cost relationship, 142–143, 145–150, 171, 180
Price formation, x
Price inflation, 94, 222–223
Price level, in business cycles, 171; influences on, 105–106, 119–120, 125–128, 130; productivity and, vi, 95–96; for products of current period, 122–123
Price support, 105, 150, 154
Prices, agricultural, v; average, v; business cycles and, 165–166, 172, 176–178; commodity, 176; in deflation, 130, 150; in inflation, 115, 123, 146, 151–153; labor and, 1–5, 94; of land, 43–50; marginal costs and, 52–53;

INDEX

Prices—*contd.*
money and, 94; and price level, 54; production costs and, 66, 99; security, 61–63; spending and, 86; stabilization of, 126; wages and, 232
Probability judgments in business, 204
Producer, isolated, 1–10, 13, 18
Production, agricultural, 41–43, 177; capital and, 27–34; by capital and labor, 38–39, 125; capitalistic or roundabout, 29–33, 55–56, 87; changes in, 67, 82–83; and consumption, 5–13, 28, 34–36, 56; current, products of, 120–123; in deflation, 130; expansion of, 5, 27–34; factors of, 64, 82, 91, 98, 99, 144; future, 98–99, 120–122; industrial, 233–234; inflation and, 115, 224; by labor alone, 36–38; and living standard, 15; machine, 29–31; over-, 5–6; past, price level of, 120–121, 130; proceeds of, distribution of, 41; purchasing power and, 119; time element in, 25–30, 33; volume of, capital and, 29; wages and, 36–38
Production costs, during business cycles, 179; differences in, 11–13, 20; interest and, 48; prices and, 66, 99; profits and, 81; total, 51
Production detours, 31, 33, 38–39, 48, 80, 101, 139
Production exchange, 34–54, 56
Productivity, of capital, 41, 55, 78, 80–82, 169; cost saving and, 59; entrepreneur and, 21–22, 24, 57–60, 77–78, 129–130; of individual worker, 33; without inflation, vi; inflationary credit expansion and, 127–128; of labor, 5, 41, 76–81, 84; of land, 48; price level and, 95–96, 127–128; and profits, 128; specialization and, 15; wages and, 4–5, 95–96
Products, 7–8
Profits, 6–7; during business cycles, 179; definitions of, 6, 16, 21, 59; deflation, 155; demand and, 58; disappearance of, 100; entrepreneur and, 21–22, 57–60; exchange and, 16–17; frozen, 58, 60; and future changes, 99; inflation, 105, 129, 153–154; inventory, 176; labor supply and, 77–78; from lagging production costs, 155; money as indicator of, 24; monopoly, 102, 154; output and, 53–54, 128; reasons for, 58–59; and wages, 89; windfall, 129, 153, 155–156
Prosperity, 65, 111, 175, 187; depression and, 134, 160, 170–173, 176, 182–183, 218–219; individual, 25; in inflation, 217–228; lasting, economic growth and, 183–184; savings during, 86; share prices in, 187–191; "volume," 128, 178
Psychological business cycle theories, 163–165, 171
Purchasing power, 119, 122, 151–154
Purchasing power theory, 147–150

Quantity theory of money, 146

Rationing, 157
Recovery, 146, 170–171, 188
Reflation, 170
Rent, 42–44, 46–47, 55, 60, 61, 156
Republican party, vi, 232–236
Revenue, equality of costs and, 56–57
Risk, 58, 62–63, 91, 175, 204–206

Savings, ix, 6, 28, 31, 38–39, 99; by banks, 118–119; capital supply and, 83–84; cost, 59; credits and, 78; during crises and depressions, 111–112, 169; deflation and, 138; income and, 85–86, 91–92; inflation and, 133, 138–139; and interest rates, 84–85, 101–102, 161; and investment, 92–93, 117–118; over-, 134, 161, 170; prosperity and, 86; quasi-, 132–134, 138, 156; reasons for, 84–87; under-, 170
Say, Jean-Baptiste, 6, 64
Say's law, 6, 64–66, 109, 160
Securities, 62–63, 100–102, 186, 210–212; (*see also* Bonds; Shares)
Sellers, deflation and, 136
Sequence analysis, 25–26, 115–116, 142
Shareholders, old, and corporation taxes, 103
Shares, 62; accumulation and distribution of, 211–212; common, x, 63, 100–104, 155–158, 186–191, 190–203, 206–207; preferred, 62, 100–101

INDEX

Speculation, 166, 172, 182–183, 199, 203, 207–209
Spending, 86, 130, 134, 136, 139, 143, 151–152, 180–182
Spiethoff, 161
Stagnation theory, 85, 87, 112–113, 124
Standards of living, 3–4; community income and, 86; low, work-hours and, 5; money and, 23; production and, 15; savings rate and, 138
Stock markets, x, 100; and the economy, 207–209; expectations for, interpersonal differences of, 199–200, 202–203, 206–207, 209–210; forecasting future of, 198–199, 203–204, 214–216; hurrying and, 157–158; during inflation, 156; and mass opinion, 212–213; offer and demand prices on, 205–206; price formation on, 192–216; secondary movements of, 164; success on, 212; typical movement of, 200–202
Strikes, 73, 89, 138, 173
Supply, credit (*see* Credit supply); current, labor and, 121–122; and demand, 3–4, 8–13, 98, 119, 121
Supply curves, 8–9, 40; of capital, 117; credit, 132–133, 145; for goods, 117; labor, 2–4, 37, 69–71, 73–74, 94
Surpluses, 6, 16, 93, 110–111

Taste, 58–59, 66
Taxes, 89–91
Total product of economy, 67, 69, 77–78, 82, 83

Under-consumption theories, 160–161
Under-employment, 93–94, 170
Unemployment, vi, 93, 229, 233–236; during booms, 96–97; during deflation, 147–150; labor supply and, 70–71; laws' effect on, 73–74; low interest rates and, 110; and price level, 123; structural, 67; union action and, 74–75; voluntary, 71, 97; wages and, 67–68
Unit costs, 51–54, 178–179
United States, 148; bank deposits in, 115; budget surpluses in, 110–111; cheap money policy of, 110; credit policies of, Republican, 232–236; depressions in, 113, 147–148, 163, 180–181; economy of, v–vii, 111, 208, 227, 229–237; inflations in, 131, 180–181, 186; labor contracts in, 146; monetary policy of, 110, 182*n*., 185, 232–236; unemployment in, 96–97, 177, 229, 233–236
Unnatural interest rate theory, 162–163
Upswing, 169–170, 226
Utility, 34, 36, 41, 42
Utility judgments, 10–11

Wages demands, 68, 96
Wage fund theory, 28
Wage level, labor supply and, 68
Wage scales, sliding, 146
Wages, 3–4, 55; changes in, 37; competition and, 21, 81; credit expansion and, 125–126; decrease in, 147, 149–150; and employment, 28, 36–37, 47–48, 96–97; excessive, unemployment and, 67; fixed, 68, 125; increases in, 146–147; labor demand curve and, 76–77; and labor supply, 70–71; money, 127–128, 147, 177; prices and, 232; productivity and, 79–83, 95–96; profits and, 89, 91–92; real, 127, 146, 177; in relation to leisure, 72; stabilization of, 126; stagnation theory and, 113; uniform, 21, 81
Waiting, 130–134; business cycles and, 164–165, 169–170; and credit demand in deflation, 136–138; and idle money boom, 157; inventories during, 136; spending and, 139; and velocity of money turnover, 135
War, business cycles and, 170, 173, 176–177, 180–181, 219; government bonds during, 156; and inflationary credits, 151; price level during, 130–131
Wealth of nations, 65
Weber, Adolf, 113
Wicksell, K., 109, 162–164
Women's labor, 72
Work day, length of, 2, 72
Workers, capital and, 27–28; and leisure, 2–3; marginal, 76–77; new, 72, 75–76; single, 1–10, 13, 18, 33, 75, 79–80
Work-hours, 1, 77–72; exchange of goods and, 15–16, 36–37; labor supply and, 70–72; marginal, 4–5; and multitude of products, 7–11; and price, 3–5